WRITING THE
PARANORMAL
NOVEL

WRITER'S DIGEST
BOOKS

WritersDigest.*com*
Cincinnati, Ohio

WRITING THE
PARANORMAL
NOVEL

TECHNIQUES AND EXERCISES
FOR WEAVING SUPERNATURAL ELEMENTS
INTO YOUR STORY

STEVEN HARPER

To receive a free weekly e-mail newsletter delivering tips and updates about writing and about Writer's Digest products, register directly at http://newsletters.fw publications.com.

15 14 13 12 11   5 4 3 2 1

Distributed in Canada by Fraser Direct
100 Armstrong Avenue
Georgetown, Ontario, Canada L7G 5S4
Tel: (905) 877-4411

Distributed in the U.K. and Europe by F+W Media International
Brunel House, Newton Abbot, Devon, TQ12 4PU, England
Tel: (+44) 1626-323200, Fax: (+44) 1626-323319
E-mail: postmaster@davidandcharles.co.uk

Distributed in Australia by Capricorn Link
P.O. Box 704, Windsor, NSW 2756 Australia
Tel: (02) 4577-3555

Library of Congress Cataloging-in-Publication Data
Piziks, Steven.
  Writing the paranormal novel : techniques and exercises for weaving supernatural elements into your story / by Steven Piziks. -- 1st ed.
      p. cm.
  ISBN 978-1-59963-134-9 (alk. paper)
  1. Occult fiction--Authorship. 2. Occult fiction--Technique. I. Title.
PN3377.5.O33P59 2011
  808.3'873--dc22
                          2010034603

Edited by Scott Francis
Designed by Claudean Wheeler
Cover photo by inhauscreative/iStockphoto.com
Production coordinated by Debbie Thomas

ABOUT THE AUTHOR

 **Steven Harper Piziks** is the author of *In the Company of Mind* and *Corporate Mentality*, both science-fiction books published by Baen Books. Writing as Steven Harper for Roc Books, he has produced The Silent Empire series for Roc and is currently writing The Brain Plague steampunk trilogy for DAW. He's also written books based on *Star Trek, Battlestar Galactica*, and *The Ghost Whisperer*, as well as the movie novelization *Identity*. When not writing, he plays the harp, wrestles with his three sons, and spends more time online than is probably good for him.

www.sff.net/people/spiziks

www.twitter.com/stevenpiziks

TABLE OF CONTENTS

PART I:
GATHERING
THE
ELEMENTS

CHAPTER 1:

The Nature of the Paranormal

Welcome to a wonderful world of weird. You can find just about anything here: lovely bones, lightning thieves, graveyard books, wild swans, half magic. The list is as endless as imagination. And you've decided to write in it. Cool!

We do have a few rules. Sorry, but there it is. You can't do just *anything*. You only get three wishes. The magical gate closes at sunset. The handsome stranger doesn't drink . . . wine. Even the supernatural world has its little ways.

Don't fret. We'll walk you through, open all the doors, and reveal all the secrets. Please keep your arms and legs inside the tour bus at all times (lest they get bitten off) and remember to tip the driver (he gets testy if you don't). And at the end of it, you'll have your own paranormal manuscript.

JUST WHAT IS A PARANORMAL BOOK, ANYWAY?

If you want to write science fiction—bear with me here—you have to create a story with some piece of extrapolated science (such as dinosaur cloning or the ability to zap a corpse back to life) that's so integral to the plot, you can't remove it without destroying the story. Remove the cloned dinosaurs from *Jurassic Park,* and you have no story. Remove the reanimated dead from *Frankenstein,* and you have no story. Science is the element that makes these novels into science fiction instead of, say, adventure or romance or gothic.

Paranormal novels work the same way. You need some element of magic or the supernatural that's so deeply integral to the story that the entire novel would collapse if you removed it. Try removing the supernatural element from *Dracula* and see how far you get. The book has a romance, but without the vampire count to move things along, author Bram Stoker would have no story. On the other hand, if your protagonist's werewolf boyfriend could just as easily be a muscular guy who loses his temper once a month right around the time he needs a haircut, you aren't writing a paranormal novel, you're probably writing a romance with supernatural trappings—and your readers will see right through it.

People have been telling supernatural stories from the beginning of human civilization. Such stories form the basis of every mythology that ever existed. These tales explain how the world came to exist, why we have earthquakes, who stole fire from the gods, where people go when they die, or anything else that needed explaining. Other supernatural stories spin grand adventures of bold heroes: Odysseus and Gilgamesh and Lemminkäinen and Aladdin. And it wasn't just the stories themselves that endured—the concepts remained as well. Who doesn't want to be swept away from this dull, mundane world to a wondrous, magical land? Who hasn't fantasized about finding a magical object of great power and having fun with it? Who hasn't fervently wished for the perfect magical lover to tell us we're irresistible? These and other supernatural concepts have hung on for generations for one reason: They're *fun* to think about.

WHAT DO PARANORMAL NOVELS DO FOR US?

Supernatural stories feed the human desire for escape. We can pretend *we're* riding that magic carpet, making those three wishes, or swinging that sword because we know (deep sigh) it's never going to happen for real.

The idea of uncovering the supernatural in your own yard is irresistible. Supernatural stories originally took place Long Ago and Far Away. This lent the stories a certain amount of—believe it or not—realism. In a time when the average person never traveled more than four or five miles from home, it was easier to suspend disbelief if the story took place halfway around the globe. *Anything* can happen in a place you've never heard of! But eventually humans invented mass communication. The world shrank, and the universe Out There became less mystical. As a result, storytellers started slipping supernatural elements into their own backyards. Bram Stoker horrified—and fascinated—the Victorians when he brought a Long Ago and Far Away vampire into modern London. (More on that in chapter two.) Stoker wasn't the first to bring an ancient monster into a modern setting, but he was the most famous, and many, many authors imitated him.

In supernatural stories, you don't need to look Long Ago or even Far Away to find adventure. You can stroll down the sidewalk or wander off the back porch. The contrast of the unknown magical with the well-worn mundane provides the charm. Winged horses and flying carpets are fun, sure, but when most people spend their time stuck in automobile traffic, a flying car sounds a lot more interesting. Heck, maybe you, the reader, will find one next.

On that note, I should let you know that this book will focus mostly on writing novels set primarily in our world, either past or present, or on novels that use characters from our world who travel to supernatural places. Although it's a supernatural genre, we'll only be making brief detours into high fantasy. If you want to write novels about armored warriors or powerful sorcerers who fight fantastic creatures in a society that never intersects with our own, you might want to check out Orson Scott Card's *How to Write Science Fiction & Fantasy*, also from Writer's Digest Books.

Meanwhile, we're going to look at the chance to use the paranormal to shake up the ordinary world—or an ordinary story.

HOW CAN THE PARANORMAL SHAKE IT UP?

I live about half my waking life in fantasy. By this, I mean I tell myself stories. I create them in my car on highway drives, I spin them while I'm jogging on that stupid treadmill, and I think about them at night to send myself to sleep. In other words, I never gave up the "Let's pretend" games most children play because the real world was never quite enough. I've wanted to explore other places—or see what might happen if something truly strange came to *this* place. Eventually I learned how to get these stories down on paper and sell them, which is how I became a novelist.

I'm not alone in this, of course. I only joined a long-standing tradition of storytellers stretching back over eons. There's something cool about adding a dash of magic to the normal world, and this coolness factor is why people write paranormal books. I'm assuming you're here for the same reason.

On the surface it looks easy—just add a supernatural element to an otherwise normal story. A detective who hunts down criminals is pretty cool. But how much cooler is it to create a detective who hunts down ghosts? Put together a group of siblings who flee the Blitzkrieg, leaving their familiar city for the strange, unfamiliar English countryside, and you have a great story. Even greater is the story of the same children fleeing through a magical wardrobe to another world entirely. The young woman who falls in love with a handsome, mysterious stranger on the run from a dark past is such a cliché that romance authors are hard-pressed to use that story line anymore. Make the handsome stranger into a werewolf on the run from his angry pack mates, and the story becomes interesting again.

But it's a little more complicated than that. (You knew it had to be, right?) Supernatural people and creatures don't just drop out of the sky, fully formed and realized, so they can step seamlessly into your story. Supernaturals need to be created, nurtured, and tended. They need to be examined, explored, and explained. Otherwise, they won't make sense.

Sense? I want a demon that breaks free from hell, falls in love with mortal women, and vows to stop the impending Apocalypse to make *sense?*

Absolutely. That's what this book is about. We're not only going to shake up a normal novel—we're going to shake it up in a way that makes people want to turn every page and stay up until three in the morning to do it.

And that's a supernatural element all by itself.

CHAPTER 2:
Elements and Elementals

The most common question writers hear is, "Where do you get your ideas?" Some authors keep a pithy or smart-alecky answer ready, such as, "I belong to the Idea of the Month Club" or "I store a trunk of them in my attic." More honest authors might answer, "I look at my bank account. It's amazing how many ideas a line of zeroes can generate."

A more useful answer is that you simply keep your eyes open. Fantasy author Mercedes Lackey once saw a small animal skitter across the road in front of her car. A split-second later, she realized her eyes were playing tricks—it was nothing but a piece of paper blown by the wind. Most people would think nothing of this and continue on their way, but Lackey is a *writer*. She played with the incident in her mind, asking herself why an animal might disguise itself as a piece of paper and what might happen if someone found such an animal. Eventually she wrote a story about it.

The easiest way to find ideas is to play the "What If?" game. What if that piece of paper really *were* an animal? What if time ran backward when I turned my watch backward? What if a vampire needed to travel quickly from New York to Los Angeles? Could he send himself by FedEx?

Another way to get novel-length ideas is to take two unrelated concepts and smoosh them together. If one of those elements is supernatural, you have a paranormal book. Neil Gaiman took the all-too-common idea of an abandoned child needing a family and combined it with the concept of supernatural creatures inhabiting a cemetery. Out of this, he got *The Graveyard Book.* Bram Stoker combined vampires with (then) modern-day London and got *Dracula.* Naomi Novik tossed dragons into the Napoleonic Wars and got *His Majesty's Dragon.* Who would *ever* have thought of that?

A writer who kept her eyes and mind open, that's who.

It's great fun to take an ordinary situation and inject a supernatural element. That's what a paranormal book is all about. So let's examine how to use some supernatural elements.

SUPERNATURAL ELEMENTS

I'm going to repeat from chapter one: You can't simply drop a bit of magic into your book and expect to claim the whole thing is supernatural. In order to qualify as a true paranormal book, your novel must contain at least one supernatural element without which the entire story would fall apart. The paranormal must be integral to the story. There is simply no way, for example, to remove the dragons from *His Majesty's Dragon* and preserve the book. Laurell K. Hamilton can't take vampires and werewolves out of her Anita Blake novels and replace them with ordinary people. The books simply wouldn't work. If you can replace your main character's broomstick with a fast car and her crystal ball with a cell phone and get away with it, you don't really have a paranormal book—you have a book with supernatural decorations.

Some books pretend to be paranormal but aren't. All the supernatural elements in Katherine Paterson's *Bridge to Terabithia* appear nowhere except in Jess and Leslie's imaginations. Edward Eager's *Magic or Not?* and its sequel *The Well-Wishers* use a well that may or may not actually be granting wishes. Peg Kerr uses parallel retellings of the folktale "The Wild Swans"—one modern, one fantasy historical—in her wonderful novel of the same title, and leaves the reader wondering if her two stories are truly connected. Some readers appreciate the magical realism and others feel cheated by it, so tread carefully if you want to go this route.

An idea for a supernatural element can hit you out of nowhere. You might be walking the dog or shopping for groceries when you realize that a magic trunk filled with an infinite number of costumes from bygone eras would make a great basis for a novel. Or, more likely, you'll be doing some reading on supernatural subjects and something will catch your eye. I always maintain that learning something new is a great way to generate story ideas. (More on that in chapter four.)

Supernatural elements tend to fall into certain categories. This is by no means a complete list, but it's pretty good. Pick one and run with it.

THE SUPERNATURAL OBJECT

This is a widget with magical powers. The classic example here is the magic sword. Excalibur springs to mind. Stories abound with people who find, inherit, receive, or even create magic rings, magic carpets, magic books, magic brooms, magic cauldrons—the list goes on. Look around your house. Any object can be made magical.

You might discover supernatural objects for your book by simply looking at the world around you and wondering what it might be like if a particular object had supernatural powers. Or an idea for an object might simply hit you over the head and demand to be used. In any case, you have to keep your eyes and mind open to receive the idea.

Supernatural objects tends to fall into two categories:

The Obvious Object

The Obvious Object's supernatural power is related to its normal function. A doll is fun to play with, but when it comes to life, it's even more fun. A motorcycle provides quick transportation, but a *flying* motorcycle will take you to the ends of the earth. A book contains interesting information, but a *witch's* book lets you cast spells.

A setting that uses a lot of casual magic might have any number of little Obvious Objects lying around. They add color to the background. J.K. Rowling makes extensive use of these in her Harry Potter books. Photographs and portraits have lives of their own. The figures in Ron Weasley's chess game move at the command of the players. A music box in Sirius Black's home plays a tune that will lull the listener into an enchanted sleep. These objects can be fun or sinister, but in either case, they provide contrast between the paranormal world and the "normal" world.

More powerful Obvious Objects can be used as plot devices for an entire novel. The children in Edward Eager's *Seven-Day Magic* discover a supernatural library book that transports them to book-related adventures, for example. On a more unusual note, Terry Pratchett uses a supernatural mail-sorting machine as the main object in his extremely funny book *Going Postal*. Once the machine gets going, it sorts letters that haven't even been written yet . . .

The Mysterious Object

You can't tell what a Mysterious Object's power is by looking at it. The magic is unrelated to the form. Magic rings fall into this category. Can you tell the difference between a wishing ring and an invisibility ring? Neither can I. And why are they rings, anyway? Why not an invisibility sweat sock or a wishing wristwatch? (I know, I know—because no one can say it.)

Other more traditional Mysterious Objects include potions, scrying crystals, magical jewelry, and Aladdin's magic lamp. Aladdin is rather startled when the djinn emerges in the original fairy tale. At the time the story was written, djinn were free-willed spirits, not wish-granting slaves, and little oil lamps were used for nothing but holding back darkness. The modern equivalent might be finding a fairy in a flashlight.

Creating a Supernatural Object

If you want the entire book to revolve around a particular object, you'll probably need a *powerful* object, one with a general or versatile power. An object that can only wash windows will have limited story potential. The children of Edward Eager's wonderful *Half Magic,* for example, discover a coin that grants half-wishes. (When one of them idly wishes the four of them could play on a desert island, the coin drops the children into the Sahara—desert yes, island no.) This versatile power has the children dealing with Merlin in the time of King Arthur, a house fire, a sister who is only half there, and a cat who can talk, but only half the time—quite the variety.

However, your supernatural object *must* have limits. A limitless supernatural object removes all conflict from your book. Your story will end very quickly if your protagonist simply has to say, "I wish all my problems were solved." (And you'll need to explain why your supposedly intelligent characters don't wish exactly that.) This means you need to work out *exactly* what your supernatural object can and cannot do in advance. Limits provide conflict, and conflict leads to plot. You may have noticed, for example, that many fairy tales allow only three wishes. The character uses the first wish to see if the magic really works. He uses the second wish to ask for something big that turns disastrous in some way, forcing him to use the third wish to set things right again. No more wishes—just in time for the story to end. "The Monkey's Paw" by W.W. Jacobs uses this limitation pattern.

Your object can have a limited number of uses, as noted above. Or it might only work under certain conditions—during the day, when the moon is full, after it's dipped in fresh blood. It might need time to "recharge" after each use, and the more power it uses, the more time it takes to charge up. It might work only for one gender or members of only one family or even only one person. It might drain energy from the user, leaving her exhausted. Or perhaps using the object changes the owner in some undesirable way, like the One Ring from J.R.R. Tolkien's *The Lord of the Rings*.

Objects can also be lost, stolen, or destroyed. Take away your hero's magic widget just before the final battle and see what happens. Or maybe the original owner comes back for it. Or it breaks, and the only person who can repair it is in a coma. Another character might unwittingly sell it on eBay. Or even worse—hand the thing over to the villain. The villain's power rises just as the hero's power drops. This is wonderful for conflict.

One thing you must *not* do is give an object a convenient new power that solves the hero's current problem. A hero who falls over a cliff can't unexpectedly discover that his grandfather's time-stopping pocket watch also lets him fly. This cheats your reader and shows poor writing. However, it's perfectly legal for your hero to find a creative new use for the device's existing power. Perhaps our hero realizes he can slow time as well as stop it, allowing him to drift slowly to the ground. The idea should be plausible within the rules and limitations you set up before you even begin writing.

Finally, an object doesn't just pop into existence. It needs a history. Who made the object, and why? What happened to the original owner? Who else, if anyone, has owned the object before now? Does anyone else know about the object? Is anyone hunting for it? Fleshing these ideas out will give you great ideas for plot development.

Just remember that in the end, the protagonist has to solve the book's problem, preferably without the object. The entire point of reading this type of book is to see how a particular character reacts to having a supernatural object thrust into her life. Your focus should be on the character, not the object. For a truly satisfying ending, the character has to win on her own.

EXERCISE

Look carefully at your surroundings. Choose an ordinary object to develop into a supernatural object. It may be any object you like.

1. Describe the object in detail, as if you were seeing it and/or touching it for the first time.
2. What's the object's history? How old is the object? Where did it come from? Who created it? Who owned it before now?
3. What supernatural power(s) does the object have?
4. How are these powers activated or accessed?
5. What limitations does the object have?

Writing the Paranormal Novel

SUPERNATURAL PEOPLE

You can also introduce a supernatural person. Does "person" have to mean "human"? Certainly not. The term *person* has a pretty broad definition in a paranormal book, but in this section I'm going to stick with mostly human-shaped people. (We'll talk about creatures later.)

As with supernatural objects, you can't just drop a supernatural character into a book without thinking carefully first. Even normal people carry around a certain amount of baggage—family history, likes, hates, hobbies, inconvenient food allergies, and so on. But supernatural people carry around an entire *ecology*. They eat, drink, sleep, and otherwise exist differently than ordinary folk. And just as with supernatural objects, you need to work out your supernatural person's abilities, complete with boundaries and limitations. Once that's done, you need to stay within those boundaries in order to play fair with the reader. Your werewolf, for example, can't spontaneously develop the ability to shoot death rays from his eyes because that ability traditionally has nothing to do with wolves or shape-shifting or being a werecreature. Yes, this is the paranormal, and nothing will stop you from creating such a werewolf, but this will probably mess with your readers' heads, and not in a good way—they may very well toss your book aside. Why? Because you aren't playing fair. (More on this in chapter seven.)

Supernatural people get to have unique motivations for their actions. This can make them both more fun and more challenging, since you have to think outside the normal human box. Immortals don't worry about death (though they may worry about being killed) and have a rather different idea of what "a long time" means. Paranormals who feed on humans or otherwise depend on humans to exist may look at people as cattle, as possessions to be protected, or as prey that might turn dangerous. Paranormals who haven't interacted with humans before the book opens may be mystified by human behavior, treat humans with condescension, or even be frightened of them. Paranormals who used to be human (such as newly minted werewolves or vampires) are often torn between embracing their new nature and hanging on to their more familiar humanity. Truly powerful paranormals may not realize that humans are sentient—or even notice humans at all.

A supernatural person who falls in love with an ordinary human is such a powerful image that it spawned an entire genre: the paranormal romance. Stephenie Meyer may have gone mega-platinum with her YA *Twilight* novels, but Dracula obsessed over Mina Harker a hundred years before Edward and Bella appeared on the scene, and Cupid fell for Psyche nearly two thousand years before that. How to write a paranormal romance would be an entire book in itself, but in short, the conflict often arises between the clash of worlds. One lover is a being of some power, often immortal, who moves in a world that is hostile or even deadly to normal people, and the other lover is an ordinary human who will one day age and die. The story revolves around how these two will reconcile their difficulties so they can be together.

When it comes to building your book, you have several types of supernatural people to choose from. They include (but are not limited to):

Vampires

The perennial favorite. The modern versions usually owe quite a lot to Bram Stoker's novel *Dracula*. Stoker himself seems to have combined fairy lore (the blood-sucking leanan sídhe), history (Vlad the Impaler), and ancient vampire lore to create his famous villain. Vampires traditionally shun sunlight, holy objects, and garlic, and need to drink human blood to live. They are immortal unless killed, usually by a stake through the heart, decapitation, or dismemberment. (Fantasy author Terry Pratchett has noted that all of these work nicely on non-vampires as well.) They usually have supernatural powers that range from super strength to invisibility to mental telepathy to shape-shifting.

Vampires started off as bad guys, but in recent decades, more and more authors have swung around to using them as protagonists. As creatures of the night—or cloudy days, in the case of *Twilight's* Edward Cullen—vampires are often portrayed as mysterious, sexy, and powerful with a strangely vulnerable side, since they can still die. Or fall in love.

When you write about vampires, you need to work out in advance exactly what they can and cannot do. The checklist below may help:

THE VAMPIRE CHECKLIST

POWERS

- ___ Extra strength
- ___ Extra speed
- ___ Shape-shifting
    - ___ Bat
    - ___ Wolf
    - ___ Mist
    - ___ Other: _____
- ___ Enhanced senses
- ___ Mesmerism
- ___ Resistance to physical damage
- ___ Flight
- ___ Wall climbing
- ___ Teleportation
- ___ Leaping
- ___ Claws
- ___ Can create new vampires
- ___ Self-healing
- ___ Telepathy
- ___ Animal control
- ___ Weather control
- ___ Immortal
- ___ Inhumanly handsome/beautiful
- ___ Other: _____

WEAKNESSES

___ Repelled by holy objects

___ Repelled by garlic (or other strong scent)

___ Must feed on blood

    ___ How often: _____

    ___ Only from a living human

    ___ Can feed on animal blood

    ___ Can feed on stored blood

___ Effect when can't get blood: _____

___ Can be hurt or killed by

    ___ Dismemberment

    ___ Decapitation

    ___ Stake through the heart

    ___ Silver

    ___ Sunlight

    ___ Fire

    ___ Other: _____

___ Can't cross running water

___ Can't see reflection in a mirror

___ Image can't be captured (photo, video, etc.)

___ Comatose during the day

___ Can't enter a home without being invited

___ Can't enter hallowed ground

___ Must rest on earth from homeland

___ Inhumanly ugly

___ Other: _____

You also need to know whether these rules apply to *all* vampires in your world or just some of them. Perhaps older vampires have fewer weaknesses and more strengths, for example, or perhaps a vampire can overcome weaknesses temporarily, especially if he's just had a big meal.

Vampires are a challenge to write about. Why? Readers may love reading about them, but the bookstores are already saturated with vampire novels. The difficulty lies in coming up with something new to say. Did you see that "Other" space in the Vampire Checklist? Don't leave it blank. Try going back to the original folklore for ideas. Plenty of nocturnal paranormal creatures out there have a hankering for human blood.

Another way to be creative is to make an unlikely character into a vampire. Instead of the usual Handsome Man or Sexy Woman or Goth Kid getting the fang, go for a different type. What about a vampire accountant? Or a vampire ranch worker? Or a vampire circus clown? Lucienne Diver's vampires made a fashion-obsessed high school girl and her chess geek boyfriend into bloodsucking undead in *Vamped* with great success. Her vampires' powers and weaknesses don't depart too far from the established folklore, but her characters are fresh and new, and that makes all the difference.

Angels and Demons

They come to Earth to steal our hearts or terrify our souls. Sometimes it's both at the same time. As agents of divine or infernal powers, they were taboo as protagonists for a long time, but lately they've been showing up as main characters in more and more novels.

A demon appears in the mortal realm, often with some sort of terrible task, but then it discovers it wants to stay here, either because it's fallen in love or because things are much more interesting here on Earth than in Hell. Some demons are trying to escape Hell, or earn their freedom from it. Many are shape-shifters, able to take on animal shapes or any human form.

Angels often finds themselves in the same situation, but mirror-reversed—sent down to Earth to accomplish some divine duty, only to realize that life down here is more diverting than in Heaven. Some angels have been cast out and need to earn their way back home.

The fun of using an angel or demon comes from mixing shades of gray. Angels and demons are supposed to be creatures of pure good or pure evil. Putting them on Earth, where almost nothing is absolute, taints their purity and forces them to deal with it, an endlessly fascinating device for writers and readers alike.

Angels and demons of folklore have an enormous variety of powers and limitations. There's simply no standard angel or demon. This means you can give them any ability you like, but it also means it's vitally important to set the limitations and stick with them.

Zombies

Zombies are enjoying a new life, so to speak. They started off as mindless monsters under the control of an evil magician, then evolved into brain-eating hordes, and have recently become . . . good guys?

The main challenge of writing zombie good guys is the ick factor. Zombies are walking, rotting corpses that eat human flesh, and it's hard to empathize with something like that. Stacey Jay gets around this by playing it for laughs in *You Are So Undead to Me*, in which a high school girl discovers she's a "Settler," someone who can end the unresolved problems that bring the dead shambling from their graves.

The other factor zombie authors have to think about is how zombies are made—and destroyed. In original folklore, they were raised by a voudon (voodoo, vodoun) sorcerer in a complicated ritual. Their main weakness (other than a bad smell and an inability to heal wounds) was salt. Flinging a handful on a zombie would de-animate it, melt it, or otherwise destroy it. Since then, other ways to create zombies have cropped up—disease, radiation, poisons, meteor strikes, even nanotechnology—and each version has its own weaknesses. Often a chainsaw is involved. Although the movie version has been around for quite some time, this type of supernatural character is a relative newcomer to paranormal novels with lots of potential to explore.

Shape-shifters

There's something irresistible about being able to change shapes. Shape-shifters get to release the inner beast and do cool things in animal shape even as they roil in angst over what terrible deeds they may have wrought. They are forced to cross the thin line between human and animal, and often face the unsettling discovery that releasing the beast brings rather more enjoyment than it should.

Werecreatures are the cursed version of shape-shifters. They *must* change shape under certain conditions. When in the cursed shape, the beast takes control, and the human side has little or no memory of what happens. Early on, many werecreatures have no idea what's happening to them, or even that they carry the curse. Some even join the hunt for the terrible beast that's begun rampaging through the town.

The most famous of these beasts is the werewolf, a human who becomes a ravenous wolf on nights of the full moon. Werewolf folklore varies. Some people become werewolves on purpose by living an evil life or through a complicated magical ritual. Others are bitten by a werewolf and accidentally become one. And some are born into werewolf families, such as the Heerkens family in *Blood Trail* by Tanya Huff. Although werewolves have the advantage of familiarity—there's less to explain and the reader is more willing to come along for the ride—they have the disadvantage of being overly familiar ground, meaning you'll have to work a little harder to make your werewolf interesting.

But there's no reason to stay solely with wolves. In her Anita Blake books, Laurell K. Hamilton uses a number of different werecreatures, including lions, tigers, leopards, rats, foxes, hyenas, jaguars, snakes, and even swans. This is the paranormal—pick an animal and run with it.

Other shape-shifters aren't actually cursed like werecreatures. They can simply take one or more animal shapes at will. Selkies from Irish and Scottish folklore are seals that change into humans, for example. They sometimes fall in love with ordinary mortals, but eventually return to the sea, leaving a sorrowful husband or wife behind. The Manitou from Peter Straub's *Ghost Story* is an evil shape-shifter that can take many forms, as can Mulgarath, the ogre villain from The Spiderwick Chronicles books by Holly Black and Tony DiTerlizzi.

Shape-shifters often have abilities beyond changing shape. Their human forms might have the sharp senses of an animal, for example, and their animals forms are often bigger, faster, and stronger than a normal animal of the same kind. Other shape-shifters can command animals from their own species. Laurell K. Hamilton's werewolves can force normal wolves to do their bidding, for example. Notice, however, that these powers usually have something to do with the type of animal involved. It wouldn't make sense to have a wereswan that can turn coal into diamonds, though you could probably get away with one that could learn to fly in human form, since swans have flying ability.

The primary idea to remember with shape-shifters is that, like all supernatural characters, they need to have limitations. If your werewolves are fast and strong and smart and impossible to kill, why don't they rule over the puny humans of the world? Answer: They have debilitating weaknesses that prevent it. Hamilton's werewolves can change form at will, but they need a lot of food right after they've changed, and when they return to human form, they fall comatose—easy prey for enemies. To make things even more challenging, werecreatures who spend too much time as animals find it difficult to regain human form. You need to make sure your own shape-shifters have good reason to stay in the shadows—unless you're writing about a world ruled by shape-shifters.

Fairies

Fairies cover a wide range of supernatural people, including elves, dwarves, brownies, dryads, gnomes, kobolds, goblins, merfolk, trolls, and more. They are often long-lived or outright immortal, and usually visit the human world from some other realm. Often, they don't change, and chaotic, ever-shifting humans fascinate them.

Fairies are similar to angels and demons in that they come in many shapes and forms, depending on their original folklore, and each type of fairy usually has its own powers and weaknesses. A leprechaun must give anyone who captures him a wish. Greedy dwarves create amazing magical objects. Trolls are strong but stupid, and they turn to stone in daylight.

Beautiful, immortal elves often fail to understand brutish, short-lived humans. Non-European cultures have fairies as well. In Japan, the mischievous *kitsune*, or fox spirit, loves practical jokes. *Tennyo* live on mountaintops and fascinate mortals with their impossible beauty. *Yosei* can change into swans and cranes.

European fairies usually fear iron and sunlight, which either cripple or kill them. There are any number of other ways mortals can ward them off, including turning their clothes inside-out, striking a church bell, or getting drunk. Often mortals who encounter fairies forget the incident later, or remember it only as a dream. Raymond E. Feist uses fairies as antagonists in a modern setting to marvelous effect in his book *Faerie Tale.*

Numerous books have used elves as major characters. Legolas in Tolkien's *The Lord of the Rings* is perhaps the most famous example, and Margaret Weis and Tracy Hickman created Tanis, a half-elven, half-human protagonist, for their Dragonlance fantasy series. Anyone who wants to use an elf as a main character will be inevitably compared to these two. To get around this, Mercedes Lackey took elves out of their traditional fantasy setting and used them as race car drivers in the SERRAted Edge series she wrote with various co-authors. The new setting and new plot went a long way toward reinvigorating an old trope. Hint hint.

And the Rest

Humans have been spinning supernatural people into their stories for thousands of years, and listing all possible types would take an encyclopedia. Ultimately, *any* supernatural person can become a character in a novel as long as you remember three cardinal rules:

1. You must know exactly what your supernatural person can do.
2. You must know exactly what your supernatural person's limitations are.
3. If you bend or break Rule 1 or Rule 2, be sure it makes sense within the mythology you've created.

And always remember that the *character,* not the magic, should be the central focus of your book. Readers want stories about people, not empty animal skins. We'll look more closely at creating well-rounded characters in chapter six.

SUPERNATURAL CREATURES

If your book can't exist without a particular fantastic beastie, you're writing about a supernatural creature. They tend to take over because they're so much fun. Supernatural creatures are distinguished from supernatural people by the amount of self-awareness. If your griffin can hold a conversation and ask where to have lunch, it's more of a person. The dragons in Naomi Novik's books are really people, for example, not beasts.

Supernatural creatures come in a variety of forms, though certain creatures show up all over the world. All cultures tell stories about dragons and giants, for some reason. Terry Pratchett points out that if turtles live on a particular continent, at least one culture there will tell stories about the world living on a turtle's back. Witches take familiars. Sorcerers summon elementals. Some creatures are just slightly more intelligent versions of their real-world counterparts, such as the owls that deliver mail and run other errands in J.K. Rowling's Harry Potter books, and other creatures are more outlandish, such as the manticore in Greek mythology.

Supernatural creatures seem to come in a couple of flavors:

Kind Helpers

These creatures are here to help our hero. They are healers or guides or protectors. They may be operating on their own or at the behest of someone else. Unlike supernatural characters, they can't communicate very well, and their help may be more instinctive than purposeful.

As a downside, the presence of a kind helper may be inconvenient. Byron the griffin in The Spiderwick Chronicles books is a powerful guardian for the children, but the kids are forced to find creative ways to hide and feed him, since a creature with a lion's body and eagle's wings would attract unwelcome attention from the authorities. This can be played for comedy or for serious conflict, depending on the tone your book is going for.

Malevolent Monsters

These creatures are out for our hero's blood. They may be working on their own, or for the villain. In more horrific stories, they may show up as hordes of single-minded animals like the weird toads in Stephen King's short story "Rainy Season." Or they might be single creatures intent on destruction, as we've seen in any number of slay-the-monster books or in the semi-intelligent Bad Thing in Raymond E. Feist's *Faerie Tale*.

The main concern in dealing with creatures of either stripe is figuring out their ecology. What do they eat and how do they get it? Do certain noises or other stimuli make them react in a particular (or awkward) way? Is your creature a pack animal or a loner? What are the form and function of various body parts? Meat eaters, for example, will have teeth (or a beak) to reflect their diet, as will plant eaters. Any creature can have claws, but herbivores usually use them for something other than fighting—digging, climbing, scratching in the dirt, etc. A good way to "build" a creature is to decide what normal animal it most closely resembles and use that as a starting point.

It *is* true that supernatural creatures might depart from the rules of nature, and readers will let you get away with it. The laws of physics simply won't let a horse grow a set of wings big enough to let it fly, but no one minds. Impossible fire-breathing dragons have become such a staple—or cliché—that some authors have their dragons breathe something else, such as ice or acid, and readers happily come along for the ride. Some authors even have fun with explaining how weird abilities work. Terry Pratchett's odd little dragons in *Guards! Guards!* eat coal and, due to a buildup of internal flammable gasses, occasionally explode. There's no reason you can't—or shouldn't—indulge in a little magical Darwinism yourself. Still, your reader's suspension of disbelief will only stretch so far. You'll have a difficult time convincing people that your slow, bumbling plant eater would need a mouthful of fangs.

GATEWAYS TO SUPERNATURAL WORLDS

If your life in this world grinds you down, escape into another one. Humans have fantasized about magical gateways for thousands of years. Stonehenge is living proof of that. The idea of a door that can transport you to a wildly different, fascinating new world is all but irresistible. The most famous of stories in this category of supernatural elements is C.S. Lewis's The Chronicles of Narnia series, in which various children find their way from 1940s England into the magical world of Narnia. Peter Straub and Stephen King flip Jack Sawyer back and forth between our world and the Territories in *The Talisman*. We all know about Dorothy's tornado in L. Frank Baum's *The Wonderful Wizard of Oz* and Alice's rabbit hole. You could also argue that any number of time-travel romances use this idea.

When the author uses this element, a character from our world steps through a gateway or is otherwise transported into another world, and the reader gets to come along. The character spends a certain amount of time figuring out where she is, how this strange new world works, and why she's there. Usually some sort of goal appears—defeat the villain, rescue someone important, restore order, etc. Toward the end, a major element of suspense arises: How will the character return home? Perhaps the gate only opens at certain times or under certain conditions, or the character needs a certain object to open the gate. Sometimes the suspense arises because the character has found romance or made close friends or otherwise found happiness in the new world, but the gate to the old one will close soon forever. Which world does she truly want?

There are great advantages for the author who writes this type of story. Since the main character is a total newbie to the fantasy world, the author has the perfect excuse to explain anything and everything. Conflict packs the story from the beginning. It lets the author create an entire new world from scratch. What's not to like?

There are challenges, however. Creating an entire world takes a lot of work, especially since you'll want to make the place as realistic (within the context) as possible. And you'll have to figure out exactly how the gate works. Is it a one-time thing or does it repeat? Does the gate stay open? If so, for how long? Can someone control it, or is it a "natural" phenomenon? If it can be reopened, how can this be accomplished? Can a traveler take anything with her through the gate, or does she arrive naked? If someone returns through the gate, does she arrive at the same place as she left? Has a similar amount of time passed, or has time done something else while the character is gone? Like everything else in your book, the gateway needs to be consistent with itself.

BECOMING AN ARCHITECT

A vampire and a werewolf fight a dragon for a magic ring while a demon tries to steal the fairy treasure and open the mystic gate. Or is that too much? How do you decide how much of the supernatural to include in your book?

It's really a matter of taste, of course. A single supernatural element can be enough to generate an entire novel. One magic character, a psammead who grants one wish per day, easily drives the plot of E. Nesbit's classic *Five Children and It*. At the opposite end of the spectrum are the Harry Potter books, which use every supernatural element imaginable.

There is a rule of thumb: *The more realistic you want your book to feel, the fewer supernatural elements you'll want to include.* It may sound counterintuitive to talk about realism and the supernatural in the same breath, but the rule makes a great deal of sense. Nesbit's five children get a single wish per day at the beginning of each chapter, and then spend the rest of the chapter dealing with the real-world ramifications of the wish. When they ask for gold, they have a hard time spending any of it because no adult believes that children their age would have so much money—a real-world problem. When they wish for wings, they have great fun at first, but then discover that other people are afraid of them. Robert wishes to be bigger than the local bully, but forgets that the adults back home will find him monstrous. The kids are often hot, hungry, or scared soon after each wish, and the novel is surprisingly gritty for an Edwardian-era children's book.

The five kids have access to one supernatural element, but their world is quite realistic. And that's what Nesbit is writing about—the intersection of the real world with the supernatural one. (A subtler theme in the book is that magic is forbidden and you monkey with it at your peril.)

On the other hand, J.K. Rowling rarely allows Harry to worry about food or clothes or money once he enters the wizarding world. The Hogwarts School of Witchcraft and Wizardry feeds its students to bursting, Harry is heir to a considerable fortune, and invisible house elves take care of the laundry. Even when Harry and Hermione go on the run in *Harry Potter and the Deathly Hallows*, they live in relative comfort in a magic tent. The few times normal people notice anything supernatural going on, agents from the Ministry of Magic wave their wands to make them forget all about it. Rowling doesn't even try to be realistic, but she doesn't need to—she isn't writing about how the real world intersects with the paranormal. She's writing about death, conflict with authority, and the search for immortality.

Also, the more elements you include, the less time you'll have to explore each one. If you want to create and explore an intricate culture of demons and angels, you'd best not include genies, werewolves, and vampires in your world. The more supernatural elements you include, the *less* you're actually writing about each one.

But world building is something we're taking up in the next chapter.

EXERCISE

Read the following mundane plots and add a supernatural element to each. Or, if you like, add more than one.

1. The ink has barely dried on Theresa Garibaldi's graduate degree when she gets the news—her ailing mother has died. Praying her elderly Toyota would hold it together for the cross-country trip, Theresa drives back to her childhood town for the funeral. Now temporarily ensconced in the tiny, cracker-box house

Writing the Paranormal Novel

she grew up in, Theresa begins the process of going through her mother's things. Stashed in a locked steel box in the attic crawl space, she is stunned to find a series of letters that reveal her mother was not her birth mother. She stares at the letter in disbelief as a loud knock pounds at the front door.

2. Robbie Graves, age thirteen, is a popular kid with a lot of friends. Well, actually they're acquaintances. Robbie feels he's never had a true friend. He's learned that a lot of kids think he's cool mostly because his dad is on that TV show. Last week, a family moved into that house on the edge of town. They're weird. They dress weird, they have weird haircuts, and they drive a car with weird stickers on it. And their daughter Thelmoline is weird, too. The kids in school pick on her, but Robbie likes her, and they become friends. But being friends with Thelmoline isn't easy. She says strange things. She disappears for days at a time, and then shows up at school with no explanation of where she was. And she spends most of her time in a tree house she built herself in her backyard. Robbie sets out to find what's wrong.

3. Ingrid Fell swears a pact with her best friend Helen—they won't date for thirteen months because men suck. They even sign a contract. Not even an hour later, Ingrid slams straight into the most breathtaking guy she's ever seen. He helps her up with profuse apologies and introduces himself as Lucas, but everyone calls him Lucky. It turns out Lucky is moving into the apartment just up the hall from Ingrid, so she runs into him often. And every time she does, something good happens. She chats with him while picking up her mail and finds her tax refund. She runs into him at the store and wins fifty dollars in groceries. She pauses to talk to him at the coffee shop and hears the DJ announce the thirteenth caller will win free concert tickets, so she dials—and

wins. Lucky is handsome, nice, and a great guy. Even worse, every time Ingrid sees Lucky, he asks her out, but the contract hovers over Ingrid's head. How long can she refuse?

4. Greg Travers isn't a private investigator. Not really. But he does have a knack for helping people solve their problems. He can't seem to turn anyone down, either—if someone asks for help, he has to ride to the rescue. One Saturday morning, Greg is looking forward to a day of sweats, pizza, and video games when Pete, an old college buddy, shows up, unshaven and smelling like a sewer. He needs a place to stay for a few days. Greg can't bring himself to refuse. That night, a terrible commotion wakes up Greg. He rushes into the living room where Pete was sleeping on the couch. He's just in time to see Pete being dragged away by two strange men. One draws a gun and fires at Greg, who dives for cover.

CHAPTER 3:
The Paranormal at Large

Nothing can exist in a vacuum. Not even the paranormal. This means that you can't plunk Ranadar the Elf into your story without figuring a few things out. First of all, it doesn't seem very likely that Ranadar is the only elf in existence. (Even if he is, he still had to come from *somewhere*.) And if other elves exist, it seems likely they'd interact in some way, which at least hints at a society. If that's the case, what kind of society do elves have? Who, if anyone, is in charge? Do they have gender roles—or even gender? Do they form family groups? What is elven etiquette like? And, most importantly, how do elves fit into the rest of the world?

To take this a little further, the existence of elves may indicate that other magical races exist. What about pixies, goblins, sprites, and gnomes? Is one of these races more powerful than the others? How do they get along? Do they trade with each other? Speak the same language?

In other words, if elves run Poughkeepsie, does that mean dwarves rule Pittsburgh?

We'll start with the big questions and work downward to the smaller ones.

SECRET VS. SUNLIGHT

The first issue to resolve is whether the supernatural in your world is a secret force or if it's a well-known phenomenon. Which one you choose will have an enormous impact on your book.

THE SECRET SUPERNATURAL

This is the most common paranormal world, especially in a modern Earth setting. Magic and supernatural creatures remain hidden to most normal people, and the majority of the population spends its entire life completely unaware that magic is real. Meanwhile, a small group of people moves within hidden supernatural circles. Often, the protagonist is a normal person who discovers these supernatural circles and is drawn into the secret world. In darker books, the supernatural controls the mundane world in a super-secret conspiracy.

This setting has a built-in draw. The world starts off comfortable and familiar—it's ours, after all—until the author whisks the lid off her metaphorical cookie jar, revealing an enticing treasure within. The reader feels pulled into "the know" and is made special right along with the protagonist. The most famous secret world setting is, of course, in J.K. Rowling's Harry Potter books, but a horde of other authors compete for the title: C.S. Lewis, Stephenie Meyer, and many, many others.

The secret supernatural is also, in some ways, the easiest setting to use. You're not changing the normal world at all. It carries on as normal, since it knows nothing of what's really going on. Sure, vampires may be secretly running the FBI, but everything *looks* normal. Cars, phones, TV shows, computers, schools—all are unchanged. A fair amount of conflict in these stories revolves around ensuring everything *stays* normal. After all, if the general public found out vampires were real and sucking blood . . . well, there are a lot more mortals than vampires, and mortals can walk around in daylight. They also have tanks and other inconvenient weapons that can wipe out public vampires. Other magical creatures and people are in the same boat—forced to keep things quiet lest a much more powerful government or powerful corporation should get hold of them and their powers.

Secret History

A variant of the secret setting is the secret history setting. Here, we're operating in the historical past—ancient Ireland, colonial America, the Ming

Dynasty of China—with a twist: Magic works and has incorporated itself into history as we know it. The Seelie and Unseelie Courts really battled over Ireland. Witches wreaked havoc in Salem. Dragons secretly ruled behind the Chinese throne. But somewhere along the line, magic faded, resulting in the world we know now, and no one these days seriously believes those old stories. This is a fun one to play with, too. For example, maybe William, Duke of Normandy conquered England in 1066 so readily because he had supernatural help that history didn't record. Keeping things consistent with what we know of history while telling a paranormal story makes for a satisfying challenge. C.C. Finlay does a beautiful job of secret history with his Traitor to the Crown books, set during the Revolutionary War.

THE SUNLIT SUPERNATURAL

The contrasting idea is to blow the supernatural all out into the open. Paranormals operate in the bright of day—those who can, anyway. Everyone knows about magic and magical creatures, and they're simply a part of everyday life.

This world takes a little more work. You'll need to figure out a number of factors, most notably the impact of your supernatural elements on history and culture. To do this, we'll need to back up a little bit.

Old vs. New

Actually, this is something to consider in a secret setting as well. You'll need to know if supernatural elements have always existed in your world (*old*) or if they were introduced some time later (*new*).

In an *old* setting, humans have always had access to magic, and/or supernatural creatures have always lived in their world, perhaps in secret, perhaps out in the sunlight. You'll have to decide what supernatural elements exist, of course (check chapter two), and work out the impact on history and culture. You might decide to keep things as close to our own history as possible by deciding that if all the major movers and shakers in history had access to magic, everything would come out pretty much the same, but still sneak in a few fun surprises for the reader. Maybe Ben Franklin was actually a dwarf, explaining his almost casual propensity for invention, and hotheaded Andrew Jackson had some goblin blood in him.

Or you can plunge ahead and alter history hugely. When Orson Scott Card wrote his Tales of Alvin Maker books, set in Colonial America, he made enormous changes to American history by giving the Native Americans enough magical power to keep the Europeans on the eastern side of the Appalachian Mountains. Since he didn't write anything past that time period, however, he didn't have to worry about what impact all this would have on the twenty-first century.

In a more modern context, Piers Anthony uses the idea that magic and science evolved side by side in his Incarnations of Immortality series. So does Philip Pullman in the His Dark Materials trilogy. In this kind of world, people are just as likely to have a magic carpet as a gas-powered car, magic wands are as common as guns, sorcerers compete with senators for political power, and no one bats an eye.

We get a *new* supernatural setting when some sort of event introduces a supernatural element into the world for the first time—or for the first time in living memory. The Apocalypse is coming for real, and as a result, demons and angels are walking the Earth again. Some fool opens a gate sealed by Solomon himself, awakening True Magic once again. Two orphans find the only dragon left in the world and wake her from her thousand-year slumber. This setting forces not only the protagonist but the entire world to deal with the new supernatural element.

PERSECUTED, EQUAL, OR SUPERIOR?

Humans divide the world into "me" and "not me," "mine" and "not mine." Out of this divide, we ultimately get family ties, property rights, and war. None of this would change in a world where the paranormal is natural. It's difficult to imagine a new world in which many sentient species would get along perfectly well, when the single sentient species on *this* world can't even get along with itself. So if you're writing in a setting in which humans share a world with nonhuman sentient beings such as elves or vampires, you'll have to work out how well the various factions get along—or don't. And you'll need to work out what the hierarchy is.

Persecuted

In this kind of world, the paranormals are a persecuted minority, a species that humans hate and/or fear and want to exterminate, enslave, or otherwise control. (Perhaps deservedly so.) This seems to be the most likely outcome if, say, vampires were revealed to the world. It doesn't feel likely that any government would want bloodsucking murderers to wander freely within their borders.

Perhaps the paranormals live in their own strictly controlled enclaves, or are flat-out imprisoned. They might also live among the ruling humans as servants or slaves. Or maybe they're hidden, always on the run. (This last one works out well in a secret supernatural world as well.) Stephen King's *Firestarter* is based on this idea.

Equal

Another possibility is that paranormals are considered largely equal to humans. This sort of setting raises a great many considerations. Do the paranormals live side by side with humans, or do they have their own neighborhoods/cities/countries? How do humans interact with their supernatural neighbors? Does everyone get along fairly well, or does tension exist? What role do the different species play in the government? The legal system? The educational system? Entertainment?

Obviously, this setting requires a fair amount of world building. J.K. Rowling does quite a lot of it with her Harry Potter books, and the magical side of her world often seems more real than the mundane side.

Superior

The paranormals have taken over. Humans exist as a subjugated class, perhaps in a post-apocalyptic setting. The conflict will probably revolve around a human trying to expel the paranormals, escape them, or otherwise find a way out from under the thumb of the supernatural rulers.

Robin McKinley wrote *Sunshine* with such a setting. In her book, voodoo wars have decimated the human population, and vampires control a large chunk of the world. Other supernatural creatures control the rest of it, and the few remaining humans are caught in the middle. This setting is fun to explore because humans are normally supposed to win and stop the paranormals from taking over, but this type of book assumes the opposite, that humans have already lost and are now just trying to hang on.

CULTURE

Put two people (or beings) together for an extended period, and they'll create a culture. Assuming any supernatural people you create aren't unique or extremely widespread, they'll create a culture, too. This applies to worlds where the supernatural is a secret and to worlds where the supernatural sits in the sunlight. Since culture helps determine behavior, you'll need to settle a few cultural details about your paranormals so you can predict how they'll behave. Besides, readers love watching a character who is introduced to the supernatural world by being thrust into it (such as someone who is turned into a vampire and discovers an entire hidden world of them) and who has to learn about this new way of life the hard way.

Creating a culture for your paranormals will also lend richness and depth to your supernatural characters. When the reader first encounters your werewolves, for example, they may behave strangely or unexpectedly, but they'll behave *consistently*. This is because you, the author, have a deep understanding of their culture and have figured out why they're acting so strangely from a human perspective.

Imagine an elf who had never seen a human before somehow arrives in a human household just in time for a very strange sight. The parents spread fat and sugar over a rounded pastry, set it on fire, and place it right in front of their young daughter. (Isn't that dangerous?) Everyone sings a ritual song, and then the girl extinguishes the flames by blowing them out. (Isn't she spreading disease?) The pastry is divided up, and everyone eats it. How strange!

An author who created the scene would know perfectly well what everything is for and what is happening. The reader would find this culture strange and compelling, continue reading to find out what the deal is, and eventually learn the significance of the cake and candles. Next year, when the birthday came around again, the reader (now in the know) would know what to expect and understand why everything was done.

An enormous number of elements make up a culture, more than we can explore here, but in general you'll want to consider at least eight primary elements when creating a culture.

GOVERNMENT

Sure, the local humans may live under a particular government, and the paranormals may go along with it, but that doesn't mean the paranormals wouldn't also have their own rulers who enforce their own laws. In a secret supernatural world, the paranormals may hold mortal law in contempt as something to be flouted or ignored. Or they may find it an inconvenience to be skirted. Or they may see it as an outright threat. On the other hand, paranormals in a sunlit supernatural world may be an open part of the legal process.

Regardless, someone has to be in charge of your supernatural world. If your paranormals choose their leader or leaders, they use a *democracy*—and you'll have to decide how these leaders are chosen. If your paranormals live under the rule of a single person, they have a *dictatorship*, whether the leader is evil or benign. (Lord Vetinari of Terry Pratchett's Discworld books is a prime example of a benign dictator.) If a single group of people remains in charge all the time, such as an eternal council or single political party, you have a *totalitarian* government. A *monarchy* uses a single ruler who keeps the power within one family. In a *parliamentary* system, the people choose members of a political party to rule. In a *republic,* citizens vote for leaders to rule for a limited time.

There are many others. A *gynarchy* is rule by women only. An *oligarchy* is rule by a tiny elite. *Plutocracy* is rule by the rich. *Feudalism* combines monarchy with a dash of oligarchy, and mixes in a dollop of rule by the warrior class. The *rule of law* sets the law itself as the supreme power in the land.

Even small groups have governments, though they might not realize it. Look at families. Some are oligarchies, run by Mom and Dad. Some are gynarchical dictatorships, run by Grandma, who makes sure all branches of the family stay in line. And some are republics, giving even the children a voice in what happens. So if your paranormals have any kind of group identity, it's quite likely they'll have some kind of government, complete with a leader or leaders, however informal.

As the author/creator, you should know how this ruling body is selected. You can use all the usual tools available to modern humans—election, right of birth, ballot stuffing—but let your paranormals add their own twist. A "fight to the finish" might mean a *real* fight. The term *dictator for life* holds powerful connotations when the dictator—and his subjects—are immortal. European folklore, for example, holds that King Oberon and Queen Maeve rule the fair folk forever, and they appear in a number of modern paranormal novels, including Raymond E. Feist's *Faerie Tale*.

Additionally, this person or group will create laws, which must then be enforced. This might be done through simple peer pressure or by a draconian police force. You probably won't need to work out every single rule or law that governs your paranormals, but work out enough so you know what restrictions your people work under—and how these laws will affect their behavior. For example, your mortal protagonist may be startled to discover that his new vampire girlfriend won't kill, or even nibble on, the muggers who try to knife them in a dark alley one night, even though she clearly has the strength of a small freight train. Only later does he learn that the Vampire Council has declared harming mortals a capital crime, since vampires need to avoid mortal scrutiny. As the author, of course, you knew this from the beginning.

ECONOMY

Economy is based on ownership—who owns what (or whom). You probably learned in high school that we have three kinds of ownership. In a *capitalist* system, citizens own their own businesses and property and must buy what they need from each other. In a *socialist* system, the government provides most of the bigger services such as education and health care, and citizens own everything else. In a *communist* system, the government owns nearly everything, including housing and food production. In a *stewardship* system, all ownership is temporary; the world owns everything. If you can come up with a fifth kind for your paranormals to live under, use it. You'll probably win an award. But economics don't stop there.

In an openly supernatural world, you may have to deal with the idea that different species find value in different things. Elves traditionally don't care about money, but do value undeveloped land—and the natural beauty that comes with it. Dwarves care about nothing but precious metals that they can work. And we all know what vampires want.

In other words, economics are about more than money. Economics are about resources and how they are distributed. Resources can be physical objects like food, clothing, cars, wood, and computers, or they can be intangibles, such as services and diplomatic favors. Terry Pratchett and Neil Gaiman worked out a very strange barter economy between heaven and hell in their book *Good Omens* when both sides understood that infernal corruption and divine inspiration were both going to happen no matter what, and there was no reason for angels and demons to inconvenience each other. If a demon realized he was going to be on the same side of town where a mortal was scheduled to be inspired for a good deed, the demon could happily take care of it, provided his angelic counterpart was willing to make a man covet his neighbor's wife for a moment or two while the demon was tied up in traffic. The cosmic balance is maintained, angels and demons keep their schedules with a minimum of fuss, and everybody wins.

Different species have different desires—and access to different resources—which can make for an interesting economy. What might vampires be willing to pay for dwarven blood? If elves play the most beautiful music ever heard, what would humans do in order to attend a concert?

Might a modern-day dragon hoard classic cars instead of gold? Working with these elements adds depth and reality to your supernatural world.

SPIRITUALITY

Spirituality is a powerful force in the real world, and there's no reason it shouldn't be one for your paranormals. This isn't to say that your werewolves must all worship the moon goddess and bow to a complex pantheon of forest spirits. But you *should* at least be aware of how your paranormals view eternity. Immortals don't fear old age, but many of them can still die, and they have a long time to think about what might happen afterward. Some paranormals have firsthand experience at it. Others—angels and demons leap to mind—have their origins in spirituality, and in that case, you need to know exactly how the spirituality works.

Spirituality also lays down rules for behavior, which in turn develops character. Rules about good and evil, marriage, sex partners, treatment of children, religious rituals—all these and more are dictated by spirituality. There's often overlap with government.

Finally, you'll need to know your individual character's *attitude* toward spirituality. Fundamentalists follow every spiritual rule and law with terrifying zeal, and might even kill in the name of spirituality. At the other end of the spectrum are characters who scoff at the very idea of a spiritual world, even in the face of the sort of evidence only a paranormal novel might provide. Most characters will probably exist somewhere in the middle, but you need to know where they land.

FAMILY AND COMMUNITY

A paranormal novel is an excellent place to explore alternate family structures and the impact they can have on people. True, your paranormals may very well come from a family structure similar to humans, but there's no reason they have to.

Families have pecking orders, divisions of labor, customs, traditions, in-jokes, rivalries, oral histories, black sheep, and in-laws, and all of them can benefit from a supernatural twist. Tanya Huff took the idea of a wolf pack and merged it with a human family to get the very strange Heerkens clan in *Blood Trail*, for example. In her book, brothers and sisters grow up with a close, near-telepathic bond. But when the girls reach sexual maturity—and go into heat—the boys have to be sent away so their relationships don't become incestuous.

And *family* doesn't have to mean *birth family*. It can mean any group of people that interacts as a family would. Humans form family units through marriage, adoption, deep friendship, and even circumstance. When your main character wakes up as a vampire one evening, she may discover she's joined an extended clan of undead, whether she likes it or not.

Families band together to form communities with extended customs, traditions, conflicts, and friendships all their own. In a modern setting, these communities can keep in contact with each other easily enough through electronic means. Octavia E. Butler created a wide-reaching vampire-and-human community in *Kindred*. Her vampires both feed off and safeguard their humans, physically and financially, while maintaining an intricate set of relationships with each other. The entire book revolves around the main character's relationships within her community.

ART AND RECREATION

When people have spare time, they play around and make stuff. Supernatural people, especially the immortal ones, have a *lot* of spare time. What do they fill it with? Bored people with power become . . . dangerous.

Supernatural people who live within another culture might continue to use the recreation of the normal people around them, but how much fun can it be to play basketball against normals when you can jump fifteen feet into the air? Paranormals also may feel that the social boundaries laid down by mortals are unfair or simply don't apply to them, which has an impact on the sort of art they produce and the kind of recreation they enjoy. Art and recreation can be a piece of the background, such as the terrifying vampire theater in Anne Rice's novels, or it can become the center of the story, such as the magical wine making in Laura Anne Gilman's Vineart War books.

FOOD

Any foodie will tell you how culture and food feed each other. People eat what's available to them, which shapes their culture. The culture, in turn, shapes attitudes toward food. When new sources of nutrition show up, cultures integrate them according to already established cultural norms—or the people may simply refuse to eat them, based on their culture. Grasshoppers, for example, are perfectly edible for humans. Yet few Americans, who see insects as disgusting, are willing to eat them, while they're routinely enjoyed in Africa and Asia, where insects are seen as little snacks with wings.

Supernatural characters are famous for having rarified diets. Many of them hanker after human flesh or blood. Others simply need a *lot* of food. Feeding the dragons in Naomi Novik's *His Majesty's Dragon* and its sequels, for example, turns into a major problem. Will Laurence spends considerable time figuring out how to feed a growing—and ravenous—baby dragon when the infant Temeraire hatches unexpectedly at sea.

In the same book, we learn that English dragons eat their meat raw. Later in the series, Temeraire discovers that Chinese dragons enjoy meals prepared by high-class chefs. He acquires a taste for foreign cuisine and ultimately begins to realize how badly British dragons are treated compared to their Chinese counterparts. This leads him to try and start a revolt among English dragons, with Will Laurence as a reluctant cohort. And it all begins with food.

Your own book can benefit from addressing this issue. It goes beyond what paranormals eat. How the food is acquired is equally important, especially if the food is rare or valuable or considered strange by others. And some food (such as human blood) is illegal. Once food is acquired, someone must prepare it. Who? In human culture, women are largely in charge of food preparation. Is it the same among elves? In India among the Hindu, eating food prepared by someone from a lower caste makes the consumer impure. Do the fairies feel the same way about food prepared by humans? And, of course, many stories mention the hazards of eating supernatural food. Persephone is forced to stay in Hades after eating six pomegranate seeds, and mortals who consume food in the realm of the fair folk are doomed to remain there forever.

Eating has a culture all its own. Among humans, people consume their meals seated at low tables, perched on high stools, and lounging in front of a television. Formal meals of state are different from casual meals with family. Festival meals are special, with their own foods and traditions. And some foods are forbidden. Exploring the food rituals of your supernatural characters will enrich them, make them seem more real—and can also help move the plot forward.

TOOLS AND TECHNOLOGY

Okay, so you worked out what magical powers and limitations your weretigers have. You know they're powerful hand-to-claw fighters, they have to transform into tiger form once a month during the full moon, and can change into a man-tiger form the rest of the month, but only after sunset. You know that they're waging a constant underground war with an ancient clan of mummies that have secretly taken over New Haven, Connecticut, and there's going to be a major turf battle tomorrow night. Your weretiger protagonist, an information tech geek recently turned into a sexy werecreature, is both psyched and nervous because this fight will be his initiation into the Blood Stripe Clan.

So the question is, do the weretigers have grenade launchers?

Seriously. If the weretigers have underground contacts and they really want to take out the mummies once and for all, what's stopping them from getting their claws on a few well-placed grenades and wiping them out from a safe distance? Yes, I *know* you want to create tension, put your protagonist in danger, and move the story forward, but you've got a serious plot hole here. The technology for long-distance combat is widely available on modern Earth, and you've established the weretigers operate an underground war, meaning they'd have access to all kinds of illegal stuff. Giving them grenade launchers would only make sense. Or maybe the weretigers could hack into the mummies' computers and wreak havoc on their financial records, destroying their stranglehold on New Haven's government and rendering them vulnerable. Your information tech protagonist would certainly have the know-how. Why are your weretigers heading into an iffy face-to-face fight when modern society presents them with so many more surefire options?

You'll need to decide what technology your supernatural people have access to, either because they developed it themselves or because they live in a society that developed it for them (say, ours). Technology, remember, is any kind of tool, not just a piece of electronics. A rock becomes technology if you use it to crack a nut. And if your paranormals come from another world entirely, you'll need to decide what technology they developed.

Technology can be subdivided into *weapons, transportation, medicine, production,* and *communication.* There are other subdivisions, but these will do for our purposes.

Weapons

This includes both offensive and defensive tools. Body weaponry such as fists and claws are the most basic ones, and from there we progress to sticks, sharp sticks, stone blades, and metal blades. (Past that, and you're getting into science fiction—another topic entirely.) Projectile (thrown) weapons start with rocks and progress to spears, bows, crossbows, catapults, and eventually to chemical-driven projectiles such as bullets. And don't forget gunpowder, dynamite, plastique, nuclear bombs, and other explosives.

Many handheld weapons can also be used for defense—you can both attack and parry with a sword—but eventually it occurs to someone to invent the shield, then armor, then chainmail, and then Kevlar.

You'll need to know what weapons your supernatural people have access to—or are willing to use. It's quite possible your paranormals have a cultural aversion to a particular weapon. Perhaps the weretigers in the above example find killing enemies from a distance cowardly and dishonorable, a "weakness" the mummies intend to exploit.

Transportation

How do your paranormals get from Point A to Point B? In human cultures, foot travel always comes first. Water travel develops next, when it's available, and people who figure out how to domesticate large animals often realize they can ride—either on the animal or behind it. The invention of the wheel leads to the cart, and here the technology stops until someone figures out internal combustion, which allows automobiles to exist. Hot-air balloons and blimps appear on the scene at some point, along with airplanes and jets and the space shuttle.

Magical talents can jiggle this process at any point. It might not even occur to teleporters to ride slow, plodding animals. Paranormals who can fly might develop different methods of mass air travel quickly, or take advantage of airborne creatures. Naomi Novik's dragons try to fly almost before they can fully walk, for example, and their humans ride right along. Dragons transport messages, too, and are the backbone of the swift courier service.

Medicine

In the normal world, medical technology started with herbs and hope. It progressed to cloth bandages and stitches, then to germ theory and vaccines, and now it's gone into a dozen different directions: cloning, gene therapy, magnetic resonance imaging, laser surgery, silicone implants, Botox, and a thousand other inventions. Paranormals can change all that. They may be more or less fragile than humans. They may heal faster (always a plus if you want to hurt your hero but have him up and running a few pages later), which may inhibit medical research—why bother learning how to stitch wounds when they close on their own within moments? And some paranormals may be able to heal others magically, which might halt any desire to develop medical technology altogether.

On the other hand, your paranormals may be vulnerable to diseases or conditions that don't bother humans—and they might develop their own ways to get around it. After all, humans figure out how to solve many of life's problems, so why shouldn't intelligent paranormals? If sunlight fries your vampires, might polarized sunglasses and a good slathering of SPF 30 sunblock remedy the situation? Mercedes Lackey's elves in her SERRAted Edge books are poisoned by iron and steel, which makes driving a race car problematic for them. They solve this difficulty by using advanced plastics and special polymers in place of most of the metal. Your paranormals should be equally resourceful to be believable—unless they're supposed to be less intelligent than humans.

Production

How do people make stuff? Humans used to make everything individually, by hand. Then the production line was invented—and not by Henry Ford. The Egyptians used it in mummification thousands of years before Detroit was even founded. Later, machines added to—or took over—the production lines. Farms and animal husbandry were also affected. Hunting and gathering were replaced by small farms, which were replaced by large, industrial farms. Humans worked alone in the fields and hunting grounds at first, but then animals aided them, and finally machines arrived on the scene. The rise of mass production changed the face of the planet, bringing us to the edge of environmental disaster. You'll need to decide where your paranormals are on that continuum (though perhaps your people are wiser than we are).

This topic may seem boring, but it bears thinking about. Someone has to make that suit of armor, that magic wand, that cloak of invisibility. Are these items unique? Rare? Common? Mass-produced? What if your vampires figured out a way to raise humans in their version of a high-density feedlot? Applying principles of production to your book can open up entirely new plots or lines of thought.

Slavery

Another production issue to consider is slavery. Many cultures practice it. The availability of cheap, intelligent labor has a tremendous impact on a culture, and people who grow up with slaves—or *as* slaves—think very differently from people who grow up in emancipated cultures. If your paranormals view humans as a lesser species, they may very well keep humans as slaves, either openly (in a sunlight supernatural world) or on the black market (in a secret supernatural world).

Most people think of nineteenth-century American slavery when the concept comes up, but many other types of slavery exist. People once sold themselves into slavery to pay debts. There's temporary slavery, sometimes called *indentured servitude*. Ancient Greece maintained a series of laws about the treatment of slaves, including what they must be fed and how much they must be paid. Medieval European serfs were basically slaves who were tied to a place instead of a person.

Just as in reality, humans aren't above keeping slaves in paranormal fiction. Isn't Aladdin's genie his slave? And, as I've already pointed out, the English essentially enslave the dragons in Naomi Novik's books. Mercedes Lackey and Andre Norton explore the concept of paranormals and slavery in their Halfblood Chronicles books. A less-than-idyllic set of race relations creates conflict and tension, which leads to more interesting stories, so don't be afraid to introduce such problems.

Communication

The transmission of ideas and information has an enormous impact on culture. New ideas transform people, energize them, and motivate them. It's why dictators try so hard to control the flow of information. Communication started with the invention of language itself. Then came people who traveled from place to place, carrying information and ideas. Written language appeared. The printing press started up the idea of mass communication. The telegraph and telephone introduced instant long-distance communication. Radio and television trotted out long-distance mass communication. And then came the Internet . . .

Paranormals can add new wrinkles to communication and communication technology. Humans don't communicate much by scent, but animal-based paranormals might. Tanya Huff's werewolves use scent quite a bit in their communication. Stephenie Meyer—and many other authors before her—made her vampires telepathic. These possibilities have major ramifications on the story and you'll need to consider them in your own work.

Communication technology actually provides one of the thorniest problems for many authors. Although it may be fun and interesting to give your main character a telepathic bond with her pack mates, or arrange for your lovers to find a set of rings that let them hear each other's voices whenever they want, you'll have to address the issue of isolation. At some point, you'll probably want to isolate your protagonist and get her into severe trouble with no hope of rescue. If she has a telepathic bond/magic ring/cell phone, you'll need to explain why she can't simply shout for help. And no, I'm afraid claiming she's "too proud to call for assistance" won't carry you through—readers won't buy that one, especially in a life-or-death situation. There should be a compelling, believable reason why your character can't call her friends or the cops. (More on this in chapter seven.)

This, by the way, is why many modern authors spend enormous amounts of time creating characters who forget their cell phones, fail to recharge the batteries, wander out of service range, drop their phones, break them, lose them, or otherwise find themselves without a working connection. One little call to 911, and Pauline Peril's problems go *poof!* The same problem will apply to characters with a supernatural method of communication, so you'll need to build in reasons why Pauline can't call the cavalry. Perhaps the person at the other end can't "hear" her, or the magical power has a limited range, or her captor has a way to block the magical ability, or . . .

A Final Thought

Technology doesn't always develop evenly in all areas. The Egyptians, for example, developed fantastic methods of production, but their medical technology stagnated, mired down by tradition. Your supernatural people could quite conceivably come from a society that has advanced in one direction but slowed in another. We see slavery as a backward, primitive idea, for example, but other cultures see it as normal, even essential. Your fairies may be advanced healers who never developed writing and are puzzled by the very idea of "words that stay."

POP CULTURE

We've always had a popular culture. We just didn't know it until the 1960s. (The term "popular culture" actually dates back to World War II, but no one paid attention. We were rather occupied.) Pop culture changes people, and people change pop culture. The difference between pop culture and "regular" culture is that pop culture changes *fast*.

Assuming you've set your paranormal novel on some version of our world, you'll have two facets of pop culture to consider.

The Impact of Pop Culture on the Paranormal

Normal humans obsess over the latest episode of *Popular TV Show*. They listen to Popular Female Music Star. They connect with friends and family through Popular Social Network. Trends in clothing, hair, slang, movies, video games, and more surface, spread, and sink with devastating speed.

Why shouldn't paranormals experience the same thing? Vampires connect with potential blood donors online. Werewolf cubs argue hairstyles with their parents. Sirens sing rock music. Paranormals may well take things further and form their own pop culture. Fairies with the ability to fly might develop club dancing that goes beyond anything humans might conceive. Sorcerers with mind control powers might possess ordinary humans and wear them like suits of clothes, with certain types of people falling in and out of fashion. Young mediums (media?) develop their own subculture, complete with slang, while talking with dead teenagers. Esther Friesner edited a number of anthologies set in supernatural suburbia that explore these ideas, including *Witch Way to the Mall*, *Strip Mauled*, and *Fangs for the Mammaries*, if you want to see some examples in short stories.

The Impact of the Paranormal on Pop Culture

The essence of pop culture is its malleability—and there's no way to predict what might mold it next. The public's attention is notoriously fickle.

Today's hot trend is tomorrow's bargain bin. Remember boy bands? Beanie Babies? The Macarena?

In a secret supernatural world, magical elements may be behind a given idea's popularity. Who's to say fairies weren't quietly boosting Tickle Me Elmo? And perhaps the "I've fallen and I can't get up" commercial was an unconscious reference to werewolves and their prey. Anne Rice, of course, put her vampire on stage in a popular rock band in *The Vampire Lestat,* creating a fictional music sensation that bled over into the real world for a short time.

In a sunlit supernatural world, you can easily imagine the impact of the paranormal on pop culture. Although there might be much to fear from the supernatural, people would also flock to it, especially if it turned out to have good fashion sense. Music, TV shows, movies, food—all these industries and more would rush to incorporate cool supernatural elements into themselves if such elements revealed themselves to the world. Can you imagine real-life fairies showing up and McDonald's *not* using them to promote their Happy Meals? Me neither.

One way to explore the ramifications is simply to take an element of modern culture and add the supernatural. The fashion industry is built around expectations of impossible beauty. What would happen if you added impossibly beautiful elves to it? Reality TV shows pit ordinary people against each other in strange contests. Imagine pitting two rival clans of werewolves against each other. Hollywood complains that agents suck blood from the studios. What would a vampire agent be like? Running with an idea in this direction is a great way to explore theme as well. (More about that in chapter twelve.)

BUT WILL I USE ALL THIS?

Absolutely not.

Every writer creates reams of notes that no one else will ever read, forms ideas no one else will ever hear, writes histories that will never see the light of day. And so will you.

Writing the Paranormal Novel

A couple years ago, I took a research trip to Ireland. For ten days, I wandered Dublin and County Meath. I crawled through Stone Age tombs, and climbed over ruined castles. I drove on the left, drank Guinness, and got lost in Irish bogs. I learned how to behave in an Irish cathedral, start a fire with dried peat, and speak with an Irish accent. But I didn't learn *everything* there was to know about Ireland—or even about Loughcrew, the small, fairly obscure tombs I'd come to study. I didn't learn how immigration works, or how to use the Dublin train system, or how to open a bank account. But you can be sure that all these things existed while I was there! The banks and trains and immigration system all operated quietly in the background, and I barely noticed.

You're essentially taking the reader on a ten-day tour through your world. There's plenty they don't need to see but which *you* need to know about. Your deeper knowledge of the world will keep the world consistent and stop you from making mistakes in the way your characters react within your setting.

CULTURAL CHECKLIST

Have you considered each of the following areas when creating backgrounds for your supernatural characters?

TYPE OF WORLD

__ Secret Supernatural

   __ Secret History

__ Sunlit Supernatural

   __ Old (Long-Existing) Supernatural

   __ New (Recently Arrived) Supernatural

SUPERNATURAL PEOPLE ARE:

__ Superior

__ Equals

__ Persecuted

CULTURE

___ Government (Type: _____)

    ___ Formal

    ___ Informal

___ Economy

___ Spirituality

___ Family and Community

___ Art and Recreation

___ Food

___ Tools and Technology

    ___ Weapons

    ___ Transportation

    ___ Medicine

    ___ Production

        ___ Slavery

    ___ Communication

___ Popular Culture

    ___ Impact of pop culture on the paranormal

    ___ Impact of the paranormal on pop culture

CHAPTER 4:

Seeking the Paranormal

The McNamara Federal Building in downtown Detroit doesn't look like it's full of people with guns. It's a tall, gray block of a skyscraper with a really ugly sculpture out front made of smashed-up cars set in an arrangement vaguely similar to Stonehenge. I parked my car and dropped quarters into the meter. For once, I was wearing a shirt with a button-down collar, slacks, and decent shoes instead of my more usual torn jeans and ancient T-shirt. Under my arm I carried a zippered leather folder.

You want to look nice when you're interviewing the Federal Bureau of Investigation.

When you enter the lobby of the McNamara Federal Building, all your stuff goes through an X-ray machine and you go through a metal detector. The guards are polite, friendly, and watchful. A creaky, shuddering elevator takes you upward, past the Treasury Department and the IRS, to the twenty-sixth floor and the FBI.

In the elevator foyer are posted pictures and descriptions of the FBI's Ten Most Wanted. Osama bin Laden still tops the list, in case you were curious. You have to pass through another metal detector to get into the reception area. This one doesn't give you the chance to empty your pockets, so your keys and change set off the alarm. (I rather suspect it's less for safety and more to alert the receptionists, who are behind bulletproof glass, to your presence.) I walked up to the bulletproof glass with a polite smile on my face and my card in my hand.

The things I do for research.

"But wait!" you say. "I'm writing a paranormal book. I'm making it all up. Why do I need to do research if it's all fake?"

Sorry—even the fake stuff is real. Terry Pratchett once teamed up with artist Stephen Briggs to create *The Discworld Mapp*, an atlas of Pratchett's famous Discworld. When the project came out, Pratchett was startled to learn that British bookstores had shelved it in the non-fiction section. Why? The stores maintained that although the thing was a map of a fictional place, it was nonetheless a *real* map. So it *isn't* all fake, and you *must* do research. Research can separate a good manuscript from a great one—and mean the difference between rejection and publication.

When you say *research,* most people think of a pale person sitting at a table paging through a stack of musty books with one hand and taking frantic notes with the other. Sometimes this is the case, and we'll talk about that. And there's also this Internet thing, which is supposedly putting books out of business. We'll talk about that, too. Books can't answer direct questions, though, and often as I'm paging through some dusty tome trying to find out just when the ground was broken on Ann Arbor's first cemetery, I find myself saying, "This is the sort of thing I could find out in less than ten seconds if I could just *ask* someone." So we'll talk about that. And other resources, to boot.

THE IMPORTANCE OF RESEARCH EVEN IF YOU'RE MAKING IT ALL UP

First of all, when it comes to your world and your magic, you're not really making anything up. You're creating the illusion of reality, and that means you need a logical starting point, a real-world reason for the reader to start believing your illusion. If you make mistakes in your world building, knowledgeable readers will trip over them and be reminded that they're reading a story. You don't want them to remember they're reading a story.

You want them to stay immersed in the book and forget that they're reading anything at all.

The more realistic you make the rest of your world, the more likely the reader will go along with the impossible elements. Become familiar with how a castle is constructed, say, and how people with swords *really* fight (as opposed to how they do it in most movies), and how to make bread in a commercial kitchen. Using real principles of bread baking and castle building and sword fighting lend verisimilitude to your world, even if you're adding magic to it. In other words, your supernatural baker may have magic to help him, but the whole process will feel more real to your reader if you use actual commercial baking as a starting point. And that means you have to look up how it's done.

Also, in a book set closer to home, you might want to use existing settings. Having your main character stroll down a real street in a real town and stop for a bagel at a real bakery adds extra reality to your book and helps the reader suspend disbelief once the impossible supernatural elements show up. It's somehow easier to believe, for example, that an angel will take on human form and fall in love with a human man if the two bump into each other at Zingerman's Deli on Washtenaw Avenue in downtown Ann Arbor just after a University of Michigan football game. Not only do the details of the real setting give you the extra dash of reality, but Ann Arbor natives will also love seeing their town immortalized in print, which will boost local book sales. This means you'll have to look things up, though—a lot of people live in Ann Arbor and they all know that Zingerman's is actually on Detroit Street, not Washtenaw. Mistakes like this will call attention to the fact that they're reading fiction and yank them out of the story. Research will help you get those small details right.

LOOKING BEYOND THE SETTING

There's more "real-life" stuff to look up besides places. When you're creating a new supernatural culture (as we did in chapter three), the best place to look for inspiration is a human culture. Fairies might be similar to ancient Celts. Vampires might run their underground society on the medieval feudal model. Werewolves might hold gladiator contests similar to those of ancient Rome. It's fairly easy to use an existing human culture as a starting point for your nonhuman people. You can research and modify the original culture to suit your purposes. Once you decide that werewolves indulge in monthly public battles much like those in the Colosseum, you can read up on life in ancient Rome, cull from it what works for your book, and mold it into a shape that suits you. This will make your werewolf fights feel more authentic to human readers, since humans ultimately invented the system.

The idea of trying to make a completely unrealistic creature more real may seem strange, but that's what you're going for—that illusion of reality. Your reader has to set aside quite a lot of disbelief to accept a bunch of people who change into ravening wolves during the full moon and who create underground societies during the days between. They need some human qualities to balance out the weirdness. (And don't worry about finding the weird. There's nothing so strange that some human society somewhere hasn't tried it, smoked it, or regretted it the next morning.)

True, you might want to create some truly inhuman paranormals— and why shouldn't you?—but this type of character is best used as a secondary character, not a main character. A completely inhuman main character wouldn't interest human readers much. There'd be no common interests, no way for the reader to empathize with such characters, and you want your readers to empathize with your main characters.

REAL SUPERNATURAL CREATURES

We all know vampires aren't real. But the folklore behind them is. Bram Stoker knew that very well. His Count Dracula was an amalgam of Irish folk tales and Eastern European vampire lore. Some of it he used: Vampires drink human blood; vampires can't bear garlic and holy objects; vampires can only be killed by decapitation or sunlight. Some of it he ignored: Scatter millet seeds on a vampire's coffin, and he'll spend the entire night counting them; vampires can spontaneously rise from long-dead corpses; vampires can't cross running water. And some he created out of thin air: Vampires can climb walls like a spider; vampires crumble to dust when killed; vampires can't cross a circle drawn in the dirt with a holy wafer in the center.

Here's the thing: A hundred wannabes copy Bram Stoker instead of using the original folklore. Why? They don't do their research. They rely on vampire lore gleaned from movies, half-remembered stories, and episodes of *Buffy the Vampire Slayer.* In other words, they got their material secondhand and thirdhand and think they're creating something new. But would a professional chef use someone else's recipe? Or recycled ingredients? Certainly not! And neither should you. The same principle goes for the folklore behind genies, angels, demons, zombies, werewolves, fairies, and the ghosts from a hundred different cultures.

Besides, after a thousand carbon-copy Hollywood creatures, something that comes from actual folklore with an actual background comes across as fresh and fascinating on the page. So do some serious reading. It'll show in your writing.

IDEAS AND RESEARCH

Finally, one of the best places to troll for new ideas is among new ideas. Ask any number of authors how often they stumble across something new in a bit of research that leads them to a new piece of writing.

As just one example, I was taking a course in British literature and was thumbing idly though the forty-pound Norton anthology the professor made us buy. By sheer chance, I came across "The Chimney Sweeper," a poem by William Blake. He wrote it in pre-Victorian London to protest the plight of climbing boys, little kids who were forced to crawl into dark chimneys and scrub them clean. The image of these children, slaves in all but name, creeping through black hell every day, refused to leave me alone, and I finally went to the library to look them up. (This was pre-Internet.) The more I learned, the more powerful and dreadful the images became. I started to wonder . . . modern children fear the monster under the bed or the creature in the closet. But these boys spent their days in chimneys and slept in piles of ash. No beds, no closets. What would their monsters look like?

I conceived of a skeletal man in a black topcoat and top hat who slid into the tight places, brushed his cold fingers against climbing boys' faces, and caused the accidents that the boys were so prone to die from. He started chimney fires, jammed your knees against your chest so you suffocated, and broke chimneys away from houses so you fell five stories to the courtyard, encased in a brick coffin. And Dodd, my protagonist, was the only person who could see him.

I finally wrote "Thin Man," a story that included several images from Blake's original poem, and sent it to Marion Zimmer Bradley. She bought it and used it as a cover story for *Marion Zimmer Bradley's Fantasy Magazine*. Fifteen years later, I was invited to submit a story to a steampunk anthology. Dodd slipped back into my mind and wouldn't leave. I realized I really wanted to know what happened to him after "Thin Man" ended, so I wrote a novelette called "The Soul Jar." It appeared in *The Shadow Conspiracy* several months later. All because I learned something new.

But it was more than that. I didn't just stumble across something new—I went out and *looked* for it. I learned quite a lot about climbing boys and their living conditions. I learned how they got in and out of the chimneys and what their brushes looked like. I learned why the chimney sweeps shaved the boys' heads and who gave the sweeps permission to steal the boys from orphanages and workhouses in the first place. Only then did the story truly take shape.

Not all books and stories work this way, of course, but if a project ever gets stuck or you've hit a dry spell, a bit of research can bump things forward with amazing efficiency.

WHERE DO YOU GO?

This may sound like a weird question to bring up in the Information Age, but it isn't. When I'm not writing, I teach high school English and the occasional graduate school course. I regularly assign research projects, and

I've learned the hard way that I can't just turn my students loose to look things up, and I don't just mean my ninth graders. Why? Because they head straight to the computer and ignore everything else—a terrible mistake. Let's look at some really good resources first.

THE LIBRARY

Obvious, right? But a lot of people don't know how to use a library very well—and many others dismiss the library as outdated or a waste of time in a day when the Internet gives us so many research tools. However, even a small, local library can offer several advantages the Internet simply can't match.

First, Google is not your friend. (I'll cover this in more detail in the Internet section on page 62.) You've doubtless already figured out that if you enter "vampire" into Google—or any other search engine—you'll end up with hundreds of millions of entries, most of which are movies or Wikipedia. (Another site that's not necessarily your friend.) Most libraries, however, subscribe to a host of research databases, including ERIC, SIRS, Gale, and others. These databases gather magazine articles, scholarly journals, newspapers, electronic books, and more. They winnow out the useless junk and categorize it for you. And they're usually free for library patrons. All you need to do is register for a password. At the library.

Second, the libraries have people on staff who can help you, who *love* to help you. These people are called reference librarians, and they *live* for those odd questions. Their eyes positively light up when someone walks up to their desks and says, "I'm looking for information on Japanese fox spirits. Can you point me in the right direction?"

Third, the local library is *the* place to go if you're looking for local history or local folklore. They're likely to have old newspapers, yearbooks, photo albums, maps, letters, diaries, and more. And if you live in a city with an actual historical library in it—heaven! Historical librarians know *everything*. Use them. They love it.

Finally, when you go to the library, you're more likely to work than become distracted. Hey, you made a special trip, perhaps even through bad weather, so your mind-set is likely to be *I'm here to get things done*. You won't be tempted to check your e-mail, post something on your favorite social network, or play a "quick" game of solitaire. You'll get your work done.

AN INTERVIEW

Reading has its advantages, but it has limitations as well. You can't ask a book a question. It won't bring up information you didn't think to ask. It can't clarify anything. A real person, on the other hand, instantly overcomes these limitations and may even hand you information you didn't realize you needed.

But just how do you find someone to talk to? And how do you ask? Won't he get mad that you're bothering him? How much do you pay her? What's the etiquette at an interview? These are some daunting questions, so let's take them one at a time.

The first step, obviously, is finding someone to consult. Sometimes you just get lucky. My first book was about a man suffering from what psychologists call dissociative identity disorder (DID). (That's multiple personalities to you and me.) I read everything I could get my hands on, but there were a lot of things the books didn't say. As it happened, my wife was taking a psychology class at the time and she mentioned my book to the professor. He was fascinated! DID, it turned out, was his specialty. When I heard about this, I hurried to call the psych department to confirm his office hours, and I went down to see him the following day. As I said—lucky.

Luck, of course, doesn't work all the time. A more reliable way to find contacts is simply to ask all your friends and family if they know anything about the field you're researching. You'd be surprised at some of the contacts you can find this way. ("Didn't you know your great-uncle Ben worked as a lumberjack for fifteen years?") Even if this doesn't yield a direct contact, it can lead you to the friend-of-a-friend system. When I first expressed interest in contacting the FBI, for example, a friend of mine told me his parents knew an FBI agent assigned to the Kalamazoo Field Office.

You can also do cold contacts. This involves getting hold of people you've never heard of (and vice versa), and it often calls for some preliminary research. I was working on a supernatural piece that involved advanced botany, and the friend-of-a-friend system was proving a dead end. I live in Ann Arbor, home to the University of Michigan, so the next obvious step was to hit the botanical laboratory.

The department's Web site wasn't very helpful, so I was forced to go down to the university for a quick visit. The botanical department receptionist was quite busy and verged on being rude, so I didn't tell her I was a writer looking for information. Instead I asked for any flyers or booklets about the biology department, since the information I needed didn't seem to be online. The catalog she gave me to look at (she said I couldn't keep it) listed all the professors and their specialty areas. I copied down several names and phone numbers, thanked her sweetly, and left. Over the next few days, I made phone calls until I located a researcher who was working on a botanical DNA project and was able to make an appointment for an interview.

Do I get nervous calling people I don't know? Very much so. I need the information, though, so I force myself to push those phone buttons. I have a tendency to babble when I'm edgy, so I often write out what I want to say in advance in case I start blithering or stuttering. When my source picks up the phone, I simply say (or read), "My name is Steven Harper. I'm a novelist, and the book I'm currently working on involves botanical DNA. I heard you would be a good person to talk to about this. Would you be able to answer a few questions?"

A note here: Always introduce yourself as a novelist, never a writer. The word "writer" is often associated with "starving" or "wannabe" or "failing." The word "novelist," however, has a more brisk, down-to-earth connotation. It boils down to the preconception that writers are artists (and therefore slightly suspect) while novelists are businesspeople. If you're doing research for a short story, say instead, "I'm working on a short story for submission to _____." And name the magazine you intend to submit the story to. This makes you sound more businesslike—you already have a market in mind.

So you've completed the preliminary research and are making the call. What if the contact is rude or unwilling to talk to you? The situation can still be salvaged: "No problem. Sorry to have bothered you. Could you perhaps recommend someone else I could talk to? I'd really appreciate it."

Let's assume, however, that your contact is willing to talk to you. Most of them will be. Really. You are a writer—er, novelist, something many people find endlessly fascinating. You're also giving them a chance to lecture you about their fields of expertise. Major bonus! People *love* talking about themselves and their work, especially if what they say has a chance of ending up in print. They also appreciate a novelist who wants to get the facts right. My mother is a retired nurse, and she can't stand medical shows because they never get hospital procedure right. As a teacher, I feel the same way about shows set in high schools. Any novelist who asked us about how either profession *really* worked would be greeted with a certain amount of enthusiasm, if not cake and ice cream. Finally, most people find it flattering to be seen as an expert on a topic. So don't worry that you're bothering people. The vast majority won't mind in the slightest.

If you only have a few quick questions, a phone consultation will often do. ("It'll only take about five minutes. Is now a good time or should I call you back?") If you need something a little more elaborate, ask if you can make an appointment for an interview. You need to be flexible and operate at their convenience, of course. Remember, they're doing *you* a favor.

Some people will offer to consult via e-mail. This can work well if your contact is in another city or overseas, making telephone calls expensive and personal interviews impossible (though Skype and other Internet programs can overcome this). The problem you may run into, however, is that people often give too little detail in e-mail. They may be willing to go on for several minutes in person, but only give a terse, one-sentence answer if they have to write it down. Be prepared to reply with a polite request for more information.

Now let's assume you've set up an interview. That brings up the question of mechanics—what to wear, what to bring, and so on. If you're talking to a total stranger in an office setting or in a private home, you'll want to dress up a bit. I normally never wear slacks, but you can bet I did when I talked to the FBI! On the other hand, if you're going to be in a barn talking to a farmer about the care and feeding of horses, your best bet is blue jeans, boots, and a flannel shirt. If you aren't sure, err on the side of dressiness.

Bring whatever method of taking notes you prefer. I take a digital recorder, but I always ask permission to use it. I also have a notebook and two pens in case one runs out of ink. (Asking to borrow a writing implement looks unprofessional.) Lastly, I bring my card. If you don't have one, I really recommend getting some printed. Many computer programs will also let you print your own. Overall, cards are quite inexpensive, and handing one out adds a businesslike touch. If you don't have a card, write your name, address, and phone number on two or three 3 x 5 cards and bring them instead.

Write out a list of questions in advance. You don't want to waste your contact's time while you hem and haw over what else you want to ask. Besides, pre-writing the questions is a more professional approach, and you are a professional.

What do you offer to pay your contacts? As a rule, nothing. Instead, tell them that you'll put their name and title on the "Acknowledgments" page and send them an autographed copy of the book when it comes out. For a short story, you send an autographed copy of the magazine. And always, always, always send a thank-you note after the interview:

> Dear Ms. Smith,
>
> I just wanted to thank you for taking time out of your busy schedule to speak with me. Your help was invaluable and will make the book [story] far more accurate than I could on my own. If you think of any other information to add, please don't hesitate to contact me.

By the way, if you interview your contact over a meal or in a bar, you are expected to pick up the tab, even if the contact was the one who suggested the idea. It's a tax deduction, so save the receipt!

Sometimes it takes a little work to get what you need, but you can't give up. When I first contacted the friend-of-a-friend FBI agent, he told me I had to talk to the Special Agent who dealt with the press. This Special Agent referred me to the main press office in the Washington, DC headquarters. I contacted the office there and was told to fax them a copy of the questions I wanted to ask and that someone there would call me back to answer the ones whose answers weren't classified. I did this and got quite a lot of information over the phone. But I still wanted to see inside the Detroit Field Office. I made several phone calls to the McNamara Federal Building, but none of them were returned. I finally drove down there, zippered folder in hand, to see if showing up in person would net me a better response.

It did, though only a little better. I briefly met with a Special Agent, who told me I would have to clear a visit with Washington, DC first. So back home I went for another round of telephoning. Eventually, I got the interview I needed with the Special Agent in Charge at the Detroit Field Office.

Writing is an exercise in persistence.

THE INTERNET

Yes, yes, yes. Of course you can use the Internet for research. If you need a quick fact right now, the Internet is likely the fastest place to find it. Just remember all the standard warnings—anyone can set up a Web site, and just because it appears online doesn't make it true. (This is what makes library databases more reliable.) This especially applies to Wikipedia. A *wiki* is a Web site that anyone can edit, and this is where Wikipedia gets its name. Anyone can edit Wikipedia, and they do. This means that sometimes people unwittingly—or deliberately—insert false information into Wikipedia's entries, so tread carefully.

If you find something online and you want to make sure it's true, check a number of reputable sites and see if they all say the same thing. And make sure they aren't quoting Wikipedia.

Writing the Paranormal Novel

Also remember that Google is not your friend. (I told you I'd say it again.) Google organizes its search findings in part by popularity. Order it to search for a particular term, and Google creates a list of the sites other Internet users clicked on most often when they searched on the same term. In other words, it's search by popular vote. Again, tread carefully.

THE ART OF EXCLUSION

Rikki-tikki-tavi had it right—run and find out. There's something compelling about research, and it's so easy to lose yourself in it or get tangled up in conflicting versions of the same story or get sidetracked by fascinating tangents—which sucks up your writing time. Fortunately, it's not too hard to avoid these problems.

SET RESEARCH LIMITS

If you know you're the type who gets lost in research (and therefore won't get writing done), set a time limit—a certain number of hours per week or minutes per day. If necessary, start a timer. When it goes off, set the books aside and start writing. Remember, research doesn't get words on paper.

You must also limit yourself to the topic at hand. If you're looking up *rusalka* from Ukraine, you aren't allowed to read about Ukrainian marriage customs, Ukrainian cooking, or the history of Ukrainian icons, no matter how tempting those particular articles or hyperlinks might be. If you find yourself going off on a tangent, firmly reign yourself in and get back to your original topic. Although it's true that learning something new is a great way to generate new ideas, you aren't trolling for new ideas at the moment—you're trying to write a book. And you're under a time limit, after all.

Finally, you have to limit yourself to research that will likely prove useful. You can't call it research if it seems unlikely you'll ever use it. I once knew a woman who said she had a hard time writing because she loved watching the Discovery Channel. Why, just the other day she spent all of her writing time watching a documentary on elephants. "Who knows?" she told me. "The information might prove useful one day."

I told her to shoot her television.

This woman was using research as a pretext to avoid writing. If your research doesn't have a specific purpose or if you aren't looking for something geared directly toward what you're writing about, you're doing the same thing. I'm a big fan of learning something new to generate writing ideas, but that kind of learning has to take place on your own time, not on your writing time.

YOU DON'T NEED TO KNOW EVERYTHING

You're writing a novel, not a doctoral dissertation. It's okay to miss a few facts. If you were looking up something specific, such as the date the first dirigible crossed the Atlantic, find it and quit researching. If you need general background material for a time or place, find enough information to get going, and then *start writing your book.*

A lot of new writers think they need to finish all their research before they start writing. Nothing is further from the truth. No matter how much you learn about a given topic, there's always more, and it's too easy to fall into the research trap. Stop researching, start the book. Once you've written a chunk, pause for some more research, and then go back to writing. Keep up the pattern. Eventually you'll discover that something you wrote earlier is wrong. Don't worry about it. You can go back and make changes—that's the beauty of writing on a computer.

You won't *ever* get it perfect. You *will* make mistakes in your research. That's okay. Your main objective is to tell a compelling story that feels realistic *enough.* It doesn't need to be perfectly realistic. Besides, you could research for twenty years and some reader somewhere will still say, "Hey! That's not how it works." A few of them might even write you or accost you in the hallway at a convention or conference and go on at great length about the errors in your book. If they do, the proper response is, "Did I make a mistake? Oops." And then you walk away.

Don't let fear of facts bog you down. Better to write a book with a few mistakes in it than never to write a book at all.

WHAT TO IGNORE

Always remember that the story is king. Mark Twain famously said that if the Mississippi was in the wrong place for a story, he'd move it. In other words, if you unexpectedly come across an inconvenient fact that would wreck your story, ignore it and tell the story.

When you're researching history or folklore, you'll likely come across contradictions. People become werewolves in a number of different ways in the original tales, for example. You can cast a spell, get mauled by a werewolf, or just live an evil life. Which is the right one? Some survivors of the *Titanic* reported that the band played the hymn "Nearer, My God, to Thee" to keep the passengers calm as the ship sank, but Harold Bride, the ship's radio operator and an eminently credible witness, reported the musicians played the ragtime tune "Autumn." Which is correct? How do you handle this for your book about ghosts and the *Titanic?*

Some writers get paralyzed with indecision. Others try to figure out ways to work *all* possibilities into the book. Both approaches are mistakes. The best solution is the simplest: *Choose the one that best fits your story.* And don't apologize for it.

NEEPERY

The author term for the cool research stuff you include in your book is *neepery.* The word first showed up in the computer crowd (possibly at Caltech), spread to the science fiction and fantasy crowd, and from there slipped into writer jargon.

Neepery can take over your story. There's so much cool stuff out there. I mean, did you know that Shakespeare's close friend Henry Wriothesley, the third Earl of Southampton, posed for a painting in drag and no one knows exactly why? Or that a dime has only one less groove on its edge than a quarter? Or that a group of unicorns is called a blessing? (Though maybe it really should be called a hallucination.) There's a terrible temptation to put almost everything you find into your story. You worked hard to find it, and it fascinated you, so it should fascinate your readers, too.

Unfortunately, that's rarely the case. Unless you're writing a historical novel, neepery has only two functions: 1) to establish setting, and 2) to move the plot forward.

C.C. Finlay's marvelous book *Patriot Witch,* the first in his Traitor to the Crown series, is a beautiful example of a novel that inserts necessary neepery without bogging down the story. One method he uses is to insert a single sentence of it into an otherwise busy paragraph, like he does here:

> As they entered the coffeehouse, [Proctor] saw Emily wave to him through the panes of the window. She shimmered like a mirage through the uneven glass. A similar ripple rolled through his stomach when he returned the greeting.

The first two sentences slip us quite a lot of information. First, we now know that pre-Revolutionary Boston has coffeehouses. We're told that Boston is wealthy enough to have established its own glassmakers, but Colonial glassmaking is still an imperfect art at this point in history. And all of this information is handed over in the context of the story, which is Proctor's brief encounter with Emily and the feelings it arouses.

A moment later, Proctor enters the coffeehouse, and Finlay gives us a description of it:

> The door opened onto laughter and clattering crockery and the scent of pipe tobacco. Dozens of chairs and benches crowded the long, narrow building, with brass candlesticks on every table, though only a few of them were lit. The walls were bare, not that you could see much of them with all the people gathered—a variety of British officers, periwigged officials, and ambitious merchants, all talking over one another. Two black slaves, one laden with cups, the other with platters, ran from table to table.

A short, straightforward description that nonetheless tells us quite a lot. Tobacco is in general use. Coffeehouses are—or at least, *this* coffeehouse is—popular. There are plenty of British in Boston. Wigs are still in fashion for men. Boston is a hangout for merchants. And Finlay reminds us that slavery is still legal, even in the northern areas.

One thing Finlay neatly avoids is over-explanation. He doesn't say "ambitious merchants from London, Hamburg, and Amsterdam." He doesn't detail the wigs. He doesn't have Proctor muse about the slaves and their plight. We already know everything we need to know for the story to continue, so Finlay shuts up and moves on to Proctor sitting down at a table with his fiancée Emily and her father Thomas, who doesn't like Proctor very much. This conflict is what the scene is really about.

Finlay has clearly spent hours researching Colonial America, but he only sprinkles in enough of it to set the scene and keep the story moving, and he often puts it in the context of action. It's a fine way to use that neepery.

WRITING WHAT YOU KNOW AND OTHER NONSENSE

You may have heard the saying *write what you know*. A lot of new writers take this to mean that you need to write about an area of expertise. If you're a teacher, set your book in a school. If you lived in Romania for a year, you're in a position to create a culture based on Eastern Europe. If you coached college wrestling, use the struggles of these athletes in your writing. Writing what you know lends necessary authenticity to your writing and makes everything feel more grounded in reality, since the details will be right in ways that mere research can't grant you.

To a certain extent this is true—but only to a certain extent. Paranormal novels (and science fiction novels, to bring in our sister genre) include a great many impossible elements. I mean, there's no way for anyone to write what they know when it comes to vampires or werewolves or ghosts or magical gateways. No one understands what it's like to be a vampire. No one knows how it feels to transform into a wolf at the full moon. No one knows what a ghost thinks or how to push through to another world. So does that mean you can't write about these things?

Of course not.

The reason you—and any number of other authors—can write about things you can't possibly know anything about is that even when you aren't writing what you know, you're *still* writing what you know, and that wasn't a meaningless tautology. You're injecting what you do know into what you don't. You don't know what it's like to be a vampire, but you *do* know what it's like to be hungry, lonely, and an outsider. You don't know how it feels to transform into a wolf at the full moon, but you *do* know how it feels to be wrenched from one mood to another, what physical pain feels like, and what it's like to battle internal demons. You don't know what a ghost thinks, but you *do* know those strange and alien thoughts that crowd your mind at three in the morning when you can't sleep. You don't know how it is to push through to another world, but you *do* know how it feels to arrive in a foreign country (or at a new job or in a new school or . . .), with no idea where anything is, who's in charge, or how anything works. In the example from the preceding section, C.C. Finlay can't know what it's like to be a young witch living in the Colonial era but (I'm assuming) he *does* know what it's like to have a secret, to be in love, and to be meeting your potential father-in-law for the first time. He includes these feelings in his writing, so Proctor comes across as eminently authentic, even though his existence is completely impossible. Injecting your own human experiences into your paranormal situations will grant your story that powerful authenticity your human readers crave.

So yeah—write what you know, even when it seems nonsensical to do so.

DEALING WITH DEPARTURES

Even though the story is king, you don't quite have carte blanche to do anything you like. Yes, readers (and editors) will forgive the occasional error or departure and keep reading, but you can't willfully ignore or change well-established fact and folklore.

If you tell the readers your main character is a werewolf, she'd better turn into some sort of lupine creature at some point in the book. Writing about ghosts? Someone probably needs to be dead or otherwise separated from his body. Demons are evil spirits, angels are good ones. All supernatural creatures have a host of background baggage that the readers are well aware of, and you do need to follow it to a certain extent. Calling a bloodsucking, undead corpse a fairy will confuse the reader, as will giving your werewolves the power to walk through walls. Readers pick up a werewolf book expecting you to meet certain precedents, and you can't depart from them (too often).

But this does bring up a question. Everyone knows vampires don't do daylight. The sun strikes them dead, or burns them to ash, or poisons them, or maybe just seriously hurts their eyes. In some vampire stories, the problem is instantaneous, and in others stories it takes a while. Some vampires fall comatose the moment the sun rises, while others remain functional. Some vampires can shield themselves with heavy clothing or a blanket, and some can survive in sunlight with nothing but a pair of dark glasses. In any case, the stories all agree—vampires and daylight don't mix.

So how come Stephenie Meyer's *Twilight* vampires sparkle in the sun?

There's no precedent for it anywhere in folklore. I mean, *nowhere.* Meyer made it up completely on her own. How is she able to get away with it?

Easy. Meyer followed a simple rule (though I can't pretend to know if she did it consciously or not): *You can make one major departure per book.* Meyer's vampires drink blood, they live forever, and they have strength and speed beyond those of mere mortals, all of which comes right out of regular folklore. The sunlight sparkles are the only major departure in the first book.

Not only that, the difference shows up fairly late in the story. She establishes the other vampiric phenomena first. By the time the sparkling shows up, Edward Cullen's identity as a "regular" vampire is firmly established in the reader's mind, and Meyer is able to stray into sparkle-land. Also, the sparkle effect gives her vampires a reason to avoid sunlight, something traditional vampires do, so it's less of a departure than it appears to be.

Finally, Meyer knows her audience. Her readers—primarily girls and young women—don't want a novel about a boyfriend who turns into a monster or a pile of dust. They want a novel about a heroine who ends up with the perfect guy. Edward has to sparkle, or that facet of the story would be ruined and Meyer would lose readers.

Departing from established supernatural norms in some way is actually a darned good idea. Readers—and editors—love vampires, but they don't want to read about exactly the same type of vampire. They want to see what *you've* done with a familiar concept that's also a little different. You need to avoid the clichés.

And that's the topic for the next chapter.

CHAPTER 5:
The Paradox of Clichés

Stop me if you've heard this one. Intrepid Author finishes her first novel and, with trembling fingers, looks up Emily Editor's address at Paranormal Books and drops the manuscript into the mail. Several months of fearful, feverish waiting pass, but at last Intrepid Author receives a response. "I'm sorry," Emily Editor writes, "but I'm not interested in more novels about angst-ridden vampires who open detective agencies. Too cliché."

Crushed—or at least annoyed—Intrepid Author sends the manuscript to other editors and gets the same response: too cliché. Some time later, Intrepid Author wanders despondently into her local bookstore and nearly crashes into a floor-to-ceiling display of the latest release from Paranormal Books. Title? *Angst-Ridden Vampire Detective: Book I.* Stunned, Intrepid Author flips a copy open. The acknowledgments page reads, *And special thanks to Emily Editor, without whom this book would never have been published.*

Intrepid Author yanks out her cell phone, calls up a mafia hit man she's friendly with, and—

Oh—you *have* heard this one.

There, there. It happens. But *how* does it happen? Editors say they don't want certain clichés—or any of them—then turn around and buy novels stuffed chockablock with them. In this chapter, we'll take a look at what the supernatural clichés are, why editors do sometimes buy them, and finish with how to get away from them—and how to get away with using them.

THE CLICHÉS

Let's get a common definition first. In writing, cliché is a character concept, story, or situation that's been used so often, it's lost any ability to surprise, entertain, or otherwise engage a reader. (An overused turn of phrase like "light as a feather" is also a cliché, but we're going to discuss bigger concepts here.) With a cliché, the reader knows what's going to happen, which takes away the fun.

I certainly wouldn't say that paranormal novels have a monopoly on clichés. Romance novelists struggle mightily with the happy ending required for almost all romance novels—it's hard to keep suspense going when your readers know the heroine will end up with the hero no matter what. Horror runs the other way—the cliché is that just about everyone is going to die in some messy way, and the few survivors will regret living. Science fiction has a number of clichés about aliens and space travel. Mystery has two favorites: the hard-boiled private investigator and the amateur detective. However, supernatural tales are the oldest stories in human history, which means the ideas have had a few thousand years to simmer into clichés, whereas detective stories and science fiction haven't even reached the two-century mark yet.

Let's take a look at a few supernatural clichés. Have any of them slithered into your story?

THE TRAGIC VAMPIRE

He's handsome, he's dangerous, he's a loner. Three hundred years ago (or some other suitable length of time), he was transformed into a Creature of the Night. Now he struggles to hold onto his rapidly fading humanity. Some nights, he wonders why it's worth the effort. A century ago, Tragic fell in love with a beautiful woman, but she died (at the hands of the vampire who transformed Tragic in the first place) and he blames himself.

Currently Tragic hovers in the shadows, observing the world but refusing to take part in it. He's not a monster like the vampires out of folklore, but is instead a struggling hero. To prove how likable he is, he refuses human blood, surviving on stray cats and sewer rats and eking out a miserable existence in alleyways. But he's still handsome. Recently, however, he's encountered the Plucky Heroine (see below). She reminds him strongly (or perhaps exactly) of his long-dead lover. He quickly falls in love with her, but how can he truly be with her? As a mortal, she'll one day age and die while he stays forever young and gorgeous. Besides, his last lover died a terrible death, and her killer is still out there somewhere. The killer might target any new woman he falls in love with. If Plucky ever finds out about all this, her love for Tragic will surely turn to hatred. How can he handle all these problems and continue to deal with being an ultra-powerful, super-handsome vampire to boot?

In a variation on this cliché, the Tragic Vampire is gay, and the Plucky Heroine is a Plucky Hero, but everything else remains the same. Another variation is the Tragic Werewolf. Just substitute the word "werewolf" for "vampire" above and you have it.

The appeal of this cliché lies in the conflict between the guy who seems to have it all (looks, power, immortality, way cool outsiderness) and his "hurt" status (the tragedy of his loss). The reader, through the Plucky Heroine, hopes to comfort the hurting Tragic Vampire and bring him into the light. Metaphorically speaking, anyway.

THE PLUCKY HEROINE

Nothing gets the Plucky Heroine down. Right now, her life is indeed difficult. It might be small things: She can't lose weight or figure out how to break up with her boyfriend. It might be large things: Her new fiancé has locked her up in a drafty manor house far from her family, or she has lost her job and her apartment in the same day. But she forges ahead with relentless determination and the utter assurance that she *can* find a solution to her problems if she just tries hard enough.

If Plucky lives in the past, she invariably develops progressive ideas about women's rights, equality for minority groups, and how servants should be treated. This strange behavior is usually explained away by some sort of unusual upbringing—a single mother, an eccentric aunt, or living as the only sister among a dozen brothers.

Plucky always has one or two best friends at her side. One of them is outrageous and daring, the other quiet and thoughtful. At some point in the story, Plucky becomes separated from these friends, forcing her to solve her problem On Her Own. She also meets the hero of the story and, rather against her will, falls in love with him. She fights this because she's afraid he'll shackle her like all the other men in her life have tried to do, but in the end she realizes she can love her guy without losing any part of her plucky self.

Everyone wants to be plucky—or Plucky. She never gets depressed, and she always finds a way out of whatever problem she has. To top it off, true love hunts her down with relentless zeal, and who doesn't fantasize about being thus pursued? Hence the appeal of the cliché.

THE ENIGMATIC WIZARD

The Enigmatic Wizard stands ready to assist the protagonist of any paranormal novel, including ones set in modern day. He strokes his beard and makes prophetic pronouncements that make no sense until after the predicted event (leaving the reader to wonder why Enigmatic bothered to say anything at all). He is invariably a scholar who speaks several languages, and he hints that he may be immortal. When the plot slows down, Enigmatic can be counted on to hint at some nugget of information that conveniently sends the protagonist down the correct path. In fact, Enigmatic hints at a great many things.

Enigmatic seems to have access to a great deal of magic, but he almost never uses it, even when the fate of the world is at stake. Instead, he risks billions of lives by putting everything into the hands of an inexperienced protagonist just so the young hero can learn and grow. No one knows where Enigmatic comes from. He seems to have no family, no friends, and no life outside of helping the main character.

This character exists because he's handy. Writers use him as a repository for whatever the protagonist might need to know, and he's an easy way to nudge the protagonist in the right direction for anything else. Since he rarely uses his powers, he doesn't upstage the hero. Unfortunately, a good library or the Internet will do much the same thing.

THE TOMBOY

She is *so* not going to wear a dress. Or get married. Or do anything else a man tells her to do. She won't be hemmed in by stupid rules. To her parents' despair, she does what she wants when she wants, and damn the consequences. She says can take care of herself (even when it's obvious she can't). She *definitely* won't fall in love (until she does). The Tomboy is often called up to be a warrior against supernatural antagonists, but she has to fight for the right to do so, since she lives in a society where girls stay home. But one day, she'll overcome the vampire/dragon/demon and prove she's as good as any man.

And did we mention she's beautiful?

The Tomboy gets to break rules with spectacular aplomb. She's also the center of attention all the time—no one in her orbit has anything better to do than try to force her into his or her mold of proper behavior. The character vs. society conflict inherent in the character appeals to writers looking for an easy way to start a story, which only adds to the cliché.

THE CHOSEN ONE

The Chosen One often appears hand-in-hand with the Vague Prophecy. She's chosen by Fate or some other power to do something important, such as defeat a great evil—perhaps even a Dark Lord (see below). A Chosen One usually gets some nifty perks like warrior prowess or a magic weapon or the ability to learn new skills at impossible speed. Many Chosen Ones are reluctant heroes, and an Enigmatic Wizard must persuade her to take up arms against the evil. And nine times out of ten, the Chosen One is way, way weaker than the Dark Lord, yet somehow manages to win in the end anyway.

This cliché has a built-in method of getting the story going. The Chosen One, still innocent of her true identity, is attacked by evil forces. Fortunately, her new Chosen One powers kick in, saving her at the last minute. When the battle is over, the Enigmatic Wizard arrives to dispense wisdom. We're only on page 20, and we've already had a fight scene, superpowers, and a mystery. Cool, right? Problem is, this story has been done so often that the cool factor has worn thinner than your high school Levi's.

MARY SUE (AND GARY STU)

Mary Sue (and her male counterpart Gary Stu) has it all. She's strong, smart, and stunningly beautiful. The strength gives her fighting prowess or some other magical ability, the smarts let her into MENSA without breaking a sweat, and the beauty comes with exotic eye color. (The name, incidentally, comes from a *Star Trek* parody story by Paula Smith, in which Ensign Mary Sue, the youngest, smartest, and most capable officer in Starfleet, sacrifices herself to save the *Enterprise* and dies tragically while Kirk, Spock, McCoy, and the others weep for her loss.)

Mary Sue tears through conflict. Her strength and brains create a deadly combination that flattens everything in her way with stunning efficiency, and in her spare time, she solves her friends' problems. You may be sure she's an expert in any esoteric skill the story might require. And she *always* gets her man. Mary Sue has absolutely no flaws, not physical, not mental, not emotional.

Gary Stu characters lean toward anti-heroism. Like Mary, Gary is possessed of breathtaking looks (don't forget the exotic eye color), has more skills than James Bond, and has a body made for pouring melted chocolate over. He kills with a gun, sword, knife, or his bare hands. He does what needs to be done, and scorns those too squeamish to join him.

He rid himself of any personal flaws years ago while mastering philosophy and martial arts at a lost Tibetan monastery.

Mary Sue and Gary Stu are pure wish fulfillment for the writer, who is clearly afraid of hurting the protagonist or providing any real conflict. In some cases, Mary Sue and Gary Stu are idealized versions of the writer. Readers find such characters annoying. Flaws and conflict make characters interesting because readers, like all humans, are dealing with their own flaws and conflicts and want to see this reflected in pages of their favorite books.

THE DARK LORD

He executes his own underlings. He drops enemies into boiling oil. He snacks on freeze-dried kittens. Eventually, he'll take over the world. Or maybe he'll just destroy it. In any case, only the hero can stop him.

Like the Enigmatic Wizard, the Dark Lord has no family, no background, and no motivation. His many minions fight for him with fanatic loyalty, but where this loyalty comes from is never explained. (High salary? Benefits package with no co-pay? Matching 401(k)?) His attempt to take over the world stems from a lust for power or from a simple need to do evil deeds. Story-wise, the only reason he exists is to give the hero something to fight.

Dark Lords make for fun writing. There's something cathartic about creating on paper someone who does dreadful things we'd never even consider in real life. Unfortunately, Dark Lords make for dull reading. They're flat and unrealistic. Some writers try to counter this by taking their Lords further and further into debauchery. Except blood and gore can't replace character.

THE DREAD DRAGON

It's big, it's bad, it breathes fire, and it eats maidens for lunch. Often it can fly and speak a dozen dead languages (even though it never goes anywhere). The Dread Dragon *always* guards a treasure. It sleeps for a hundred or a thousand years at a time and then, when the story requires it, the creature wakes and hunts for food. Ordinary weapons can't penetrate its armored skin, which means the hero has to find the right magical tool to defeat it, though some Dread Dragons have a single weak spot that allows the hero to kill the creature with a single skillful shot.

Lately, a number of Dread Dragons have been transformed into Misunderstood Dragons—creatures who are not evil but merely persecuted. Humans, of course, assume that any giant lizard that breathes fire must harbor a hankering for virgin flesh, and they react with sharp, pointy efficiency. Once the hero learns the truth about the Misunderstood Dragon, he changes from dragon hunter into dragon helper, even though it means appearing to betray his own people.

Another subset of the Dread Dragon is the Mighty Steed (see below).

The Dread Dragon may not actually be a dragon. It could be any awful monster—griffin, sphinx, basilisk, kraken, take your pick. Funny how many of them turn into Dread Dragons if you look closely enough.

A big scary monster is an easy target. You know it's evil, and it has to be exterminated before it hurts someone. The appeal lies in the drama inherent in a small man fighting an enormous beast and risking his life to save someone else. The problem is that the reader feels pretty sure the monster's going to lose, so there isn't much suspense.

THE MIGHTY STEED

The Mighty Steed is more than a white charger. It's a best friend, a lifetime companion, an ally who becomes closer than any mere lover. The Mighty Steed can be any large creature—a horse, a unicorn, a dragon, a griffin. The Steed's strength and speed makes it a powerful protector, the perfect guardian angel. Everything the Dread Dragon isn't.

Best of all, the Mighty Steed can read your mind. At an early point in the story, the Steed forges a telepathic bond with the protagonist because the protagonist is there when the Steed is born, the protagonist feeds the Steed at a critical stage in its development, or the Steed simply decides the protagonist is worthy in some way. This lifelong bond cannot be broken, and if one half of the pair dies, the other soon follows. The Steed and the protagonist become inseparable, the perfect friends, even as some terrible disaster threatens their lives.

The appeal here is obvious. The protagonist—and therefore the reader— ends up with a friend who loves her unconditionally, without judgment or ridicule and regardless of flaws, who will always be there and who will die to protect her. What's not to like? The trouble is, it's been done and done and done.

THE VAGUE PROPHECY

The future is set. No way to change it. And Certain People know what that future is. These people might spout it out loud or they might scribble it on a scroll for future generations. But they never, ever say anything useful. Vague Prophesies are always couched in odd metaphors ("The hand of darkness will steal the treasure of the sky") or in deliberate double-speak. (When the oracle says, "If you go to war, you will destroy a great kingdom," which kingdom does she mean?) In any case, the protagonist is hardly ever able to figure out what the prophecy means in time to do himself any good. In the rare instances when the prophecy is actually clear ("Great disaster will befall you in the city of Paris!"), the hero inevitably ignores it. As a result, great disaster befalls him, and he spends the rest of the book trying to get out of the manure pile he dumped himself into.

A subset of the Vague Prophecy is the Self-Fulfilling Prophecy. This type of prophecy only comes true because the prophecy itself exists. The king learns his newborn son will grow up to kill him, so he orders the child killed. The executioner can't bring himself to do the dirty deed, and he sends the kid far away. Years later, the grown prince returns to his homeland and accidentally kills his estranged father. None of this would have happened but for that stupid prophecy, so why didn't the oracle just keep her big mouth shut?

Prophecies are usually handier for writers than for readers. The vague or double-speak aspect allows the writer to say, "See? I *told* you what was going to happen right up front, but you didn't listen/pay attention/read carefully enough," even though a Vague Prophecy is clearly a writer's trick. And the Self-Fulfilling Prophecy loops back on itself, making the story appear as neat and tidy as a figure eight. So tidy, in fact, that the reader knows exactly how it'll turn out.

THE GATEWAY TO ANOTHER WORLD

In the back of an attic or between two standing stones lurks the Gateway to Another World. This cliché usually begins with a kid who has a problem—dysfunctional family, school bully, terminal shyness. In a strange new place, the kid finds a gateway to a world where magic works and where the kid can become some sort of hero. The kid makes new friends, survives incredible adventures, and finds the key to overcoming the problem he had back in the mundane world. Often the kid is forced to choose whether to stay in the magical world or return to the real one, and the kid always elects to go home. Always.

The Magical Gateway cliché seems to attract children (though the occasional adult does stumble across one). For readers, the idea of leaving this troubled world for one filled with magic and adventure proves powerfully magnetic. For writers, the gateway creates automatic conflict—the door thrusts the character into a difficult situation, and the plot nearly writes itself. This makes the Gateway a major draw, one that appears again and again.

PLOT COUPONS

The hero must rush to Point A and find the Key of Kevormax (Coupon 1). Then it's off to Point B to uncover the Book of Blastum (Coupon 2). After that, he dashes to Point C and the Ring of Roonja (Coupon 3). Once the hero collects all the Coupons, he can save the world, unlock his true heritage, or slay the Dread Dragon in an earth-shattering climactic battle. In an alternate version, the hero has to find Coupon 1 in order to find Coupon 2, and so on.

Plot Coupons are a beefed-up variety of treasure hunt, which looks neat on the surface, but any writer who uses it inevitably discovers the limitation—if the hero misses even one coupon, the climactic ending be-comes a no-show, and the reader *knows* there'll be a climactic ending. This makes the story predictable.

THE HERO'S QUEST

Very few heroes get to stay home. Most leave their familiar surroundings (perhaps at the urging of the Enigmatic Wizard or as the result of a Gate-way to Another World) and head off into unknown territory to find a par-ticular object, rescue a particular person, or set the world aright. Usually a companion or two will come with. Along the way, the hero will make new friends, vanquish enemies, fall in love, and overcome at least one personal flaw.

This is the most ancient of clichés. Nearly every paranormal story uses it, and mythologist Joseph Campbell became famous for pointing out this fact. Humans seem to be hardwired to tell—and enjoy—such sto-ries, and we inevitably drift toward them like sailors to sirens. To tell the truth, you can actually get away with using this cliché because there's al-most no way to avoid it.

AND THE REST

Many other clichés run rampant through fiction: the Servant Turned Hero, the Honorable Thief, the Street Kid, the Helpful Clergyman, the Lost Ob-ject, and more. By now I think you're getting the idea. Remember, *a cliché is any idea or character that's overused and underdeveloped.*

So enough about what they are. Let's look at dealing with them.

GETTING AWAY FROM THE CLICHÉ (FOR THOSE WHO HAVEN'T CREATED THEIR CHARACTERS YET)

The first part of the above rule is *a cliché is any idea or character that's over-used.* So the easiest way to defeat the cliché monster is to avoid it entirely. Yes, you must have a likable protagonist as the center of your book, and yes, you must have at least one supernatural element. That doesn't mean you have to repeat what everyone else has done.

Okay, sure—vampires in the city have been popular for two hundred years. But with dozens of Tragic Vampire books already on the market, why would an editor want to publish yours? Answer: She probably won't. She'll figure everyone has read your story elsewhere.

If you haven't created your main characters yet, stay away from the clichés. Sure, write about vampires. The market continues to maintain reader interest, against all expectations. Just do something *different*.

I can hear the groans all the way over here. "Yeah, Steven," you're complaining. "Easy to say. What's new after a thousand years?"

Try turning the cliché upside down. Do the exact opposite and see what happens. Instead of a Tragic Vampire, what about a guy who *enjoys* being a vampire? Sure, he misses daylight and eating normal food, but the power is fantastic! Instead of a Plucky Heroine, try one who suffers from agoraphobia and has to fight inner demons every time she leaves her apartment. Forget the Enigmatic Wizard. How about a magician who keeps getting in the hero's way, who won't let him *be* a hero? ("You have no idea what you're doing, kid. Step aside.") Instead of a Vague Prophecy, use a prophecy that spells everything out quite clearly and seems to lock the hero into a dreadfully predetermined end. (You think that won't create conflict? Ha!) The Gateway to Another World that always closes after a while? Leave it open. Of course, that means things can wander through at will. Forget the Hero's Quest. Have everything happen in the protagonist's hometown. As for the Tomboy, how would she react within a family who said, "Let her do as she likes. These are modern times"? (Besides, these *are* modern times.) What about a Chosen One who isn't actually chosen, but has to compete for the position? Or a completely different *type* of Chosen One? Stephen King used a little old lady for a Chosen One in *The Stand* to marvelous effect, as just one example.

Instead of Mary Sue's hyper-competence and ultra-confidence, create a protagonist who doesn't know anything about her current situation and is forced to learn or die. What if the antagonist gathers up all the Plot Coupons right from the beginning? Forget the Dark Lord. Try the Bright Lord, the one who intends to take over the world and do right by it. He has everyone's best interests in mind. Good schools, good roads, good police department, low crime, reduced poverty, and everyone goes to the same church every week. He loves everyone, and you're next. Oh my yes, wouldn't that be *nice?* Certainly a lot more scary than anything the Dark Lord could dream up.

A more challenging method is to simply not use the clichés at all. Create different characters entirely. A vampire who was embraced during the 1960s can't quite get away from the flower-child era. A recently divorced accountant who worries about her teenaged daughter's relationship with that strange boy and whose company is talking about some serious downsizing encounters magic in the copy room. A fifth grader with a smart mouth who covers up the secret fear his mother is going to die discovers that the young woman who runs the local comic shop is secretly a magician, and she's going to train him in the magic of artwork.

Don't be afraid to strike out into new territory. The newer, the better, in fact. Editors see dozens of clichés a day, and a book that avoids them will stand out like a spotlight in a cellar.

SO WHY ... ?

If editors are desperate for new material, why do they buy cliché-ridden novels? Any number of reasons. An editor will buy a novel from an established writer with a track record, regardless of clichés, because she knows anything with that author's name on it will automatically sell X number of copies and bring in X number of dollars. Other authors might write have a writing style (voice) that grips the editor so strongly, she figures the clichés won't matter so much. (Better to have a gripping voice *and* a lack of clichés, but the one will override the other.) In yet other cases, the editor may figure there's a market for that particular book at that particular time, clichés and all, and if your book had only arrived two weeks earlier, it might have been chosen instead. A chunk of publishing is, unfortunately, pure luck.

You can, of course, make some of your own luck. Editors are always looking for the next trend, and a writer who can anticipate a trend, either by luck or design, has a much better chance of jumping to the head of the publishing line. The trick is spotting a trend. You can't do it by watching the bookstore—most novels spend a year going from manuscript to book form, and that doesn't count the time it took to write the thing. If you start a project based on bookstore trends, you'll first have to write the book—months or years, depending on your speed—and spend more time finding someone who wants to publish it, who will then take a year or more to get it into print. By then, then trend may be over. So following what looks to be a current trend is difficult.

You can, however, become aware of upcoming trends by listening to what editors and agents are saying. Attend writers conferences and listen to what the editors say they're looking for—and what type of stories they think seems to be dying. Read agent blogs and Web pages and see what they're most interested in. Hang out at online forums where writers, editors, and agents do and see what they have to say.

Hollywood has an oar to row in this, too. Read entertainment news to keep an eye on what *kinds* of movies are coming out in the next year. Have three major stars signed on to do werewolf detective flicks for three different studios, set to release the summer after next? Might be a good time to start a werewolf detective novel. Big movies start—and feed—trends.

And remember, publishing may require a certain amount of luck, but the more you try, the luckier you'll get.

GETTING AWAY WITH USING THE CLICHÉ (FOR THOSE WHO'VE ALREADY CREATED THEIR CHARACTERS AND FALLEN IN LOVE WITH THEM)

Okay, before you picked up this book, you created some characters and situations, and you completely love them. No chance of dumping them and starting over. Let me ask, then:

Do any of them fit the above list? Are any of them clichés? Be honest— no one's here but the two of us, and I won't tell.

If they are, don't worry. We can fix it, and it'll be more fun than you think.

You wanna know a secret? One of the better ways to sell a book is to get the editor all the way through the manuscript before she says, "Holy cow! It's a Plucky Heroine story and I never noticed." In other words, you can use a cliché as long as you don't *look* like you're using a cliché.

Remember the other half of the rule: *A cliché is any idea or character that's . . . underdeveloped.* Lack of development is what really makes a cliché. The Enigmatic Wizard has no family, no friends, no hobbies (reading doesn't count), no background, nothing. So develop him. Figure out where he grew up, who his best friend was when he was twelve, where he went to school, what his favorite teacher was like, how he first discovered his magical talents. Give him a family—parents, siblings, aunts, uncles, cousins. Do they know about his wizardry? If so, what's their reaction to it? Family ties are a rich source of plot, so use them. Give Enigmatic a hobby or two that has nothing to do with magic (and please, please don't have him play the violin—this has been the weirdo hobby of choice since Sherlock Holmes). Get rid of the stupid beard and put him in fashionable clothes. Hell, maybe he's a clotheshorse. And hey—Enigmatic Wizards often seem to be wealthy. If yours is, explain where his money comes from. Or maybe your Enigmatic is poor all the time because he smokes pot when he isn't chanting in chalk circles.

You can do this with any cliché character. It also works with cliché situations. That Gateway you created? The one that's the same as every other Gateway? Develop it. It didn't spring into existence, right? Who created it? And for what purpose? Is the creator still around? Is he *happy* that people still use this Gateway? Perhaps the Gateway is difficult to open—or close—and it requires certain rituals or ingredients.

Adding more detail to a cliché will make it less cliché and more realistic, like a living, breathing person. In fact, this topic is so interesting, we're going to explore it more fully in the next chapter.

Choose a cliché character or situation from the list.

CLICHÉ:_____

_____

Now remove at least one element from that cliché, two if you can arrange it.

ELEMENT 1: _____

_____

ELEMENT 2: _____

_____

Now add three new twists, updates, or otherwise fascinating facets to the cliché.

NEW ELEMENT 1:_____

_____

_____

_____

NEW ELEMENT 2: _____

_____

_____

_____

NEW ELEMENT 3: _____

_____

_____

_____

In a paragraph or two below, describe your newly redesigned concept as if it were appearing on the back cover of a book. (EXAMPLE: Brad Higgins didn't ask to be a vampire. He studied physics under Isaac Newton, for God's sake, and was the old man's most promising student. That was three hundred years ago . . .)

PART II:
SUMMONING
THE
CHARACTERS

CHAPTER 6:

Supernatural Characters

Take an ordinary person, add a dash of magic, and you have a supernatural character, right? Well . . . that's a start. You might want a few other ingredients, too. In this section, we'll discuss creating fun, well-developed protagonists with supernatural elements.

THE NON–SUPERNATURAL PART

Always keep firmly in mind that people read any novel, no matter what the genre, to find out what happens next to a fascinating set of characters. And no, throwing some magic into an otherwise dull-as-dirt character won't make her fascinating. They need to be fascinating people on their own. So how do you do that?

First, remember that *fascinating* doesn't necessarily mean *unusual*. Regular people can end up on the fascinating end of the scale. Cinderella and Aladdin start out as perfectly ordinary people, but their stories have lasted for generations. Terry Pratchett's *Unseen Academicals* relies on Glenda, a relentlessly ordinary baker. The people who buy the country home in Raymond E. Feist's *Faerie Tale* are a perfectly ordinary blended family. Charlie Asher of *A Dirty Job* by Christopher Moore is dreadfully ordinary. It's part of the point of his character.

SO WHAT ABOUT MY WEREWOLF?

I'm not saying you can't write about extraordinary people. Quite the contrary. It's just that handling intrinsically extraordinary protagonists like vampires and werewolves and wizards is a big topic that deserves its own chapter. We'll look at them more closely in chapter eight.

Two factors make ordinary people worth reading about.

ONE: FULL DEVELOPMENT WITH UNUSUAL BITS

You need to develop your protagonist, fully and completely. On one level, this means she should have a fully documented life, from birth to the present—where the character was born, where she went to school, who her childhood friends were, what her family was like back then and what it's like now, the first time she fell in love, and more. As the author, you need to know nearly everything that has happened to her. I say *nearly* because more ideas and possibilities will crop up as you write the book. Old lovers, forgotten cousins, photographs from long-ago vacations, and other detritus from the past can show up at any time to create conflict—or help the character in a moment of crisis.

All of the above are merely facts, however. You also need to develop the character's *attitudes*. Two kids survive Mrs. Futz's awful third grade class. One shrugs the whole thing off, and the other comes away hating school for the rest of his life. Which attitude would your main character have?

Glenda from *Unseen Academicals* leads an ordinary life doing an ordinary job. A homely, slightly overweight woman just this side of thirty, she runs the night kitchen at a university, reads piles of romance novels when no one's looking, and still has a teddy bear named Mr. Wobble. Except for the teddy bear, there's nothing extraordinary, or even interesting, about her. Pratchett *makes* her interesting through her attitudes. Glenda is eminently practical. She runs the night kitchen with an iron fist because she knows in her heart there is One Right Way to make pies, and that's how it shall be done. The practicality extends to keeping a close eye on her assistant Juliet, who is beautiful and therefore not quite trustworthy in practical or romantic matters, in Glenda's estimation. Glenda also sees to it that the elderly people in her neighborhood are checked on, fed, and aired out from time to time because *someone* has to do it, and if she doesn't, who will? All this endears her to the reader and makes her interesting to read about long before a hungry goblin shows up in her kitchen and things get a little strange.

Your own characters need to have the same sort of depth. This extends beyond work and hobbies. How does your main character see the world? What does she expect when something good happens? When something bad happens? How does she react to a challenge? To a loss? How does she fit into her neighborhood or other community? Knowing all this and more will allow you to write a three-dimensional character who will draw readers into a story, regardless of supernatural setup.

Take a look at the following checklist. You don't need to know everything on it, but you should be aware of most of them.

THE ORDINARY PERSON'S CHECKLIST

EARLY LIFE

___ Conception circumstances

___ Birth circumstances

___ Babyhood anomalies, if any

CLOSE FAMILY

___ Mother's bio

___ Father's bio

___ Parents' relationship at time of conception

___ Parents' current relationship

___ Siblings (bio for each)

    ___ Relationship with sibling

    ___ Has it changed?

EXTENDED FAMILY

___ List family members

___ Relationship with each

FRIENDS

___ Current best friend (bio)

___ Former best friend(s)

___ Other current friends

ROMANCE

___ First crush

___ First dating relationship

___ First sexual encounter

___ First long-term relationship

___ Important romantic relationship(s)

___ Currently involved with someone?

    ___ Nature of relationship

    ___ History of relationship

    ___ Impact of relationship on character

EDUCATION

___ Elementary

___ Junior high

___ High school

___ College/grad school

___ Attitude toward school

ENTERTAINMENT AND HOBBIES

___ Loves to . . .

___ When bored, likes to . . .

TALENTS AND INABILITIES

___ Good at

___ Not so good at

___ Terrible at

NO ONE'S THAT ORDINARY

I teach a media studies class in high school. During the unit on the tricks and traps of TV advertising, I always ask my students, "How many of you live in a normal, ordinary family?"

No one ever raises a hand.

Almost nobody thinks of themselves or their family as completely ordinary. Everyone comes from something that they feel is at least a little odd or weird or different. It might be as small as having parents who were born in another country or as big as surviving two cancer operations. It might be a desire to be a dancer in a family of factory workers or a secret talent for knitting when your brothers all play football. It might be a sister who lives in a mental hospital or a father whose job takes him out of town three days out of five. Almost no one in the real world feels truly normal.

Fictional characters feel the same way. In the above example from *Unseen Academicals*, Glenda doesn't see herself as normal. She makes the best shepherd's pie in the world, works a night job instead of a day one, and keeps a level head in a place where everyone around her seems to go bonkers on a regular basis. Charlie from *A Dirty Job* doesn't see himself as normal either. He's a single father with an infant daughter. Nothing weird in that, except he's in this position not because of a divorce, but due to his wife's death. The otherwise normal children in Edward Eager's *Half Magic* also feel they're unusual because their father died years ago.

Lots of people in the world are levelheaded and work the night shift. Lots of people have lost wives or husbands. Lots of children have lost parents. Nothing unusual in any of this. *But that's not how the characters see it.* The characters see their situations as unusual, perhaps even unique.

This is human nature. Sometimes we want to believe that we're so different, so special, that no one else in the whole world is going through what we're going through, and neither can they understand it. (This is one reason why people turn to books, by the way—to see their lives reflected in fiction.) We want to be unique.

Other times we're *sure* no one else is going through what we are, so we don't bother talking about it, even though we'd secretly like to discuss the situation with someone who knows what it's like. When I adopted my sons from Ukraine, I talked about it quite openly among my co-workers and was surprised to discover a large number of people whose families had been touched by adoption. They had either adopted a child themselves or someone in their family had done so or they themselves had been adopted. Adoption isn't the rare event everyone thinks. It's certainly not unique, or even vaguely strange, but almost everyone I've talked to thought it was because they *felt* like it was. What's more, the people I talked to were quite happy, even relieved, to talk about it. Conversation broke the isolation.

Your characters need the same notion, some part of their lives that takes them off the beaten path as they see it. It'll make them like everyone else.

BUT HALF THIS STUFF WON'T MAKE IT INTO THE BOOK!

Actually, *everything* will make it into the book. Your character may never mention that her parents divorced messily when she was eight and that her mother dated a string of men thereafter, leaving her with a subconscious uncertainty about relationships. But *you'll* know, and this knowledge will tell you exactly what to do when Victor Vampire sweeps into Norma Normal's life, all handsome and delicious—and completely transient, from her perspective. Norma herself may not be aware why she keeps breaking it off with Victor even when it's clear she loves him, but you, the author, will know because you worked it out. Her reactions will come across as more consistent and therefore more realistic. So get that background together.

TWO: THE ADDITION OF THE EXTRAORDINARY

The other factor that makes ordinary people worth reading about is watching them cope with extraordinary situations. Seeing ordinary people deal with weird situations is, in fact, the core of a whole lot of stories, but paranormal stories have the chance to get really *extra*ordinary. So once you have your regular character fully developed and breathing nicely, you add the supernatural.

This is where the fun begins. How will your protagonist react when the magic shows up? See, the readers are regular people with (as observed above) one or two things that make them feel a little different, and if you've done your job, they're empathizing with the protagonist. On one level or another, they're pretending to be—or wanting to be—your main character. The only thing they're missing is honest-to-goodness magic, and it's your duty to supply it so they can face it right along with your protagonist.

So once you establish your character's normal life, you introduce the supernatural element(s) you chose from chapter two.

How soon? Depends, really. Some authors introduce it on the first page. Lucienne Diver's protagonist wakes up as a new vampire in her underground coffin in the opening paragraph of *Vamped*. Other authors take a little longer. Stephen King and Peter Straub barely hint at supernatural events when a seagull seems to stare at young Jack early on, but don't really get going on the magic until chapter three, when Jack talks to Speedy Parkway about the supernatural world known as the Territories. More in the middle is Christopher Moore's *A Dirty Job,* which hints at magic when Charlie's wife dies in chapter one and becomes much more supernatural when various objects in Charlie's shop acquire a magical red glow in chapter two. Chapter three starts with the wonderful line, "It was two weeks before Charlie left the apartment and walked down to the auto-teller on Columbus Avenue where he first killed a guy. His weapon of choice was the number forty-one bus." From then on, a supernatural blizzard of demons, death goddesses, and hellhounds tears through nearly every page.

As a general rule, you'll want to introduce the supernatural element as early as possible. Otherwise your readers will start to wonder when the magic's going to show up, and they rightfully get upset if you hold back.

Edward Eager sums it up very well through one of his characters in *Seven-Day Magic*:

> [Barnaby] shut the cover with a disgusted bang.
>
> "I thought so," he said. "Of all the gyps! It calls itself The Magic Door, but there's not a speck of real magic in it anywhere! It's just about this boy that learns to get along with these other people by being friendly and stuff. And the magic door's just the door of good fellowship or something. Man, do I despise a book like that!"
>
> And the others could not have agreed with him more.

So get moving on the magic.

Once it shows up, *show us how the character reacts*. That's most of the fun. We want to see your main character's surprise, shock, elation, desire, fear, curiosity, or whatever other strong emotions smack him upside the head when he first realizes that selkies really do exist and he's just met one, or that the rusty old sword left to him by his great-uncle is an artifact of great power and a circle of sorcerers intends to kill him for it. It's what Bilbo Baggins felt when he picked up a ring that would turn him invisible, what Lucy Pevensie felt when she first crossed into Narnia, and what Charlie Asher felt when he realized he'd been recruited to take a job as Death. This "holy cow" response is called *the sense of wonder* and is practically a requirement of paranormal novels. We'll get into details of how to make your readers feel the character's emotions in chapter eight.

GIVING GOALS

One of the simplest ways to develop a protagonist, supernatural or not, is to ask yourself two questions:

1. What does he want?
2. What is standing in the way?

You should have at least two answers for number 1. And neither of them can be "Survive repeated attacks from the antagonist," thank you. Readers want *real* goals, ones with depth and power. In a Magical Gateway book, the goal might be to find a way home before time runs out, for example. Several smaller goals might be wrapped within that larger one: to repair the magic ring that will open the gate, to rescue the boy who knows where the magic ring is, and so on, but everything should lead back to this larger goal. The second goal may be an emotional one. Perhaps it's to find real love, or a need to overcome a character flaw. Bonus points if you can tie the second goal into the first one, forcing the protagonist to deal with two conflicts at the same time.

The answer to number 2 is probably tied to the antagonist. The ring that will open the magic gate and send the hero back home is the same one that will allow the antagonist to bring his Dark Mistress into this world, and the antagonist already possesses half of it. Or the antagonist needs the blood of an Outlander to complete the spell and has set out to capture the protagonist before he can leave. In any case, you need to throw something into the protagonist's way. This creates conflict for your book.

If you can't state at least two goals for your protagonist, chances are the character is underdeveloped, and you need to add more information about him.

SOME SUPERNATURAL PROTAGONISTS

There are many types of supernatural protagonists—archetypes, if you will. Without proper development, they can fall into cliché, but you read the previous chapter and won't allow them to do that. Let's take a look at a few.

THE REGULAR JOE/JOSEPHINE

The Regular Joe (or Josephine) starts off very much the ordinary person as outlined above, but early on in the book, he encounters the paranormal and is forced to deal with it. One caveat, however—the Regular Joe never develops supernatural abilities or powers. Ever. And he deals with the magical world using resources available only to ordinary people. The Regular Joe isn't especially strong or smart, but he knows his place in his own world, and that makes him powerful in his own way. The fun with reading Regular Joe is watching him cope with—and eventually win against—the more powerful supernatural, which is way outside of his normal worldview.

The Regular Joe is a tremendous draw for readers because it's easy to empathize with him—he's so much like us—and paranormal novels abound with examples of him. Writers like this type of character for exactly this reason, and because he's easy to hurt physically, which creates yet more conflict. We've already talked about Jack Sawyer in *The Talisman*, the children in The Chronicles of Narnia, and the family in *Faerie Tale*. Yet another is young Lewis Barnavelt from John Bellairs's *The House With a Clock in Its Walls*. There are plenty of others.

THE RELUCTANT

The Reluctant doesn't want anything to do with this supernatural stuff, doesn't want to be a hero, and certainly doesn't want to risk his life to save the world. He already has a life—a very nice one, in fact—and nothing you can do will make him jeopardize it. Let someone else handle the heroics.

Hold on. *Who's* in danger? They're going to do *what?* Well, maybe he could help a little. Just this once. And then he expects to be left alone, got it?

This appeal of this character comes from the "will he/won't he" conflict. Even though the reader knows he'll end up pitching in to save the world or fight the monsters or whatever's going on, the fun lies in seeing how he's persuaded. Moist von Lipwig is the quintessential reluctant hero in Terry Pratchett's *Going Postal* and again in *Making Money*.

THE HUNTER/WARRIOR

She hunts down supernatural blech and deals with it. She kicks butt and doesn't bother to take names—that's for lesser warriors. She might even be a little Reluctant (see above), but in the end, she'll find her way into the thick of the battle, beheading vampires, shooting werewolves, and destroying demons. (And yeah—this character might be a guy, too.)

The kick-butt Warrior started off as a guys-only thing and got a little stale. Then women edged into the club, and the archetype took on new life. Initially, writers used female Hunter/Warriors for shock value: "Look at how we're breaking stereotypes! Girls can fight, too! Aren't you amazed that a girl can fight?" As time passed, the character became more accepted, and now readers see it as normal.

A major plus for this type of character is that the writer always has a reason to get the character involved in the action—as the Hunter, she's supposed to seek out supernatural messes, and there's no need to invent reasons to force her participation. Diana Tregarde from Mercedes Lackey's *Burning Water* and its sequels is such a heroine, as is Laurell K. Hamilton's Anita Blake.

THE NEWBIE

The Newbie doesn't know anything about magic or the paranormal. He doesn't watch vampire movies or read ghost stories. He can't name a single Greek god, and his only experience with leprechauns is through a box of breakfast cereal. He certainly doesn't believe in any of this otherworldly crap. So naturally, he's the one who gets yanked into the supernatural world.

There's a sense of "Why him?" that combines with a feeling of superiority from the reader that combine to make this character appealing. The reader can agonize over why this person, who knows nothing about the paranormal and doesn't really care about it, gets to take part in a supernatural adventure while the reader, who probably knows quite a lot about magic and would happily climb over his own grandmother for the chance to see it for real, misses the chance entirely. And once the story gets underway, the reader can have the satisfaction of trying to figure out various supernatural motifs ahead of the ignorant Newbie. Some Newbies learn quickly, and others continue to stumble.

Writing the Paranormal Novel

This character creates a major advantage for the writer because he has a built-in reason for exposition—everything has to be explained to him eventually. Gina, the fashionista vampire from *Vamped* by Lucienne Diver, is a Newbie who learns quickly. C. Thomas Flood, the San Francisco vampire from Christopher Moore's *You Suck*, is a Newbie who learns more slowly.

THE SUPER

The Super is born with or granted great powers, and must learn to use them in order to accomplish some important task (like save the world). Often the whole deal comes with a time limit and an advisor who can provide a bit of training. A good chunk of the book is dedicated to the hero discovering how these powers work, but before the hero has quite mastered them, she has to face the crisis. A good part of the conflict comes from the hero's struggle to master the new powers in time and being forced into a fight too early. This character type is often combined with others, like the Reluctant or the Newbie.

Supers are enormous fun to read and write about—who hasn't fantasized about having superpowers? There's some danger in the Super, however: The more powerful the character becomes, the more difficult it is to challenge her.

Almost all vampire and werewolf protagonists are Supers. So is Harry Potter, along with Percy Jackson from *The Lightning Thief* by Rick Riordan.

THE EXPERIENCED ONE

Here we have the opposite of the Newbie, someone who knows quite a lot about the supernatural world already by the time the book opens. The character is often powerful and may be a Super, or simply have a great many supernatural contacts. A great advantage of the Experienced One is, like the Hunter/Warrior, the author doesn't have to work terribly hard to get such a character involved in a paranormal storyline.

Abraham Van Helsing is a prime example of an Experienced One. So is Anita Blake.

THE ANTAGONISTS

Not every paranormal book needs an antagonist. Most of Edward Eager's books do quite well without one. E. Nesbit's books do the same. This can actually throw some readers, who are expecting a fight between opposing forces, but as long as you have something for the protagonist to struggle against, the readers will adapt. Usually this conflict will be something that arises from a situation: character vs. nature or character vs. society. The character might have to work out how to use magic, survive in a hostile environment, or dodge a group instead of a person. Nesbit's and Eager's children, for example, try to work out the rules of magic during their adventures, and the mistakes they make cause them problems. They also have to hide their magic from the adults in their lives. Naomi Novik's dragon Temeraire deals with antagonists, but his primary conflict is a societal one—he wants equal rights for dragons in England, a country that essentially enslaves them.

However, most books call for an antagonist—the more deliciously horrible, the better—and she should be as carefully crafted as the protagonist.

We need to be clear here—an antagonist is *not* a villain. Antagonists may be evil, cruel, sadistic, selfish, or worse, but a true antagonist is never a villain. A villain is a two-dimensional character who exists only to give the protagonist someone to fight; an antagonist is a fully realized, well-developed character whose goals happen to conflict with the protagonist's. In other words, the protagonist and antagonist can't both have what they want, but we want the protagonist to win.

You need to figure out the goals for your antagonist just like you do for your protagonist. Remember those two character questions? Go back and answer them for your bad guy. If you can't, you have a mere villain, and that's bad for your book.

Also remember that even the worst people in the world never see themselves as evil. They're just . . . misunderstood. Perhaps they're trying to bring some good or order into a world that doesn't appreciate them, or they're ahead of their time, or people are just too foolish, too stupid to understand the genius of their accomplishments. Or they don't see themselves as bound by the idiotic rules of a society they didn't create and therefore don't need to obey. But evil? Certainly not. Your antagonist should have a similar view.

Supernatural antagonists have their own archetypes.

THE DESTROYER

The Destroyer seeks destruction on an enormous scale. It might be a town or city, or it might be the entire world. The actual mechanism can vary. The old-fashioned explosive disaster is one way, but other Destroyers intend to release something dreadful, such as a horde of monsters, or a dark god, or a horrible plague. Some Destroyers don't realize their plan will wipe out the world and proceed in merry ignorance. The protagonist has to stop him—or convince him to stop—before said destruction is unleashed.

This antagonist brings a serious pile of chips to the table, which can make for some powerful conflict: If the protagonist fails, millions will die. The disadvantage to the Destroyer comes if you want to write multiple books. Can you thrill the reader in Book II if you've threatened to wipe out the entire world in Book I? (Actually, you can. See chapter seven.) The Morrigan from Christopher Moore's *A Dirty Job* is an example of a Destroyer.

THE MISGUIDED ONE

The world needs guidance. It needs a firm hand. Above all, it needs *order*. And there's just one person who can provide it.

The Misguided One knows the world would become a better place if everyone would just do as she says. In fact, she's doing everyone a favor by taking over. Doesn't anyone understand the sacrifices she's making? How difficult it is to rule? Or how wonderful the world will become once we get past this difficult early stage? Any and all ends justify the means here, since they're all for the greater good. And the trains will run on time, too.

In the right hands, this antagonist becomes truly scary. After all, she's fully convinced she's the good gal—and there might be some truth to what she believes. Lilith from Terry Pratchett's *Witches Abroad* is a perfect example of this antagonist.

THE OPPOSITE

The Chosen One has a mirror image, someone the dark forces chose as their champion. He'll have special powers and abilities just as the Chosen One does, and likely will go one or two better—the forces of evil almost always have the upper hand at the beginning, otherwise the heroes would have too easy a time of it. Often the origins of the Opposite and the Chosen One are intertwined, and the two are fated to meet.

This archetype is fun to play with because it's always interesting to hold a mirror up and ask, "What would the opposite be like?" The conflict is built right in. On the downside, the Opposite falls easy prey to cliché. If you go this route, be careful that you're not just creating two empty suits of superpowered armor to pound on each other. Develop the character fully to avoid this, as we've discussed above. Randall Flagg provides an Opposite to Mother Abigail in Stephen King's *The Stand*.

THE JILTED ONE

This antagonist has a personal vendetta against the protagonist and is using supernatural means to get revenge. Although she may need to acquire wealth or power along the way, they mean nothing—revenge against this single person remains the driving force in the Jilted One's life. It might be over a love affair, sure, but it might also have something to do with another kind of loss that she blames the protagonist for—the death of a loved one, loss of personal status, not being allowed to join the Circle of Sorcery because the protagonist got the last open slot, whatever. Often this character's motivation is hidden at first. She seems to want something else, something that draws the protagonist close enough for her to reveal her *true* motivation.

Unlike many other antagonists, the Jilted One may not necessarily want to kill the protagonist. She may settle for humiliation or the loss of the protagonist's powers or even the death of someone close to the protagonist. In some ways, this makes her even more dangerous. Looking all the way back to Greek mythology, we can find the Jilted One in King Menelaus, who declared a decade-long war on Troy solely to pry his beautiful wife from the arms of that idiot Paris.

THE ONE-UPPER

The One-Upper wants more—more power, more money, more toys. Enough is never enough. Each conquest is nothing more than a stepping-stone to the next one. The One-Upper often controls vast resources or magical power, which gives him a tremendous advantage when it comes to persuading people to work for him, or corrupting them into it.

This character is tricky to write. One-Uppers exist all over the place in the real world—any number of politicians and businesspeople fit the mold—but in fiction it's easy to let them fall into caricature. Be sure you know *why* your One-Upper is so obsessed with having more. (Actually, you should know why *any* antagonist wants *anything*, but it's especially true in this case.) Perhaps he's actually insecure and afraid of losing everything because of certain events in his upbringing. Or perhaps his mother was a relentless perfectionist who never let anything he did be good enough. Count Magpyr from Terry Pratchett's *Carpe Jugulum* is one example of a One-Upper, and so is the White Witch from C.S. Lewis's *The Lion, the Witch and the Wardrobe*.

THE LUNATIC

The Lunatic has gone cuckoo bananas. Perhaps she was born, or perhaps she was made. In any case, she doesn't respond to pain or fear or love the way normal humans do, and her goals seem to make no sense. As a result, the heroes never know what she'll do next. Yet, in the end, every move she makes turns out to have a careful reason.

This is a difficult antagonist to handle well, and it requires a fair amount of research. You can't really throw a bunch of random, nasty behavior together and get a workable Lunatic antagonist—many of your readers know too much about psychology and mental health, and they'll call you on it. Instead, you'll need to find a psychological diagnosis, learn how people with that particular affliction think, and work that into the character. You can take some literary license. In fact, you'll have to—very few truly insane people would be functional enough to give a supernatural protagonist much trouble.

Also remember that while the Lunatic's actions might look loopy to everyone else, they make complete sense to *her*. This means you, the author, need to know why she's scared of butter, why she won't use the Internet on Sundays, and why she's obsessed with making zombie black cats.

A subset of this antagonist is the Raving Lunatic, the one who's gone completely round the bend. Werewolves do this every month, and some vampires do it if they get hungry enough.

Victor Frankenstein from Mary Shelley's famous novel arguably fits this type of antagonist. Jack Torrance from Stephen King's *The Shining* starts out as a Regular Joe protagonist and ends as a Lunatic antagonist.

THE SELFISH ONE

The Selfish One has some kind of personal problem and will do anything to solve it. Nothing and nobody else matters. If people have to die, so be it. If he has to ruin lives, that's fine, too. Many vampire antagonists fall into this category—the juicy need to feed rules all, and they don't care who gets hurt in the process. Some Selfish antagonists are seeking something in particular—immortality, a long-lost love, a cure—and woe to anyone who stands in their way. Or perhaps the protagonist holds the key to what the Selfish One wants, which automatically draws the two together.

The fun of writing a Selfish antagonist is that he starts off as eminently believable. We're all born with a certain amount of selfishness. Crank it up a little, add some magic, and you have a delicious supernatural opponent. Count Dracula is, of course, the preeminent Selfish antagonist, and Fay Harper from Mercedes Lackey's *Jinx High* was built from the same mold.

THE BETRAYER

She's your friend, fighting by your side to destroy the Destroyer, one-up the One-Upper, and show the Misguided One the error of her ways. Just when everything looks its worst, you discover that she's been feeding information to the enemy all along. Then she guts you from behind.

The Betrayer comes in several flavors. One kind lies from the outset, making friends with the hero for the sole purpose of waiting for the perfect moment to insert that knife. Another kind truly starts off as a friend but becomes secretly corrupted by the antagonist, who hands her the knife with a wink and a grin. A third type doesn't want to play Judas but is forced into it because the antagonist has kidnapped her sister or cornered the market on the herb that keeps her alive or threatened to feed her son's soul to ravenous ghosts if she refuses to obey—or tells the protagonist what's going on.

Betrayers provide a wonderful plot twist and a great emotional punch, especially if the betrayer is—or seems to be—romantically involved with the protagonist. However, you have to set up a Betrayer with care. To be fair to the reader, you need to weave small clues about the Betrayer's intent into the narrative before the betrayal so the reader can be surprised but also mentally add, "And why didn't I see that coming?" Finding the balance between gentle whisper and a bullhorn isn't easy, though, and a fair number of authors abandon the idea altogether, choosing instead to rely on dramatic irony instead. The reader becomes aware early on that the Betrayer is quietly working against the clueless protagonist, and the reader gets sweaty palms hoping the main character will figure everything out in time—or that the Betrayer might have a last-minute change of heart. Luke Castellan from Rick Riordan's *The Lightning Thief* and Edmund Pevensie from Lewis's *The Lion, the Witch and the Wardrobe* are both Betrayers.

THE DARK LORD OR LADY

The Dark Lord or Lady moves from the shadows. His reach extends to the far corners of the world, and his many minions do his bidding without hesitation. His vast powers are often nebulous, left unexplained or undefined. Many Dark Lords operate in secrecy—the protagonist may encounter several layers of minions before realizing the Dark Lord even exists.

Dark Lords are tricky, from a writer's perspective. They inevitably invite comparison to Sauron from Tolkien's The Lord of the Rings trilogy or Lord Voldemort from the Harry Potter series. It's also difficult to come up with plausible reasons why the Dark Lord doesn't simply send an overwhelming force of minions to destroy the protagonist once and for all. On the plus side, the nature of a Dark Lord makes him intrinsically scary and automatically a difficult challenge for the protagonist. Stephen King used the Dark Lord antagonist when he created the Crimson King, who appears in several of his novels and short stories.

THE HYDRA ORGANIZATION

Destroy one agent, and two more take its place. The Hydra Organization has enormous resources, can field an infinite number of agents, and won't rest until the protagonist has been captured or killed. It can tap phones, hack computers, track credit cards, and insert agents almost anywhere. Some Hydra Organizations are "alphabet" groups like the FBI, CIA, or NSA. Others are secret societies with occult leanings like the Illuminati or the Masons. And yet others include groups of vampire clans, werewolf packs, or circles of sorcerers. A Hydra Organization may have as its leader another antagonist such as a Dark Lord or a One-Upper. The Unseelie Court from Emma Bull's *War for the Oaks* is a supernatural Hydra Organization, as are the General Oblation Board and the Magisterium from Philip Pullman's *The Golden Compass* and its sequels.

As with protagonists, you can combine some of these archetypal traits when creating your antagonist. There's no reason you can't have a Lunatic Dark Lady or a Selfish Betrayer. Just be sure you give her as much thought and care as you give your protagonist.

SUPPORTING CAST

The rest of your characters are called the *supporting cast.* Some will be *major characters*, people who show up quite a lot, and you'll need to develop them just as fully as the protagonist. Minor characters, called *spear carriers* in theater, don't need much development. The cab driver who gives your protagonist directions can do it without a full life story, but your protagonist's love interest definitely needs one. Full development will guide you when your characters meet and interact, and character interaction is one of the factors that make a book fascinating.

NAMES

Character names must be chosen carefully. The name is the first thing a reader (and an editor) will see when the character appears, and that name creates a mental picture. *Frederick* creates a different mental image than *Freddie,* and the image *Bess* projects diverges quite a lot from the one projected by *Elizabeth.*

Naming characters in a paranormal novel can carry a few extra difficulties. Some, or even all, of your characters might come from another culture or another world, meaning you might be creating their names from scratch. It's easy to wind up with something that comes across as unintentionally silly or that's overused, which is why we need to take a closer look at the process.

NORMAL NAMES

Even characters who live in modern America and Europe need carefully chosen names. Everyone knows the trick of buying a baby name book or going to baby name sites for ideas. A few other tips:

For male characters, names with a *J* or a *K* in them (Justin, Kevin, Jake) tend to sound action-oriented and totally way cool. As a result, they've become overused in both the real world and the fictional world.

Jake shows up in a lot of books, for example. Try avoiding these unless you're really wedded to the name *Kirk* or *Jason*.

Most baby name books list each name's meaning, and I admit it's great fun to pour over such lists to see who among friends and relatives has a name with a meaning that actually fits his or her personality. The temptation is to choose character names that reflect the person's personality, too. You're writing about a guy who takes charge of any situation, so you spend half an hour looking through the baby name book until you discover the name *Derek,* which means "ruler of the people." Perfect! My advice? Don't bother. The vast majority of your readers won't make the connection, and the ones who do will probably figure the whole thing is a coincidence. It's wasted time.

When you choose a name, say it aloud two or three times and see if it works. *Elizabeth Brown* works well, but *Chris Simonson* is a little awkward. Names that end in *S* are problematic as well. *Dennis* seems a perfectly serviceable name until you give him, say, a sword or anything else that begins with an *S. Dennis's sword* may be grammatically correct, but it looks odd, and the phrase interrupts the flow of words on the page. For the same reason, avoid surnames that start with the letter that ends the first name. Say *Les Stiles* and *Bev Victor* aloud and you'll see what I mean.

While we're on the subject of letters, make sure your characters' names start with different ones. It confuses the reader if your characters are named Kevin, Kelly, Ken, and Kyle. Avoid.

Some authors try too hard with character names. Thorne, Cade, and Hunter may seem pretty cool and exotic when you're writing them down, but they ultimately come across as outlandishly ridiculous, especially if all three names appear in the same book. As a rule, you can get away with *one* exotic or weird name per novel (unless your characters come from another world—see page 109).

Finally, make the character's gender clear in the name. Yes, *Kyle* and *Sam* can be female names, but the shift takes serious mental adjustment on behalf of the reader, and you don't want that. The same goes for androgynous names like *Chris, Drew,* and *Dakota.* A name should help establish an image in the reader's head, and an androgynous name only clouds that process.

Notice that these are all guidelines more than rules. If you break them, be sure you're doing it on purpose. If you name the men in your book Justin, Jake, and Jeremy, make it part of the plot. Maybe they're triplets. If your protagonist is a woman named Kyle, part of her character should be a certain amount of weariness toward people who assume she's a man.

OTHERWORLDLY NAMES

Characters from other worlds may well need otherworldly names. (If your world is a close analog to Earth, then you may end up using Earthlike names.) Create them carefully. Your characters may be otherworldly, but your readers live on Earth. You don't want to choose names that bring your reader's eyes to a screeching halt in mid-sentence. Let's take a second to look at ways to create workable, off-Earth names.

One place to get inspiration is foreign language names, especially ones from non-Western cultures. Look at names from China, Africa, and India. Smoosh them together and mix them around to see what you get.

Another place to look is the ancient patronymic method. In Cyrillic languages, you add -*vich* to the end of a name to mean *son of,* and that becomes a man's last name, so *Mikhail Sergeievich* means *Mikhail, son of Sergei.* Similarly, in old Ireland, *mac* meant *son of (macDonald)* and *nic* meant *daughter of.* There's no reason you can't create a similar system.

Nicknames and epithets are another place to look. A redheaded guy might become known as *Eric the Red,* while his tall daughter might be *Wanda Loftus.* The family that moved here from Derry might be known as *the Derry family,* and that young man who guards the gate between worlds might just be known as *Warden.*

You can also simply string vowels and consonants together until you get something that seems workable. However, be sure to say the name out loud a few times to ensure you haven't accidentally made a joke. An elven warrior named *Tompis* from the land of *Green* might look good on paper, but if you say the names out loud once or twice, the weaknesses become apparent. Reading names out loud will also check for easy pronounceability, a characteristic all names should share.

Avoid names with odd letter combinations. English readers don't know what to do with *ii* or *qk* or *iy*. Hell, half the time we don't know what to do with *gh* and *ei*. And forget about non-English letters like *ä*, *ç*, or *ö*. Readers won't look at the name *Kôjïq* and say, "How creatively exotic!" They'll look at it and think, "How the heck do you say that? Is the whole book like this? Maybe I should read something else."

Assume that readers will mentally insert standard English pronunciation when they see your names. English readers who see *ch* simply won't think of the German or Scottish throat-clearing noise, for example. If you absolutely must use a non-English pronunciation to a name, be sure to tell the readers:

> I shook her hand and my mouth went dry. "I'm Pete."
> "You can call me Lucia." She pronounced her name with a *ch* in the middle. Sexy as hell.

Finally, avoid the Apostrophe of Doom. For some reason, a number of writers decided that sprinkling apostrophes over a bunch of names would make them really neat. This resulted in the creation of names like *K'Panna* and *Le'mann'tua* and *Hos'e'he'd the Do'of'u's*. In English, apostrophes indicate ownership (*Norman's armor*) or that something was left out (*can't*). When an apostrophe shows up that performs neither function, English readers stumble. We can't help it. You don't want your readers to stumble.

CHARACTER DEVELOPMENT

EXERCISE #1
Do a Web search on "common job interview questions" and use the results to create a list of ten interview questions. Then answer them for your character, using your character's words.

Writing the Paranormal Novel

EXERCISE #2

Write a letter from your character to you as if the character were an old-fashioned pen pal. The character should introduce himself thoroughly in his own words. (I use this one quite a lot with characters who won't "talk" to me while I'm writing.)

EXERCISE #3

Write down three facts about your character that won't appear in the book.

EXERCISE #4

Answer the following questions in detail: If your character could go back in time and change one thing about her past, what would it be? What happened? Why would she choose this event? What change would she want to make?

CHAPTER 7:

Magic and the Superhero

In chapter six of your book, the heroine learns how to heal her own wounds—which means that bullet wound you're planning for chapter seven suddenly doesn't mean much. And in a wonderful moment of angst, your hero overcame a mental block in chapter nine. Now he can send his thoughts to the heroine from anywhere on the planet—except you were planning to have the Dark Lady kidnap him, tricking the heroine into thinking he's dead. Now what?

No worries! This is fiction, and there's always a fix. In this chapter, we'll deal with supernatural powers and the unique difficulties they create for plot and characterization.

CREEPING

Superpowers are cool to write about and fun to read about, so why not give your heroine just one more? Or boost the ones she has? Trouble is, this line of thinking leads to a mega-protagonist who can do too much, which means you'll have to create an even more powerful antagonist to provide a challenge, but to win your heroine will have to become even stronger yet, leading you to create an even more powerful protagonist, who forces the heroine to become stronger . . .

Yeah.

This problem is called "superhero creep." It's plagued comic books for decades, and has more recently invaded paranormal novels. When Jerry

Siegel and Joe Shuster created Superman in 1932, he could leap really high, lift a car, and stop bullets. By the 1980s, he had a whole mess of vision powers, super breath, flight, total invulnerability to everything but kryptonite and magic, and the ability to move faster than light. Each successive writer made him a little more powerful, and a little more, and a little more. As a result, his villains had to become more powerful, too. He graduated from fighting street thugs and wife abusers to fighting world-wrecking monsters with names like Doomsday. His powers crept up higher and higher until the writers couldn't find anything to challenge him anymore and they killed him off in 1992, only to bring him back after great public outcry.

Terry Pratchett ran into the exact same problem with Granny Weatherwax, an immensely popular witch who appears as the protagonist in several of his Discworld books. One of her abilities is the power to "borrow." Her mind leaves her body and slips into an animal so she can see and hear what it does. In *Equal Rites,* her first appearance, Granny is already pretty good at it. By *Lords and Ladies,* her fourth book, she is able to borrow the collective mind of an entire beehive, something no witch has ever done, in order to face down the evil Queen of Elves. By *Carpe Jugulum,* her sixth appearance, she can put her mind into inanimate objects. Between this and other powers she's developed, Granny has become the most powerful witch in history. So what's left for her to do? Pratchett, ever the humorist, makes fun of this problem in an early scene of *Jugulum* by making Granny feel a certain amount of ennui because the world lacks challenge—until an entire clan of vampires shows up. *Carpe Jugulum* has to date been Granny's final appearance as a protagonist, and she's been relegated to supporting cast in other Discworld books, quite possibly because finding a challenge for the most powerful witch in all of history is more trouble than it's worth, especially since Pratchett has a number of other characters he can explore instead.

Superhero creep in novels usually happens because the writer doesn't anticipate the hero becoming all that popular. By the time the character's popularity has entrenched itself, the author has committed to a pattern of one-upmanship, always trying to outdo what came before. The first bad guy was going to wipe out a town, so the new bad guy will wipe out the country. This means the next bad guy has to threaten the whole world, and the one after that has to take on the entire universe. Whew! How can you follow that?

(By now you've probably figured out that this problem largely shows up in series books, and you're likely working on your first novel. How much do you need to worry about this? Plenty. First, it never hurts to plan ahead. Second, paranormal books lend themselves to series, and if you sell one, it's quite possible the editor will say, "What else you got?" So start planning now.)

One way to avoid superhero creep is to set a ceiling for yourself. Decide *in advance* what powers your protagonist will start out with and what powers she'll develop. If your main character starts off with some weak mental powers that give her unexpected flashes of the future and the ability to tell something about the owner of any object she picks up, figure out exactly how far you want take that. Will these powers develop into a full-blown ability to look into the future? The power to control people through the objects they touch? In which book will each of these powers develop? The more you have planned out, the more control you'll have over your long-term story and the less creep you'll have.

Another way to avoid creeping is to make a new power temporary. Once the situation that requires it has ended, the power vanishes, taking superhero creep with it. This takes a little finagling, though. For example: Lawrence has been blocking his own potential, refusing to tap his birthright power of Light. But in the climactic scene, Martina dies and Lawrence pushes past his own limits to bring her back from the dead. When it's over, Lawrence learns that resurrection is forbidden and he won't be allowed to do it again. The power is gone—and the author doesn't have to worry about explaining in future books why Lawrence doesn't resurrect other people, ones whom the author needs to stay dead. No superhero creep. The drawback with this approach is that if you do it more than once or twice, readers will twig what's going on and get justifiably annoyed with you. Use this method sparingly.

You can also flatly refuse to increase your character's power level. Amanda will never progress beyond future flashes and a bit of object reading, and that's it. Lawrence will have to live with minor healing powers, nothing more. Avoid the creep by refusing to go there, and work on other areas of character development instead.

THE NEED FOR LIMITS

Supernatural powers must come with limits. Without them, your characters turn into omnipotent walking weapons fairly quickly. Even gods in ancient myths have their limitations. Besides, setting limits creates conflict, and conflict creates story. All characters need something to struggle against, and limitations on their abilities provide just that.

Limits also prevent them from becoming Mary Sue or Gary Stu (see chapter 76).

This requirement, oddly, applies more heavily to protagonists than to antagonists. Supernatural antagonists are almost always more powerful than protagonists in order to keep the protagonist on his toes—a weaker antagonist isn't much of a challenge, and an equal antagonist only has a fifty-fifty chance of creating suspense. Antagonists therefore tend to have fewer limits. Note that I said *fewer* instead of *no*, however. An omnipotent antagonist isn't much fun, either—it's hard to explain why he simply doesn't wipe out the hero with a wave of his tentacle.

There are a number of ways to limit supernatural powers. Let's take a look at a few.

EXHAUSTION

Using supernatural power sucks up serious energy, and it makes the character tired. Or hungry. Or both. The more magic the character uses, the worse it gets. Eventually her powers stop working until the character has the chance to rest and/or eat. Drain things too far with something spectacular, and the character can send herself into a coma, or even die. Vampires often suffer from this one—the more power they use, the hungrier for blood they get.

This is a good one because it allows the author to drag a character through the mud and then throw everything she has into one final, self-sacrificing push to stop the antagonist. You can also scale back this limit as the character becomes more powerful. Just watch out for that superhero creep.

YIKES!

The character's ability only kicks in (or *always* kicks in) when he's startled or excited or otherwise upset. This one is a favorite among authors who create characters with mental powers. It's nicely inconvenient for powerful abilities like telekinesis (moving objects with your mind), pyrokinesis (setting stuff on fire), and teleportation (jumping instantly from place to place), but it works for other abilities, too. Not only does the character have to learn how to use the power, he also has to learn self-control so his dog doesn't pop to the North Pole every time he has a bad day.

Characters with this limitation often spend a fair amount of time working to overcome it or control the power—and when they do, watch out! Unless you remove the problem fairly early, this limitation is often best for a protagonist who you *know* will only appear once. Otherwise, you'll continually juggle flying dishes or end up with an enormously powerful character in later books.

ONLY WHEN ...

Some characters can use their powers only under certain conditions: when the moon is full, after dark, when the sun shines on them, when they're drenched in blood, when they're singing a particular tune. Folklore is full of limitations like these, so if you get stuck, do some research.

The wonderful part about this limit is the chance for suspense. Will the sun rise (or set) in time for the character's power to kick in? Will she be able to remove the gag so she can sing? Will her outstretched fingers reach the sunbeam before the goons notice? This one is also less prone to creepage.

THREE TIMES

The character can only use a particular power a certain number of times. Or there's a time limit on the power—it'll only work for so long. After that, the power stops working for a specific amount of time, or even forever. Wishes work like this, often coming in sets of three. Other powers might just need to "recharge."

The advantage of this one comes from added suspense similar to the previous "Only When" category, and from the author being able to force the character to operate *without* his supernatural power and find creative ways to resolve the conflict.

YOU CAN'T …

The character can't use her powers for certain actions, either due to a vow or because the source of the power won't allow it. A healer, for example, might have sworn to use her power to help, never to harm, or perhaps the source of her healing power has made it clear that if she ever *does* use her power to harm, she'll lose it or pay some other dreadful price. Or perhaps it's simply impossible to use the power for anything but its intended effect.

This can create a bit of wonderful conflict—if faced with an extreme situation, will the character break away from the requirements or stay true to it?

POWER CORRUPTS

The more the character indulges in the power, the more it corrupts him. This problem tempts many vampires—drinking blood makes them powerful, but killing people weakens their connection to humanity. The same goes for characters who summon dark gods, demons, or other nether powers.

This limitation creates some powerful conflict, but it's hard to carry it past more than two or three books. A character can teeter on the edge of corruption only for so long. Then it gets repetitious.

PAY THE PIPER

The paranormal carries a price. The character might have to pay in blood every time she casts a spell, or kill something, or do a return favor for a higher (or lower) power, or anything else you can think of. The more power you want, the more you pay. Good guys pay the price themselves; bad guys make others pay for them.

This limitation, the notion of the sacrifice, flows through a lot of paranormal literature and is as old as human civilization. It works well—there's only so much one person can give, and the bad guys, who can make others pay, gain a nice advantage over the protagonist.

RECIPE REQUIRED

There's no quick magic. Everything requires long preparation and ritual, with exotic ingredients and much chanting in weird languages. Even a small interruption will ruin the spell, or cause a catastrophe.

This is a huge limit on power. Magic tends to be for special occasions. You can't have a supernatural face-off or do quick spells. On the other hand, you don't have to worry about cleaning up after people who can fling lightning bolts down Madison Avenue.

HOW TOUCHING

Mind powers or magic only work on people the character can touch. Forget long-distance telepathy. And the character will have to be creative in order to find ways to make physical contact with people he needs to "read." Antagonists who are aware of this limitation will go out of their way to avoid touching people, making the protagonist's job even harder.

There are a number of variations on this. The power might work only as long as the "reader" is touching the other person (requiring him to think fast), or the character might need to touch the person once to establish contact and not need to do it again thereafter, or touching other people might send the reader an overload of information that's difficult to sort out, or the character reads other people *every* time he touches them, making some social situations (including sex) awkward, embarrassing, or painful.

GET OUT OF MY HEAD!

This one's generally for supernatural mental powers: The character's abilities switch on unexpectedly, or are always working on some level. She's always reading the surface thoughts of the people around her, and it's driving her crazy.

This is a facet of the *Yikes!* category (see page 116). The character may or may not learn to rein in her telepathy, but meanwhile she'll certainly have a difficult time of it.

BLOCKED!

Every power has its opposite. Every strength has its weakness. Your main character has developed a long-range telepathic link with her boyfriend? Big deal. Your antagonist has a way to block it, or temporarily sever the link, or—better still—has found a way to use the protagonist's new telepathy as a two-way street, attacking her through the link and bludgeoning her into unconsciousness. And that new insta-healing power? Turns out if you use it too often, it causes unexpected mutations. We can restore that severed arm, but it might turn out to be a little rubbery, with suckers on. So heal carefully.

YOU WANT IT WHEN?

The character's power works when only it wants to. There's no pattern to it, no rhyme, no reason. The character lives with an ability that shows itself at odd moments, often inconveniently.

This limitation is one to use sparingly, since it's obviously an author dodge. The power shows up whenever the writer wants it to, which removes suspense, and it can become a major cheat if it appears just in time to pull the character out of a difficult spot. The ability to see the future is usually coupled with limitation—someone with the power to control his precognition completely would ruin almost any story. Readers know that and are willing to accept it in this particular case, even though they know it's kind of a cheat.

SYSTEMS OF MAGIC

The major advantage of writing a paranormal novel is the freedom it grants you. You're dealing with magic and the paranormal. Some of it—telepathy, psychokinesis, etc.—might technically be more science fictional, but for all intents and purposes it's still magic. This means you can do anything you want, and you have no special-effects budget. Create impossible monsters; have characters do impossible things. Tear a hole in the fabric of the universe, suck something through, and mend the rip, all in one scene.

But you still need to know how it all works.

The trouble with being able to do anything is that you can do anything. When something troubles your magician main character, why can't he just chant the right spell, reconfigure the nature of causality, and make everything The Way It Should Be? This gets back to the need for limitations, of course, but it also points out the need to have a system for magic.

Before you start writing the actual book, you need to know how magic works. Like science, it has to have rules, and those rules *must* remain consistent throughout the book—or books. If you decide that werewolves must remain human in sunlight during chapter one, you can't suddenly have William the Were shape-shift at noon in chapter ten to rescue his girlfriend. When unexpected magic saves the day instead of the character, the readers feel cheated.

The Greeks had a name for this: *deus ex machina*. It means "god out of the machine." When ancient playwrights realized they'd written themselves into a corner and there was no way for the characters to resolve their various problems, some of them got out of it by lowering a god character on a pulley (the machine) onto the stage. The god would do some hand-waving and poof! All problems vanished. Such endings were immensely unpopular with audiences back then, and they remain so today.

Writing the Paranormal Novel

Keep in mind that your readers live in a world that works with logic and consistency. Your readers can't break the laws of physics or the laws of causality in the readers' world—levers and light switches always follow the rules, and a consequence can't precede its cause. (In other words, your car can't be crushed before the accident, and you can't fail a test before you take it.)

The same applies to rules of magic. Readers need logic and coherence in fantasy because their world also has logic and coherence. You can set up whatever rules you want, but once you've created them, you have to stick with them. When your magic works the same way all the time, it's called *internal consistency.* Maintaining internal consistency develops your world and makes it feel real. Internal consistency keeps up that illusion of reality I mentioned earlier.

You're already dealing with magic, a chaotic force in fiction that does what you, the author, tell it to. When you invite the reader into your paranormal story, you're also telling the reader to trust that your world will make a certain amount of sense. Violate that trust, and the reader walks away.

So let's look at ways to make some magic.

THE SOURCE

First, you need to know where magic power comes from. A number of alternatives present themselves. Magic could be intrinsic in living things—everything alive has a certain amount of magic power in it, and magicians can draw off that power. Maybe magic power can be recharged through rest or other means, or maybe the drain is permanent. Or magic could be associated with a place, with power piling up in some places and other places remaining virtually dead. The idea of ley lines puts magic into rivers flowing around the globe, and magicians tap into that power. The limitation is that a magician caught more than a few yards away from a ley line can't do much—no power.

You should also know if magic has a "flavor." Is there good magic and evil magic, or is magic a neutral force like electricity? Or perhaps magicians are divided up by the elements, able to control air, or earth, or fire, or water, and they can't control any other substance. Or whatever else you want to come up with.

Divine and infernal sources are another place to get magic, though such effects are more properly called miracles. Angels and demons, of course, can perform a number of miracles, but often humans with sufficient faith can pull them off as well.

Sometimes magic leaks in from other worlds, with gates or rifts allowing power to stream through. Or it's all alchemy, with specially brewed potions and teas that give magical effects. Or all magic must come through supernatural objects that are fiendishly difficult to create. Or it's a combination of the above.

Your magic-wielding characters may not be aware of the exact source and nature of magic, but as the all-knowing author, you should be. Your knowledge will give the world that internal consistency we mentioned above.

THE WHO VS. THE WHAT

You'll also need to know *who* can do magic. In a world of so-called "cookbook magic," anyone can cast spells if he knows the right words and has the right ingredients, which makes books of magic very valuable indeed. Another way to go about it is to allow only certain people to cast spells, people born with a special spark or talent for magic. Or perhaps magic is restricted to members of a certain gender or certain family lines. Maybe this is further divided so certain families have access only to certain types of magic. Gender-based magic has been around for a long time as well, though the female healer/seer has been done an *awful* lot, so you'll have to work a lot harder to make that sort of character interesting, and you might be better off doing something else with her altogether.

There's also the question of *what* can do magic. In some settings, magic is restricted to magical beings. Only fairies, elves, demons, vampires, werewolves, ghosts, and similar creatures have intrinsic magical powers. Humans can't cast spells—against the supernatural they have only folkloric weapons such as garlic and silver for defense. However, there's no reason not to have a world of magicians *and* magical creatures, if you want! As always, just make sure you have the rules laid out in advance so you can keep your magic consistent.

THE COST

Magic rarely comes free. Otherwise magicians and magical creatures would rule the world. Be sure you've chosen appropriate, consistent limits, as we've discussed above.

THE IMPACT

One final consideration is the overall impact of magic. Sure, there might be (should be) a cost to the individual, but what about the impact on the big picture? If a magician uses a lot of magic in one place, can she drain the magic permanently? What will that do to future magicians who want to use that place? If these little "dead zones" don't heal themselves, what's the impact of thousands of years of magicians creating thousands of little dead spots all over the planet? Is there a supernatural version of global warming?

Are there long-term costs to the magician herself? Some paranormal stories give magicians longer—or shorter—lives. Other systems of magic give sorcerers physical effects, like odd hair color or cumulative skin markings or even animallike characteristics. Perhaps using a lot of magic attracts the attention of Other Powers, or lets other magicians track the position of the caster like a supernatural GPS, something you wouldn't want an enemy to be doing.

What about magical fallout? In a big battle, what happens to deflected power or failed spells? This could be the supernatural version of nuclear waste, creating unintended side effects ranging from small mutations in local plant life to accidental tears in the space–time continuum.

Taking a step back and looking at the overall impact of magic creates an opportunity to explore your world on a whole new level—and possibly create new story ideas.

CHAPTER 8:
Keeping It Real

No matter how wild and weird your paranormals get, you're always writing about humans. Even when you're writing about elves, vampires, werewolves, and wicked little pixies, you're writing about humans.

This isn't a bad thing.

First of all, you can't avoid writing about humans because *you're* a human. (Your eventual editor probably won't be—mine's a lava-snorting demon—and with any luck your agent will be a vampire, but you—you're human.) No one can completely step outside his own humanity far enough to write a completely inhuman character.

Nor should you want to do so. Your readers are humans, too, and won't be able to empathize or identify with a being who thinks and reacts in a completely inhuman manner. Vampires started out as bad guys because they were inhuman monsters, with needs and desires humans couldn't understand—and neither did they wish to. Later authors began to give vampires their humanity back. Vampires began to obsess over love partners, yearn for the past, and fight to control the inner beast. These are difficulties we humans understand because we go through them, too. The delicious and dark paranormal twist added to the struggle made the story even more compelling. As vampires became more and more human, they drifted away from being antagonistic and some even became full-blown protagonists. Nowadays, you're hard-pressed to find a vampire book in which the bloodsuckers are all bad to the blood. They became likable once they became human.

Your supernatural characters need to follow the same rule, so let's go through some ways to keep your paranormals human, even when they're not.

THE INNER BEAST

All humans fight the Inner Beast. It's that interior voice that tells us to lie, steal, cheat, hit, kick, punch, yell, shout, threaten, smash, crush, and kill. Some of us are better at ignoring it than others, and some days even the best of us give in to it, but everyone knows what it's like to fight it.

Many supernatural characters fight the Inner Beast, too, but with a thousand-volt boost, and human characters who are transformed into supernatural characters (as opposed to characters who are supernatural from birth) tend to get zapped the most. This only makes sense. People generally fear the unfamiliar and cling to the familiar. Humanity is familiar, and a human who is changed into a vampire or werewolf or ghost most likely wouldn't want to let go of that familiar humanity to embrace this weird new existence, and certainly not if becoming a vamp/were/ghost requires the character to do something that, as a human, he would have found repugnant, like behead puppies or snack on friends, no matter how alluring the new activity may have become.

Supernatural beings such as vampires and werewolves continually deal with new hungers that are far more powerful than the normal ones we humans live with. (It's puberty all over again.) As humans, we've all dealt with being surrounded by food and feeling hungry but knowing we mustn't eat, either because Mom said we'd spoil supper or because we're dieting or because the food belongs to someone else. It sucks. Sometimes we just deal with being hungry. Sometimes we eat anyway and damn the consequences.

Victor Vampire deals with this problem on a whole new level. He's surrounded by delicious food every moment he's awake, the most wonderful, ambrosial food imaginable, food he could pluck from the street as easily as a child picks an apple. But he mustn't. Either because he'd attract the attention of the authorities (and strong as the vampire may be, enough determined humans could eventually bring him down), because the prey he wants is someone he shouldn't kill for other reasons, or because the vampire is trying to hold on to his fast-eroding humanity, and drinking human blood Would Be Wrong. The conflict between Victor's hunger for blood and his need to avoid fulfilling it creates a powerful paranormal situation—and it's one human readers can still relate to.

The only trouble with this particular conflict is that it's been explored quite a lot, and you'll need to present it in a new way. You can use a new type of character, like Anne Rice does in her vampire books. (Back when she first did it, the idea of a gay vampire as a protagonist was a new one, and Claudia, the little girl vampire, is a perfect example of a vampire who is ruled by the Inner Beast.) Or you can use a new voice, like Lucienne Diver does in her Vamped series. (Editors love this approach, and we'll talk about voice in chapter twelve.) Or you can try new relationship structures, like Tanya Huff does in her Blood books. (The Inner Beast forces her vampires to snipe at and fight with each other in death, even if they were lovers in life, and her werewolf families, as I've pointed out elsewhere, have to split up sibling sets when the sisters go into heat so they don't try to mate with their own brothers.) Or you can explore some other facet of the struggle.

FADING HUMANITY

Some "converted" paranormals feel their humanity slipping away. They succumb to the power of the vampire or the werewolf or the spiritual world. Every time they use their new powers, a piece of their former life slips away, and they find themselves less worried about their former friends, relatives, and lovers. For some paranormals, this creates conflict. They don't *want* to lose their humanity, but keeping it seems to be mutually exclusive with their new state; they can't be both human *and* supernatural. What to do? Terry Pratchett explores this idea in *Unseen Academicals*, although his human character is actually a goblin named Mr. Nutt who discovers, much to his dismay, that he's turning into an orc—or that he's always been one. Still, Mr. Nutt is a very human goblin, and we're with him all the way as he deals with the fear and difficulty of his transformation.

Believe it or not, this is a very human conflict. Change is forced on all of us throughout our lives, even if we don't want it. A big one is puberty, which changes our bodies, the way we see other people, and the way we see the entire damn world. It's scary, it's freaky, and it's glorious all at once, and there's no way to stop it. Other breathtaking, scary changes explode into our lives—falling in love, falling out of it, finding a job, getting married, having a child, getting divorced, dealing with a death in the family, moving to a new town and swearing we won't lose contact with old friends even though we know it'll happen—and every one of these changes us in unexpected ways. Sometimes we become more powerful, sometimes less so, sometimes we grow up, and sometimes we learn things we'd rather have stayed ignorant about. In any case, we deal and keep moving.

Forcing your paranormals to deal with their own magical changes (loss of humanity) makes them feel more human to the readers because the readers have gone through their own version of it, and it makes such characters more sympathetic. So don't hesitate to force it on them.

COMMENTING ON HUMANITY

Not all supernatural characters were once human. Elves, dwarves, selkies, angels, demons, and others may have partially human form, but they don't think or act like humans. As I've pointed out above, nonhuman protagonists do have to be human enough for readers to identify with them and like them. However, nonhuman characters also need to explore their nonhuman side. One way to do that is to use them as contrast between humans and nonhumans.

Nonhuman characters provide you with an opportunity to comment on human existence or point out the silly, foolish, and outrageous. As outsiders, nonhumans take nothing for granted and look at humans from a different point of view. This allows them to see our foibles, and since they're outsiders, they can mention these flaws out of scorn, naïveté, or curiosity. I already used the example of the elf attending a birthday party and finding it confusing. To take it a little further, he might ask the family questions about what's going on:

> "Why did you set the pastry on fire?" Ranadar asked. "Only a moment ago you told me you teach your children that fire is dangerous."
>
> "We're not setting it on fire," Melissa explained. "The candles are symbolic—one for each year of Hailey's life."
>
> "And she gets a wish when she blows it out?"
>
> "Exactly."
>
> Ranadar shook his head. "I don't understand. Magic doesn't work in this world, and I heard you tell Hailey there's no such thing as elves or witches or ghosts."
>
> "Well, that's true," Melissa hedged. "But—"
>
> "So you lied to her when you said her wish would come true?"
>
> A flush crept across Melissa's face. "Now look—"
>
> "Mommy," Hailey asked. "Can I blow out the candles now?"

Cultural clashes between humans and nonhumans actually serve to highlight humanity and make the nonhuman characters more fun to read about.

Nonhumans might find human ways disgusting (to be avoided), intriguing (to be watched), or even seductive (to be joined in on). They might want to keep their ways and customs separate from human pollution, or they might be sucked in against their will. The humans change the nonhumans, the nonhumans change the humans, and the transformation makes for a fun story.

The interaction and absorption of human and nonhuman ways is another facet of the supernatural Terry Pratchett explores extensively in several of his books. His dwarves, for example, are quite literal-minded. As a result, the language of humans, "with its unthinking reliance on metaphor and simile, is a veritable minefi—a complete morass—a fog of incomprehensi—very difficult" for dwarves. (This is from Pratchett's *The Discworld Companion,* with Stephen Briggs.) Additionally, dwarves don't get along well with outsiders—except for the ones who move to Ankh-Morpork, a supernatural combination of Victorian London and modern-day New York City. There, dwarves become model citizens, once a few incidents of hacking-at-the-knees with trolls are smoothed over. Ankh-Morpork dwarves still find humans confusing and difficult, but they also find their modern way of life quite seductive. Some of the more daring female dwarves start wearing makeup under their beards, stirring up quite the scandal back home under the mountain and raising questions about equal rights for everyone, regardless of what they wear under their chainmail. Ultimately, all of it is commentary on human behavior.

THE IMPORTANCE OF EMOTION

Not even the stoniest Creature of the Night can operate without emotion. Or maybe they do—who knows for sure? If they do, I don't want to know about it. Your fictional creatures, however, need to emote because the human readers do. It forges a connection between your character and your reader.

Despite this fact, one of the most common comments I write on student manuscripts is, "How does the character feel about this?" or "What is her reaction?" It's easy to narrate events, much harder to show internal reactions. But as a writer, you need to show us these reactions. Knowing how the characters feel draws the readers into the story.

So how do you do it? Here's a primer. (Incidentally, I'm going to use several basic grammatical terms in the following section, ones all writers should be familiar with. If you come across a term you don't know, definitely pause to look it up in a grammar book or online.)

STATE EMOTIONS DIRECTLY
You can tell the reader exactly what the character is feeling:

> Nick felt nervous.
>
> Jessica was so proud.

Although it's concise and direct, this actually is the weakest way. For one thing, you're *telling* the reader what the character is feeling instead of *showing* it, and it's almost always better to show the readers something rather than tell them about it. Second, this method uses linking verbs, which make for dull sentences—the character is existing, not acting. Use this method sparingly, if at all.

HINT AND CONFIRM: ACTION, ADJECTIVES, AND ADVERBS

Action makes for more compelling reading than mere existence. Combining it with a few emotional adjectives or adverbs lets us in on the character's emotional state. You can use an action to hint about a character's emotional state, and use a descriptive (an adjective or adverb) to confirm it.

> A nervous sweat broke out on Nick's face.
> Jessica proudly tossed her head.

In these examples, note how the action hints and the descriptives confirm. Sweat breaks out—a hint that Nick is nervous—and it's a *nervous* sweat, which confirms. Jessica tosses her head—a hint that she's proud—and she does so *proudly*, which confirms.

This is another method not to overuse, however. Adverbs that end in *-ly* get fingered as repetitive quite a lot, and if your adjectives outnumber everything else in your sentence, you're heading into what's called *purple prose*. Passages like *Harold crept through the dank, twisted passages, wondering how he'd ever overcome the deep, turgid terror of his frightened soul as his heart pounded hard and timidly within the dark cavity of his chest* overwhelm and annoy the reader. Use balance and moderation.

SNEAK IT IN WITH FIGURATIVE LANGUAGE

Figurative language includes simile, metaphor, hyperbole, and personification. Using any of these to set up emotion gets you bonus points (if you do it well) because, in addition to drawing the reader into your character's emotional state, they make your writing more interesting.

> Nick slipped into the room, nervous as a mouse in a hawk's nest.
> The wall of Jessica's pride surrounded her in an iron fortress.

This method is generally strong, though too many similes and metaphors in a row will bug the reader. Similes especially stand out, since they all use *like* or *as,* so you don't want to use more than one or two per page. Again, balance and moderation.

DESCRIBE THE PHYSICAL SENSATIONS

Emotions create physical, visceral sensations. Everyone has experienced a pounding heart, sweaty palms, or a tight stomach. Weirdly, describing these symptoms can actually bring out a similar, if lower-key, response in the reader, which makes this a good method for getting across a character's emotional state.

> Nick's mouth dried up and his hands shook. He found he couldn't sit still, and his toes seemed to tap on their own.
> Jessica threw her head back and strode across the podium, a proud, well-earned smile on her face. Thunderous applause boomed through her very bones.
> I looked over the edge of the cliff and my insides turned to liquid.

While this works very well, notice that it's an indirect method. You're implying what the character is feeling instead of letting the reader know directly. Physical sensations *add* to emotions. They don't replace them entirely. Don't be afraid to combine this one with some figurative language or a well-placed action sentence that shows us the emotion.

MAKE THE EMOTIONS DO THINGS

This method combines several of the above methods. It actually turns the emotion into a temporary character who acts on the person you're writing about.

> Fear turned Nick's hands to ice and his heart jerked inside his chest like it was trying to jump out.
>
> Pride swelled Jessica's chest and put a jaunty spring in every step.
>
> Bright happiness filled me with golden sunshine as I ran down the steps to meet him.

This is one of the strongest ways, though like any method, it gets repetitive if overused. In other words, vary the method of getting your character's emotional state across. But *do* get it across.

How often? It depends. Emotion slows down action scenes, so you'll want to use it sparingly, and lean more on the method that describes physical sensation. Romantic scenes, naturally, tend to drench themselves in emotion. As a rule, whenever something significant happens to the character, include an emotional response to the event.

USE THE SETTING

Readers want dialogue the most. In second place comes action. Description rates a distant third. This creates a dichotomy for us writers—we have to describe the setting here and there so the readers know where they are, but perversely, the readers aren't very interested in getting the information from us. One way around this is to force your setting into double duty as an emotional mirror.

Our emotions color our perceptions. The sunniest, loveliest summer day feels dreadful and cruel when you've been dumped, and a nasty, drenching rainstorm feels fine and refreshing when you're in love (as Gene Kelly famously pointed out). Whenever possible, your setting should provide insights into the emotional state of your viewpoint character. This can be tricky, but with a little practice, it can become second nature.

Below we have an example of a perfectly good setting description. Unfortunately, it comes across as dull:

Writing the Paranormal Novel

> Chris looked out across the wide, shallow river. The water rippled over rocks and sand beneath the noonday sun. Birds sang overhead and animals made rustling noises in the undergrowth behind him. A brown picnic basket sat next to him, and Chris caught a faint whiff of potato salad. He wrapped his arms around his knees and waited.

The narrative is nice enough, but nothing happens, and we have no idea what Chris is feeling. Let's try the exact same scene, slightly reworded:

> Chris glared across the wide, shallow river. Chilly water tore over hard rocks and rough sand beneath a harsh noonday sun. Birds shrieked overhead and small rodents rustled in the undergrowth behind him. A prickly brown picnic basket sat next to him, and Chris caught a rancid whiff of potato salad. He coiled his arms around his knees and waited.

An entirely different feel. Adjectives like *chilly, hard, rough,* and *prickly* tell us that something's wrong. Even the potato salad is unhappy. Whomever Chris is waiting for is in for a bad time. We can do this again yet another way:

> Chris gazed across the wide, shallow river. Warm water rippled over smooth rocks and soft sand beneath a gentle noonday sun. Birds twittered overhead, and tiny animals made rustling noises in the undergrowth behind him. A brimming picnic basket sat next to him, and Chris caught a sweet whiff of potato salad. He hugged his knees with his arms and waited.

Chris's emotional state is entirely different. Now he sees the water as warm, the rocks as smooth, the sand as soft. The basket is comfortable instead of prickly, and the salad is sweet. Whatever's coming up is something to look forward to. The setting tells us this—or rather, Chris's *perception* of the setting, as the author presents it, tells us. And this presentation makes for more compelling reading. Your paranormal settings should do the same whenever possible.

Rewrite the scene below as if the viewpoint character hates the place. Make any necessary changes, but all the elements of the original scene should remain.

> Sarah stepped into Grandma Nell's old parlor for the first time in fifteen years. The same threadbare carpet with its pattern of cabbage roses stretched over the floor. Dim light filtered in through the curtains, which were closed against the sun. A long couch sat along one wall, the same couch where Grandma Nell had presided over afternoon tea every day at four. Two easy chairs flanked a coffee table. Pictures of relatives, the same photos Sarah remembered, hung from the walls. In one corner sat a single wooden stool. Sarah ran her fingers through the dust that coated the top. How many times had she sat quietly in that corner?

Now rewrite the scene to show the viewpoint character is *fond* of the place.

THE SENSE OF WONDER

The most powerful emotion in your arsenal is the *sense of wonder*. Your readers don't get to visit fantastic worlds, talk to supernatural creatures, or travel in underground societies, but your characters do, and your readers want to experience all these things through these characters. They want to be startled and astonished, amazed and thrilled. However, since you're telling the story through the eyes of your characters, your supernatural creations are only as fantastic as your characters *feel* they are. If a unicorn strolls onto Bob's suburban back lawn and he accepts the event with bland calm, any chance of wonder if ruined. Your description of the unicorn may be gorgeous and make the creature shine with unearthly light, but Bob's blah reaction cues the reader that a unicorn is nothing special. If Bob reacts with wonder, fear, or amazement, the readers will feel these things too, and experience that sense of wonder that draws them to the paranormal genre.

Even a character who is used to strange events can feel wonder when confronted by the paranormal. Just because something has become part of normal life doesn't mean it's lost beauty or power. Most of us see rainbows and thunderstorms and rock concerts on a fairly regular basis, but each one is still pretty amazing. I've participated in decorating my house for the winter holidays forty-four times now, yet it somehow never gets old. Even "regular" supernatural events should remain filled with wonder.

Ginn Hale demonstrates this quite clearly in *Wicked Gentlemen*. Belimai Sykes, who is part demon, has been able to fly since he was a child. Hale writes:

> I pushed my window open and leaned out. The moon spread its light across my face and bare chest. Wind rolled up through my hair and stroked my skin. When I had been a child, every night had seemed as lush and wondrous as this. . . .
>
> Taking a deep breath, I threw myself out into the open air. Wind whipped over my bare skin and through my hair as I plunged downward. I smelled the filth of the ground below wafting up toward my face. A rush of terror and exhilaration shot through me.
>
> With a twist of my body I veered up . . . I swept up over a factory roof and caught hold of one of the tin chimneys. My momentum whipped me around it twice. When I let go, I went spinning off like a top.

Notice how Hale uses every part of the action to feed into the sense of wonder. The sensual description of the night makes it sound like a lover (an emotional use of setting I mentioned in the preceding section). Sykes rises above the filthy smells below—a bit of symbolism—with a rush of emotion. Once fully airborne, he doesn't simply fly. He veers, sweeps, whips, and spins. Even though Sykes has flown hundreds of times before, the sense of wonder remains clear—and we're right there to experience it with him. This thrill is one of the main reasons paranormal readers pick up these books, and it's the author's job to deliver.

CAREFUL WITH THAT METAPHOR—IT'S LOADED

Writers love figurative language, as well we should. A well-placed simile, metaphor, or bit of personification lends life to a dead paragraph, makes a sentence jump, sprinkles starlight over a page. But when you're writing a novel filled with supernatural events, you need to exercise a bit of caution. Figurative language in a normal novel is always taken to be metaphorical, but in a supernatural setting, the metaphoric might be normal. For example, you could perfectly well start a military with the opening hook "Pete shaded his eyes as a dozen metal dragons roared across the sky." The reader will know that the character is involved with the Air Force and you're describing airplanes with a bit of metaphor.

However, the same metaphor used at the beginning of a paranormal book can confuse the readers. They already know from the cover art and the blurb on the back of the book that your novel has magic in it, so they're ready to believe that a flight of real dragons is coasting over Pete's head with a roar. If the "dragons" turn out to be a metaphor for jet engines, the readers are wrenched around and rightfully annoyed for it. Be sure your wonderful figurative language is clearly figurative.

THE PERFECT FLAW

There's that guy. You know whom I'm talking about. He's handsome. He's rich. He's talented. He has the perfect job. And a perfect wife. He even smells nice.

Don't you just hate him?

By all rights, you should like him. I mean, there's nothing to dislike. Not one, tiny thing.

And that's the problem. *We* have flaws. Imperfections. Problems. And we tend to resent people who don't seem to have any. Why should *he* have it so good when I'm dealing with a mound of debt, weight problems, and a bad relationship with my cat?

For the same reason, readers usually don't empathize with fictional characters who have no flaws. First of all, such characters are unrealistic and unbelievable—no one can be completely perfect. Second, as I noted above, we resent people who seem to have it all. And lastly, flaws make characters *human,* which is what you're striving for in a supernatural character. Paranormals are already at least one step removed from humanity, making them less empathetic for human readers. You don't want to leave out those flaws that make them human.

Incidentally, by *flaw,* I mean *personal* flaw, an internal problem that makes the character's life difficult. Walter Werewolf's bad reaction to silver is not a flaw, it's a weakness—there's nothing the werewolf can do to overcome it. Walter's gambling addiction, however, is a flaw—he doesn't *have* to gamble, but he does anyway, even when he can't afford to lose the money. This complicates his life or otherwise makes it difficult. It's a flaw as opposed to a weakness *because the character has a choice about it.* No one is forcing Walter to gamble; he sits at the poker table knowing full well that if he loses, he won't make his tuition payments and will have to drop out of law school.

A proper flaw also gives the character some kind of *real problem.* Sorry, but creating a Mary Sue and then claiming she's flawed because she refuses to step on sidewalk cracks won't cut it. What reader would see this as a real problem? The flaw has to severely restrict, threaten to harm, or otherwise bring major difficulty into the character's life. The flaw also has to cause the character emotional distress, either directly ("I can't stop gambling, and I hate myself for it") or indirectly ("My wife left me because of my gambling habit, and I don't know what to do"). Anything less and you have a paper tiger, not a flaw.

The most famous supernatural character with a flaw is Odysseus from Homer's *The Odyssey.* At the beginning of the story, Odysseus is too proud of the way he has conquered Troy and refuses to acknowledge the gods' role in it, so Poseidon curses him to roam the seas forever. Later, when Odysseus manages to blind the Cyclops and sneak out of the giant's cave, he can't keep his mouth shut. Pride makes him bellow his true name, which reveals his exact location to both the Cyclops and Poseidon, getting Odysseus into more trouble. (The Greek word for this is *hubris*.) When Odysseus finally arrives home, he wants to burst into his palace and be welcomed by his long-suffering wife Penelope, but he discovers invaders have taken over his home. They'll slaughter him the moment he steps through the door. Will he proudly rush in anyway, or sneak in through the back? Odysseus grinds his teeth and enters his own palace disguised as a beggar, his pride finally overcome. As a result, the gods take his side, and he wins back his kingdom.

Although Odysseus is impossibly strong, a fantastic swordsman, and clever beyond imagination, the entire story is driven by a flaw—his pride. This pride also makes the otherwise impossible Odysseus more believable and more human.

In a more modern story, Jack Torrance from Stephen King's *The Shining* has two major flaws—he's an alcoholic who can't overcome writer's block. When Jack and his family move to the haunted Overlook Hotel for the winter, the ghosts in the Overlook force Jack to confront his two flaws. Unlike Odysseus, Jack loses the struggle. He starts drinking again and obsesses over his inability to write. Eventually he goes nuts and attacks his family. Jack's flaws provide the hotel ghosts with hooks into his soul and ultimately drive the story. If Jack had no flaws, the ghosts wouldn't have been able to touch him and the story would evaporate. His flaws also make him thoroughly human and sympathetic. Right up until he reaches for the roque mallet to go after his wife and son, we're rooting for him, hoping he'll tell the ghosts to shove it. Why? Because we've been there. Our ghosts are inside our heads and they might be telling us to eat that extra box of chocolate or skip work this week instead of urging us to chug scotch and kill our kids, but we've been there. Jack's struggle just has that paranormal twist to it. Your characters should undergo a similar journey.

Speaking of multiple flaws, your character will likely have them. Real-world people have multiple flaws, after all, and realistic characters should deal with them, too. (In addition to being too proud, Odysseus couldn't keep his toga zipped, and it cost him several years' travel.) You don't have to riddle your characters with flaws—too many is as bad as too few—but two or three is a good number to play with. It's enough to seem realistic but not so many that the character is dragged into an existential abyss.

Remember that the key to a perfect flaw is that it exists because of the character's *choice*. It needs to be something the character could overcome easily enough, if only she had the mental or psychological wherewithal. Ideally, you should force the character to confront the flaw multiple times throughout the book, and the flaw should hold her back. Really good writers work the flaw into the main plot of the book. At a key moment, usually close to or even during the climax, the character should be forced to confront the flaw in a way that will decide how the story will end. If the character overcomes the flaw: happy ending. If the flaw overcomes the character: tragic ending. Either way, your supernatural character will feel more human.

Terry Pratchett's young witch Magrat Garlick has a number of flaws in *Lords and Ladies*, but her biggest problem is that she can't seem to stand up for herself. Ever. At the masterful climax of the book, when the Queen of the Elves is about to kill her, Magrat sees the Queen bring down a close friend, and she forces herself to stand up. Having overcome her flaw, Magrat finds the strength to face down the Queen and defeat her. Pratchett resolves the main plot and a character development subplot in one stroke, which makes for riveting reading.

PART III:
CASTING
THE
WORDS

CHAPTER 9:

Thinking Big and Small: Arc, Plot, and Subplot

When I'm not writing, I teach ninth-grade English, and every year I draw the plot mountain on the board. Remember that? It's coming back to get you now, like a zombie rising from a damp graveyard. A diagonal line rises upward, peaks, and slopes back down on the other side. The upward line is the *rising action,* the peak is the *climax* (pause while everyone titters), and the downslope is the *falling action* or *resolution.*

This version works fine as an introduction to basic literature. It doesn't stand up to real scrutiny because it's extremely simplistic. As a writer of the paranormal, you need to be aware of your plotting and how it works. Paranormal books have their own quirks and problems when it comes to plotting, however, and we'll talk about those as we go.

We'll start with the big stuff.

ARCS

I pointed out in chapter eight that paranormal novels lend themselves to series. Maybe it's that once you start combining the real world with the paranormal, the stories just keep on coming. Or maybe it's that supernatural elements mixed into the mundane world create so many fascinating ramifications, a single novel can't explore them all. Or maybe readers of paranormal novels are the type that can't be satisfied with a single book about the characters and settings. Or maybe it's a combination of all these things.

Whatever the reason, if you're writing a paranormal novel, it's not a bad idea to assume you'll write more than one with the same characters and setting. That means you need to plan now, and think about what sort of arc you want to explore. An *arc* is a long-range story, and it can apply to a plot, a setting, or a character. Laurell K. Hamilton develops Anita Blake in a *character arc*. Over several books, Anita gains strength and power and deals with her increasingly complicated love life, but the books don't have a single story line that ties them together. J.R.R. Tolkien ran several multi-book *plot arcs* in *The Lord of the Rings* with Frodo trying to slip into Mordor to destroy the One Ring and Aragorn running interference for him. The entire story isn't fully resolved until *The Return of the King,* the final book. C.S. Lewis runs a *setting arc* in The Chronicles of Narnia series. The readers see the creation of Narnia in *The Magician's Nephew,* explore several places and points of interest in Narnian history with a range of characters in several other books, and watch the world end in *The Last Battle.*

There are divergent philosophies about arcs. One philosophy says it's better to know in advance what sort of arc you want to explore. Advance planning will give your long-term story focus. It won't wander off in strange directions and get out of control. Tighter planning will create tighter writing. Planning will also allow you to slip clues and foreshadowing into early books about events that will happen in later books. You'll also have fewer inconsistencies in your books, since you already know what you're doing.

The opposing philosophy says arcs should grow organically. Advance planning only kills creativity and locks you into a story line that you may later decide you don't like or you discover doesn't work. The more you write, the more you develop as a writer, and your later ideas will be better ones anyway, so it's best to leave yourself open to using them.

I think a middle ground between the two works the best. You should definitely have at least a general idea of where you want to take your

Writing the Paranormal Novel

characters, setting, and long-term story, if for no other reason so you can tell your editor what your future plans are. You don't need every detail nailed into place, however. Leave yourself open to new possibilities that occur to you along the way. Writers live for those "Oh! That would be fantastic!" moments, and you don't want to seal yourself off from them.

As a rule, plot arcs tend to require a little more planning. Long-term plotting requires you to drop clues and foreshadowing that lays the groundwork for future scenes. If it's important for a character in Book II to know the details of a graveyard scene, you have to make sure he was there at the cemetery in Book I. J.K. Rowling is the modern mistress of long-term story arcs. A number of carefully constructed bits of plot show up in the first Harry Potter book that turn out to be important in the seventh and final one, not the least of which are the details of what happens on the night Lord Voldemort kills Harry's parents.

On the other side of the coin, character arcs tend to be a little more organic. You might have it in mind that Jessica and Norman, who don't like each other much in Book I, will finally get together in Book III, but exactly how they'll get there is something you'll explore along the way. Really, the answer is to use whatever works best for you.

SERIALS VS. STANDALONES

At one time, the standard advice for writing a multi-book series ran something like this: Write the first book to stand alone. Write the second book to end in a cliffhanger. Write the huge third book to resolve the cliffhanger. The reason for this pattern was because a publisher might buy the first book and wait to see how sales went before offering a second book. If no offer came, readers of the first book wouldn't be left hanging. If an offer *did* come, it would likely involve at least two more books, so a cliffhanger ending was a good strategy to "remind" readers to buy the third book.

This strategy no longer holds true so much. You can certainly use it—go right ahead—but it's not the near-requirement it once was. Feel free to explore other structures in your series.

Some authors write *standalones*. Each book can stand by itself as complete, and readers can enjoy the books in whatever order they find them. Long-term stories tend to be character or setting arcs instead of plot arcs. The advantage to this type of series is mostly to the readers. They can pick up any book in the set and read it without worrying about what came before. This is a tremendous plus in an age when books rarely stay in the bookstore for more than a few months. Few things frustrate readers more than grabbing an intriguing-looking novel and realizing it's the second in a series, with the first one nowhere in sight. The disadvantage is that you can't use a long-term plot arc, and you'll also have to sneak in all the exposition about how magic works in every book, since you can't assume the reader read it in a previous volume. (More on exposition in chapter ten.) Terry Pratchett's Discworld books are standalones, as are Christopher Moore's urban fantasy books. Several of Pratchett's and Moore's novels share characters, in fact, but they can still be read in any order.

Other authors run *serials*. These books are more tightly bound together, with a strong plot arc, and readers who try to drop into the middle of the series will be confused because the author assumes everyone has read the previous material and doesn't stop to explain what's come before. The advantage here is that the author can present a long-term, complex story that won't fit in a single volume. The disadvantage is that anyone who can't find Book I won't be able to catch up, and if the publisher lets the first volume go out of print or the bookstores stop carrying it, later readers are out of luck. Many serials come in sets of three, a trilogy, but if a serial is successful enough (i.e., sells enough copies and makes enough money), the publisher may ask for more. C.C. Finlay's Traitor to the Crown books and Anne Rice's first three vampire novels are just two examples among hundreds of paranormal trilogies out there.

PLAYING WITH AN ARC

When creating a story arc, you're an artist stepping back to look at the entire painting all at once—you're surveying the big picture. This means your story arc needs to be *big*. And *big* is relative. It's certainly *big* if the character saves the world from an invading army of ghosts. But it's also *big* if the character does so by overcoming a decades-long hatred and mistrust of his mother in the process. The latter may not be big to anyone else, but it's certainly big to the character.

In a long arc, a character often goes from a position of weakness to a position of strength. A magician's apprentice grows into his power until he's the equal of his former master. A young woman escapes her abusive husband in Book I, starts her own business in Book II, and establishes herself as a woman of wealth in Book III. A new werewolf is saddled with the Beast in Book I, learns the extent of his powers in Book II, and gains control of himself in Book III. You should create your own supernatural protagonist with this sort of long-term growth in mind.

In addition to long-term growth, character arcs must also provide continual small bits of growth. The character needs to have small personal setbacks and victories within the overall arc so the reader can watch the character change and evolve. For example, a werewolf fighting to keep the Inner Beast under control might initially lose that battle big time and do serious damage to the people around him (setback), spend some time dealing with the guilt and recriminations (victory), gain some control over the Beast (victory), lose it again (setback), and finally admit he can't do it on his own and join Beasts Anonymous (victory). Mercedes Lackey uses this arc in her Diana Tregarde books. Diana, a paranormal investigator with some magical abilities, suffers from nightmares and panic attacks related to her earlier cases. As the novels progress, she slowly gains more and more control over herself (victory), though she backslides from time to time (setback).

Another story arc can involve stopping a hugely powerful antagonist. The hero starts off far too weak to confront the Big Bad Guy directly, but fortunately, said BBG either doesn't know the hero exists or doesn't view the hero as much of a threat, and the hero ends up fighting someone who works for the BBG instead. (In some arcs, the hero thinks he *is* fighting the BBG, then learns the guy he barely managed to defeat is a mere minion, and the real fight is just getting started.) As the protagonist works his way up the bad-guy ladder to the BBG one book at a time, he slowly gains power and over-comes flaws—part of that "going from weakness to strength" thing—until we get the final showdown. Harry Potter follows this sort of arc, with Harry battling the minions of Lord Voldemort until the seventh novel, when the two of them finally square off for a wizardly smackdown.

A different arc uses a long-term goal. The character needs to accom-plish something that can't be done in a single book. Like most long-term goals, it's broken up into several short-term goals that are handled over multiple books. The smaller stories along the way may veer off in some in-teresting directions, but the character is always working toward this goal. Naomi Novik's Temeraire series runs this way. Temeraire wants to change the way the English treat dragons, while Will Laurence wants to win the war against Napoleon. The search for ways to accomplish these goals takes them to Europe, China, Africa, and Australia. They resolve several short-term goals along the way—bringing more dragons into England to fight Napoleon, finding the cure for a plague that threatens the English dragon population, forcing the English army to grant the dragons certain rights and privileges, rousting Napoleon from England, and others. All of these short-term goals feed into the long-term ones, allowing Novik to continue her story lines over multiple books.

ARCS AND LADDERS

One problem of the arc was mentioned back in chapter six: how to chal-lenge the hero. Conflicts are supposed to escalate, in theory. If you threaten to destroy the world in Book I, you naturally have to go further and threat-en the entire universe in Book II. So what's left for Book III?

The ever-escalating arc is actually a trap, and you don't have to fall into it. True, you can try to increase the stakes every time, but this tires the readers after a while—and takes on an air of ridiculousness. The solution is actually to scale back. After your hero has saved the world, tone things down and threaten just the main character. It won't matter to the readers

Writing the Paranormal Novel

that the threat is smaller. By now the readers are vested in the fate of the protagonist, and they'll be on the edges of their chairs if you go after this beloved hero—or someone close to him.

Naomi Novik, to return to her again, uses this technique to great effect. (I'll be revealing the outcome of some of her novels here, so if you haven't read them and don't want them spoiled, you might want to jump down to the next section.) In *Empire of Ivory,* a plague is decimating the English dragon population. Temeraire and Laurence barely manage to uncover a cure in Africa, only to discover that the English government intends to use it on their own dragons and then infect Napoleon's dragons with the original disease. Temeraire is horrified—all European dragons, including those allied with the English—will eventually die. More dragons fall ill, and Napoleon's superior forces amass across the English Channel. The stakes are enormous—thousands of dragons' lives. Eventually, Temeraire and Laurence commit treason by sneaking into an enemy camp and giving Napoleon's army the English cure. A terrible fight follows, and Temeraire is led to believe Laurence is killed. The book ends.

Novik raises the stakes in the next book, *Victory of Eagles.* Napoleon conquers England and occupies it. We've gone from threatening the dragon population to threatening all of England. Temeraire, newly reunited with Laurence, leads the fight to throw Napoleon out. In the end, they succeed. After nearly destroying England, where can Novik go for another novel?

She scales back. In *Tongues of Serpents,* the next book, Temeraire and Laurence have been charged with treason and transported to Australia, even though they saved England. The new conflict initially surrounds the characters we've come to love. We share their outrage at the injustice, and Novik doesn't need a worldwide disaster to get us interested. Threatening characters themselves is quite enough.

THE LITTLE THINGS

One vital part of an arc is small satisfactions. You can't plan to drag out an arc without resolving *anything.* Readers need something to cheer about along the way to the final ending. Each book should have its own satisfying resolution of some goal or conflict so the reader doesn't feel too strung along. In other words, each book in a series needs to have its own story that gets resolved, even if that story is part of a larger arc. To refer to Harry Potter again, the first six books in the series ends with Harry defeating an antagonist of some kind and wrapping up a major story, even though the ultimate goal of defeating Lord Voldemort remains unresolved. The reader is anticipating the next book, yet still feels satisfied with the current one.

So how do you make sure the reader feels satisfied with the plot of the current book? Let's zoom inward a little and take a look.

THE RULE OF THREE

The number three rules. Seriously. How many paranormal stories can you name in which stuff comes in threes? You know—three wishes, three bears, Red Riding Hood notices three things about the wolf, and so on. And as I noted above, paranormal books often come in sets of three. In fact, let's do a quick exercise about this:

EXERCISE

On a piece of scrap paper, list all the instances of sets of three you can think of from myths, fairy tales, and other stories in sixty seconds. Go!

SCORING

0–3: You need to read three more books of myths and fairy tales.

4–9: You've threed up some time for reading.

10+: Threedom is yours!

Even now that the exercise is over, more trios are probably occurring to you. They keep showing up the more you think about them. There's a reason for this: Humans like stories that come in threes. It's a natural rhythm.

The first event tells you what's going to happen, or creates an event. The second event sets a pattern. The third event breaks the pattern and resolves the problem.

Possibly no paranormal story illustrates this better than the German version of "Cinderella." (The American version has been shortened considerably and made nicey-nicey.) In the story, we have three girls—two stepsisters and Cinderella. The first stepsister is cruel (this is the event), the second stepsister is cruel (set the pattern), and Cinderella is nice (breaks the pattern). The king announces three balls. Cinderella is forced to sneak out to go to the first one (event). She sneaks out to the second (pattern). She leaves her golden shoe behind at the third (break). When the prince arrives at Cinderella's house with the golden shoe, the first stepsister tries it on, but it's too small, so she cuts off her toes to make it fit, but the prince discovers the ruse and refuses to marry her (event). The second stepsister tries on the shoe and cuts off her heel to make it fit, but the prince refuses to marry her as well (pattern). Cinderella tries on the shoe and it fits, so the prince marries her (break).

Adding another stepsister to the mix would overburden the story. By the third foot-chopping incident, the reader would be thinking, "Okay, we get it, we get it." Removing one of the stepsisters wouldn't work, either—the events wouldn't build very far and the story would be cut too short, so to speak. Three is often Just Right. Goldilocks certainly thought so, too.

In any case, this is why so many fictional events come in threes. It simply makes for fine storytelling. Not *every* set of events needs to come in threes, of course, but it's a good pattern to keep in mind, both when you're looking at the overall book and when you're looking at individual scenes.

PLOT

If you back up and look from a distance, the plot structure for a novel looks like a smooth mountain with one side shorter than the other. (Rising action, climax, and falling action, incidentally, come as a set of three.) Once you get closer, however, you can see that the structure is a little more complicated. It's actually a fractal pattern, a bunch of little mountains that form the slope of the main mountain, climbing steadily upward toward the peak. In other words, there are conflicts within conflicts, climaxes within climaxes, and resolutions within resolutions. We can take the structure from big to small.

AT THE NOVEL LEVEL

Every plot starts off with a main character who has a problem, called a *conflict*. It has to be a major conflict. Minor conflicts—paper tigers—aren't enough to hang a novel on. And since you're reading this book, it's going to be a *supernatural* conflict. If the character's difficulty has nothing to do with the paranormal, you've pushed the supernatural elements into the background and you aren't writing a paranormal novel. You should always be able to sum up the protagonist's conflict in a single sentence that uses action verbs:

> A girl from Kansas accidentally lands in a magical country and has to figure out how to get back home. (*The Wonderful Wizard of Oz* by Frank L. Baum)

> A young man in the New World uncovers a magical conspiracy to destroy the colonies and must choose between his Loyalist fiancée and his own growing powers of witchcraft. (*The Patriot Witch* by C.C. Finlay)

> A high school teenager moves to a new town, where she unexpectedly falls in love with a teenaged boy who turns out to be a vampire. (*Twilight* by Stephenie Meyer)

Take note of the prominent supernatural elements in all three of the above examples.

Being able to create this active sentence grants you two advantages: It ensures your plot has focus, and it gives you a quick way to sum up your book to an editor or agent who asks, "What's your book about?"

Now that you've established your protagonist's conflict, you're going to spend three or four hundred pages showing us all the interesting adventures he has trying to solve it. And you're going to make it difficult for him. In fact, you're going to make him walk over metaphorical hot coals and broken glass to find the solution to his conflict. Characters need to *earn* their happy endings (those who are getting one), or it's not worth the effort to read about them. This idea is personified in *Pinocchio,* by Carlo Collodi. (The book, a very paranormal novel, is quite different from the Disney movie of the same name. Pinocchio squishes the talking cricket in chapter four, for one thing.) Pinocchio wants to become a real boy, but he has to *earn* that position, and he goes through some pretty awful times to do it, including being turned into a donkey and getting swallowed by a mile-long shark. During this journey, he sees other people suffer and learns empathy for others. In the end, he gives all his hard-earned money to the hospital where the blue-haired fairy has fallen ill and hurries back to his basket-making job to earn more for her, at which point he's proven he's changed from a selfish marionette into a kind person, and he becomes a real boy. The blue-haired fairy always had the power to turn Pinocchio into a real boy, but that ending wouldn't have been at all satisfying because Pinocchio wouldn't have *earned* it. Your characters need to earn their endings as well. The more they work and suffer, the more satisfying the ending will be.

This means that when you start plotting your book, Greg the Protagonist can't head out to solve his problem and then immediately do so. You need to throw roadblocks in his way and force him to work around or through them. There's a general pattern to this:

1. Greg has a conflict.
2. Greg tries to solve the conflict and fails.
3. Greg tries to solve the conflict a second time and fails again. The conflict gets *worse.*
4. Greg tries to solve the conflict a third time and puts everything he has into this ultimate, last-ditch solution.
5. Greg succeeds (happy ending) or fails forever (tragic ending).

You may have noticed that this pattern comes as a set of three also—Greg tries to solve his conflict twice, and the third time is when he finally breaks the pattern and wins through or fails forever.

When you're looking at the overall plot for a novel this pattern becomes very broad, so be aware of it for your own book to keep the story from wandering. In *Pinocchio,* the pattern runs like this:

1. Pinocchio wants to become a real boy. (Conflict.)
2. Pinocchio tries to earn humanity by going to school and learning, but allows the Fox and Cat to sidetrack him. (He fails.)
3. Pinocchio wanders the world looking for other ways to become a real boy, but he only becomes less human, loses his father Geppetto, and learns his behavior has made the blue-haired fairy ill. (Conflict grows worse.)
4. Pinocchio impoverishes himself to pay the blue-haired fairy's medical bills and rushes back to work to earn more money for her. (Last-ditch solution.)
5. Pinocchio's compassion has made him into a real boy. (Happy ending.)

You'll notice that number 3 above is actually longer and more complicated—it takes up most of the book, in fact, and encompasses dozens of scenes. But we're looking at the plot from a distance.

This pattern also appears in Christopher Moore's *A Dirty Job.* (Warning: The analysis gives away part of the ending.)

1. Charlie Asher, a shy single father, discovers he's become the new Death, but doesn't know anything about his position. (Conflict.)
2. Charlie tries to learn how to be Death, but can't figure out how it works because someone else takes the instruction book. (He fails.)
3. Charlie tracks down the book and learns how to be Death, but in the process he attracts the notice of several ancient gods of death who want to destroy him and his daughter. (Conflict grows worse.)
4. Charlie overcomes his shyness and faces down the forces of darkness with his daughter at his side and gives his life—sort of—so she can live. (Happy ending—mostly.)

You should be able to create similar steps for your own novel. Now, let's zoom in a little closer and look at the novel plot in its smaller pieces.

RISING ACTION

The upside of the plot mountain starts low and rises higher to meet the climax, and we introduce the paranormal along the way. It's divided into pieces.

THE HOOK

You're in a bookstore, just browsing. A title catches your eye. Idly, you lift it from the shelf and read the back cover. Looks interesting. You flip to the first page and start reading. Huh. Not bad. You set it back on the shelf with a mental note to get it later.

Another title gets your attention. Back cover also seems interesting. You read the first page. And then the second. You're sprinting halfway down the third when you remember the dentist appointment you've been avoiding. A moment later, you've paid for the book and are looking forward to reading more of it in the dentist's waiting room.

What was the difference between the two books? The second had a stronger hook.

The *hook*, or opening scene, needs to grab readers from the first sentence and not let them stop reading. You do this by showing the readers something so fascinating the idea of putting down the book becomes unthinkable.

Most novels arrange this with some sort of conflict. In fact, every editor I've ever spoken to has said that, with extremely rare exceptions, the author needs to introduce some kind of conflict in the first chapter, on the first page if you can arrange it. (It doesn't have to be the *main* conflict, but it does have to be *a* conflict.) You want this because conflict hooks readers more than description, character development, pretty language, or nearly anything else an author can use, and you definitely want to hook the reader at the beginning, before she has a chance to set the book down. The literary example everyone uses for this is *Paradise Lost* by John Milton—a paranormal story if there ever was one. Milton starts his story with Satan and the other rebel angels falling into Hell with their wings on fire. He starts in the middle of the action (called *in media res,* for Latin lovers), forcing the reader to keep reading in order to find out what the deal is, and his hook set the gold standard. Plenty of conflict, plenty of reason to keep reading.

Lucienne Diver follows in his footsteps for her rather more modern novel *Vamped.* Her opening paragraph reads:

> I'm here to tell you, rising from the dead just purely sucks. I woke in a blind terror. Literally blind . . . my eyelids tried to flip upward like cartoon window shades as consciousness kicked my butt, but they got nowhere fast. Something was holding my lids shut.

The conflict is clear and straightforward—the protagonist is rising from the dead in terror and something is holding her eyes shut. Three points of conflict in as many sentences. You'll also notice that Diver doesn't begin with Gina's (the viewpoint character's) actual death at the fangs of her vampire boyfriend. Starting there would force Diver to explain too much. It's much more interesting to show Gina come back to unlife and dig herself out of her own grave. The details of how she got there can wait until after the reader has become hooked on Gina and her situation.

Writing the Paranormal Novel

Christopher Moore opens *A Dirty Job* like this:

> Charlie Asher walked the earth like an ant walks on the surface
> of water, as if the slightest misstep might send him plummeting
> through the surface to be sucked to the depths below. Blessed with
> the Beta Male imagination, he spent much of his life squinting into
> the future so he might spot ways in which the world was conspiring
> to kill him—him; his wife, Rachel; and now, newborn Sophie.

Moore has two things going for him in his very first sentence: humor and
conflict. Humor grabs people with its own merits. Moore also nails the
reader with some conflict: a simile that shows Charlie's fear and caution
toward the world. What, the reader wonders, could make Charlie act this
way? Moore follows up in the second sentence, hinting that the world is
out to kill him, his wife, and worst of all, his newborn daughter. And what
the heck is a Beta Male imagination, anyway? We've all heard of an Alpha
Male, so we can probably guess something about a Beta Male, but the lack
of information is a tease calculated to pull us forward. Works, too.

Not everyone likes to hit the ground (or grave) running. Emma Bull
bravely starts *War for the Oaks* with a one-paragraph description of a
shopping mall. Fortunately, she ends the paragraph with the line, "But
late at night, there's a change in the Nicollet Mall." Two paragraphs later,
she dives into a conversation between two supernatural entities, one with
a voice like earth and one with a voice like water:

> "Tell me," said the water voice, "what you have found."
> The deep voice replied. "There is a woman who will do, I think."

Even though Bull starts with description, by the end of the first page we
have some conflict—a mall that changes after sunset for unknown reasons, and a pair of magical beings involved in a mysterious conversation.
It's quite enough to reel the reader in. Your own novel should start with a
similarly strong hook.

But starting with conflict isn't quite enough for a paranormal novel.

CUE THE PARANORMAL

Here's the other thing: *Notice the presence of the paranormal at the outset.* All three of the example books introduce or at least hint at some supernatural element within the opening conflict. Diver gives us someone who's come back from the dead. Moore shows us a world that's out to get one specific person. Bull hands us a pair of elementals. All these elements appear on the first page.

You're writing a paranormal novel. Your readers picked up your book expecting the paranormal. It's therefore your job to deliver the paranormal. It doesn't have to be on the very first page, but it's not a bad idea. At the absolute latest, some sort of supernatural element should show up in the first chapter. You don't want readers to wonder when the show's going to start, yawn, and put your novel down in favor of some quality time with the PlayStation.

BUILDING

As any novel progresses, the conflict needs to *build*. By this, I mean the protagonist's problems need to get worse before they get better.

One mistake I see among beginning writers is the linear plotline. The character encounters a problem, solves it, encounters a bigger problem, solves it, encounters an even bigger problem, and solves it. The writer thinks the bigger problems make the story climb a plot mountain when the book is actually traveling in a straight line.

A better way to build the conflict is to force your character to multitask. Problem A shows up, and while the character is working on solving it, Problem B lands in his lap. He works on both and manages to solve Problem A and is halfway through Problem B just as Problem C smacks him. He juggles B and C, solves B just as Problem D arrives. Or maybe he doesn't solve B yet and he has three things going all at once.

Here's where paranormal novels have an advantage—they have a built-in way to build that plot. The main character's normal life can be giving her difficulties, and then this supernatural problem intrudes, which only makes the normal life problem worse, which makes it harder for her to deal with the supernatural problem. And so on. Moore uses this structure in *A Dirty Job*. Charlie is dealing with the difficulties of raising his daughter and running a small business as a recent widower when he's forced to become Death. Before he can entirely get the whole Death thing under control, the demon attacks start up. Before he can figure all *that* out, a set of hellhounds appear and take over his house, which makes it difficult to run his business and take care of his daughter. And so it continues. Your protagonist should juggle multiple problems, too.

Another method for ratcheting up the tension is good old-fashioned *complication*. This is when a conflict gets worse instead of better. The hero tries to solve this problem, but something else gets in the way and makes things worse yet—or perhaps just more complicated. And since you're writing a paranormal novel, you can use supernatural complications. Greg wants to make up with his fiancée and persuades her to meet him at a restaurant, but on his way to this assignation a vampire attacks him. He wakes up in a Dumpster with a new set of fangs and ten angry text messages from his girlfriend. Greg's first problem has just gotten worse. Hamlet arrives home from boarding school, eager to see his girlfriend Ophelia, and discovers his father has died and his mother married his uncle Claudius. While Hamlet is dealing with his feelings about this, the ghost of his father appears and demands revenge—he was murdered by his brother, who stole his throne. Hamlet must pretend he's insane in order to get proof from Claudius, but abruptly discovers this makes his relationship with Ophelia difficult. Hamlet tries to learn more about the murder from his mother, but accidentally kills Ophelia's father, which drives Ophelia mad. Complication piles on top of complication, difficulty upon difficulty, as Shakespeare's most famous supernatural play progresses, until the explosive, tragic ending becomes all but inevitable.

This, incidentally, isn't to say that your protagonist should have no victories along the way. Throwing problem after problem at your main character with no hint of solution will turn your book into a depressing lead paperweight. You need small successes here and there that bring the protagonist a little closer to solving that big problem. Hamlet manages to confirm to himself that Claudius did indeed murder Hamlet's father. Hamlet can't act on the information directly, but it's a small victory nonetheless. Claudius tries to send Hamlet to his death in England, but Hamlet manages to deflect that plot. Small victories along the way ensure the reader won't feel bogged down by tragedy and have moments to cheer about.

TWISTS AND TURNS

For any novel, predictability spells doom. Predictable stories are dull. Reading one is like climbing onto a roller coaster only to discover it's just the same commuter train you ride to work every day. Where's the fun in reading a new book when you can see the ending coast toward you like a familiar station?

The reader should not be able to guess how the book will end—or if the ending is clear (such as in a romance, where an upbeat ending is a foregone conclusion), the reader shouldn't be able to figure out how on Earth we're going to get there. Careful plotting requires at least one *plot twist*—unexpected change in direction—that throws the reader off the trail. Multiple twists are better, since they keep the reader guessing continually.

Paranormal novels have an extra supply of plot twists. The protagonist can discover new facets of the magical world or learn a new aspect of his supernatural abilities—or discover a new weakness. The Betrayer antagonist is always good for a plot twist, of course, and then there's the Black Moment, which we'll get to in a minute.

J.K. Rowling, famous for her plot twists, keeps them coming in big ways and small. In *Harry Potter and the Sorcerer's Stone,* Harry confronts Draco Malfoy, the school bully, in a scene that in most books ends with the bully winning. (Gentle warning if you haven't read the novel yet—we'll be talking about the ending in this paragraph.) It's early in the book, and the bully *always* wins early in the book. Malfoy flings another student's treasured object, and Harry flies after it on his broomstick. In a surprise twist, Harry discovers a natural talent for broomstick riding and is quickly recruited to Seeker on the school Quidditch team, a plum position. In another twist, Harry believes Professor Snape has been working against him, but at the last moment, he discovers Snape has been helping him all along, and the real antagonist is actually shy, retiring Professor Quirrell.

Hamlet stabbing Polonius through the curtain is a major plot twist in *Hamlet*. Richard Grace turning out to be Mulgarath the ogre in disguise is a plot twist in The Spiderwick Chronicles. Jack Torrance siding with the ghosts and turning on his family is a plot twist in *The Shining*.

Plot twists do need to make sense. You have to set them up so the reader can say, "Oh! I should have seen that coming. Why didn't I?" A plot twist that comes out of nowhere is called a *tomato surprise*, because the so-called twist is about as effective as throwing a tomato into the reader's face and shouting, "Surprise!" Readers don't like tomato surprises, and you should set up your plot twists.

Rowling shows Harry able to command his broomstick better than the other students before he goes off on his unexpectedly skillful ride. The incidents when Professor Snape seems to be hurting Harry are later explained to be misinterpretations of his helpful actions by Harry, who dislikes Snape, while several clues that Professor Quirrell is attempting to hurt Harry are sitting right there in the open. The audience realizes Hamlet has good reason to think Claudius is behind the curtain in *Hamlet*, but only a second before Hamlet does the deed. Mulgarath is established as a shapeshifter early on. Jack Torrance's psyche hangs by a thread for quite some time, and since he seems to be the protagonist, we're thinking he'll win in the end. Fortunately, we're wrong. All these plot twists are unexpected, but they all make sense within the story.

THE BLACK MOMENT

At or just before the climax of any story or novel should come a dreadful, terrible point in the narrative when everything looks lost. The protagonist has been separated from all friends and other support. The antagonist has stolen the magic sword or killed the protagonist's best friend or finished the spell that will release the dark god into the world. It's all over. There's no way the antagonist can win.

This is your *black moment*. Almost every paranormal book has one. It heightens suspense to unbearable levels at the climax and keeps the reader up until dawn to finish the story, the intent of every author. The black moment can be as enormous as something that will spell doom for the entire world, or something as small as meaning the protagonist will never accomplish a personal goal such as crossing through the gate back home, ridding himself of a curse, or finding true love. Whatever it is needs to be deathly important to the protagonist, which makes it important to us.

The black moment forces the protagonist to use that final, gut-wrenching, all-or-nothing attempt (which also, if you're doing your job right, forces the protagonist to confront that Perfect Flaw that's been plaguing him for the entire book) to win in a way that neither the antagonist nor the reader saw coming.

The black moment and its solution comprise the ultimate plot twist. You set up an out for yourself earlier in the book and you take it, sending your protagonist through one final wringer in the process so when he wins in the end, the reader cheers—or if he loses tragically, the reader weeps.

Terry Pratchett ends *Lords and Ladies* with a heart-stopping, drawn-out black moment in which the Queen of Elves has killed Granny Weatherwax and is turning her considerable power on Magrat, who has never been able to stand up to anyone. Even after the climax is resolved, the black moment continues—Granny Weatherwax is still dead. Mulgarath flings Mallory and Simon off a balcony and starts changing into a dragon to kill Jared. J.K. Rowling ends her entire Harry Potter series with a tremendous black moment. The unstoppable Death Eaters break into Hogwarts, and Lord Voldemort kills Harry. How on earth will the characters get out of this? These black moments make the books impossible to put down, and you want to make sure your own book follows suit.

SCENE BY SCENE

We're zooming in even closer now to look at individual scenes. That Rule of Three above still applies as we move inward, and so does that plot mountain.

Any scene in which the main character needs to accomplish something is actually a short story within your book. In the scene, you need to have rising action, complication, climax, and falling action. This is part of that fractal pattern I mentioned earlier—little plot mountains that make up the big plot mountain. This structure pulls the readers along because those little mountains are continually moving toward a climax, hitting one, or just recovering from one.

The pattern you generally want to follow is the one with Greg's conflict a few pages back. It works at the novel level and it works at the scene level. At the scene level, we might have Greg trying to break into a house one night. (Greg has a conflict.) He tries the door and windows, but they're all locked. (Greg tries to solve the conflict and fails.) Greg tries to pick the front door, but his picklocks break off in the keyhole, permanently jamming the lock. Meanwhile, a police car has turned down the block. (Greg tries to solve the conflict a second time and fails again. The conflict gets *worse*.) Greg dashes around to the side of the house and sees a basement window. He kicks it open, breaking it, and squeezes in, though he slices his arm badly and leaves blood on the glass. (Greg tries to solve the conflict a third time and puts everything he has into this ultimate, last-ditch solution.) The police car's headlights sweep the place where Greg was lying as he drops into the basement. (Greg succeeds.)

This structure shows up in *A Dirty Job*. Charlie, still uncertain about this whole Death thing, is walking down the street when the three-in-one death goddess Morrigan threatens him from the sewer grating. (Charlie has a problem.) This frightens Charlie, but he keeps his cool and cheerfully reminds Morrigan that he spent the night in bed while she got to sleep in a sewer. She calls him more names. (Charlie tries to solve the conflict and fails.) At the next block, Morrigan threatens to torture and kill Sophie, Charlie's daughter. This turns Charlie's stomach, but he manages to snarl a threat back at her, which serves to make her angrier. On top of it all, people on the street have begun to notice Charlie is talking to himself. (Charlie tries to solve the conflict a second time and fails again. The conflict gets *worse*.) Finally, Charlie plants himself and the souls he's recently collected outside a sewer grating as bait. When Morrigan's arm snakes out to grab him, he stabs her and flings bagful of lit M-80 firecrackers into the sewer. (Charlie tries to solve the conflict a third time and puts everything he has into this ultimate, last-ditch solution.) The firecrackers explode in the confined space, temporarily incapacitating Morrigan. (Charlie succeeds.)

I should add that this is not a hard-and-fast rule, and not every single scene will run this way, but it *is* a compelling structure for both small scenes and big novels.

SO WHAT ELSE IS GOING ON?

You'll need more going on in your book than just the protagonist's attempt to save the world. People deal with multiple problems in the real world, and fictional people should deal with the same situations. Secondary conflicts within the main conflict are called *subplots*, and you'll want two or three of these. Subplots add breadth to your world and depth to your characters by letting you explore facets of both that may or may not have anything to do with the main plot. It's the little things that make a person's life interesting—and more realistic. You can use subplots to heighten tension, contrast two characters, add to the main plot, and more.

One of the more common—and expected—subplots is the romance. Sure, Greg has to figure out how to survive as a vampire and stop the werewolf rampage from destroying the city, but he also needs to sort out his feelings toward his fiancée Kelly, especially since he's been feeling oddly attracted to Isabel, that South American vampire who turns up whenever he needs help. Diver's vampire fashionista Gina in *Vamped* is mainly interested in stopping a vampire queen from undead-ing Gina's entire high school, but Gina also deals with boyfriend difficulties, all of which is further complicated by the fact that both her current and ex-boyfriends are now vampires, too. Glenda from Terry Pratchett's *Unseen Academicals* watches her best friend fall in love, and she becomes quite surprised when it happens to Glenda herself.

None of these romances are the main story. Paranormal readers enjoy watching the main character slip, fall, or be dragged screaming into a relationship, but they don't want it to be the primary focus. If the protagonist's relationship makes up your paranormal novel's main plot, you're writing a *paranormal romance,* a slightly different kind of book.

Not all books *need* a romance. *A Dirty Job* doesn't have one for Charlie Asher. Terry Pratchett's Granny Weatherwax deliberately turns one away in *Lords and Ladies.* So it's not a requirement, even though it's quite common.

Romantic subplots are usually resolved after the main climax of the book. Greg barely defeats the alpha werewolf in life-threatening combat, and only when it's over does he admit to Isabel that he loves her, for example. Ron and Hermione, and Harry and Ginny get married only after Lord Voldemort and the Death Eaters have been dealt with at the end of the Harry Potter series.

Another subplot revolves around those character flaws I mentioned in chapter eight. Will the character manage to overcome the flaw? If so, how? What impact will all this have on the character? Sometimes a character flaw will take center stage and becomes the main plot, but that's called a *character novel.* It might be a paranormal novel, too, but the structure is different than what we're talking about here.

Character flaw subplots are usually resolved *during* the main climax. This is because you, the author, have cleverly set things up so your main character will be forced to confront this flaw in order to achieve her goal at the climax. A protagonist with a fear of heights will naturally find herself fighting for her life—or the life of someone she loves—atop the Empire State Building. A main character who has trust issues will be faced with the choice of trusting someone and succeeding or drawing away from the other person and failing. In *Harry Potter and the Sorcerer's Stone,* Harry is forced to confront his own secret desire for parents in the Mirror of

Erised at the same time he confronts Professor Quirrell and the fledgling Lord Voldemort at the book's climax. The combination makes the scene even more gripping—there are *two* issues to resolve, and if Harry fails at either one, the story will end in tears. The tension heightens, and the reader can't put the book down.

Running jokes or other nagging problems are yet another type of subplot. That annoying little demon the main character forgot to banish and who now hangs around on top of the refrigerator. The police detective who won't leave the werewolf protagonist alone. The main character avoiding a doctor's appointment. The aforementioned hellhounds become a major subplot in *A Dirty Job,* for example, and Charlie's attempts to get rid of them become a running joke as well.

This kind of subplot can be resolved whenever the author wants. In a series, they may never be resolved, especially if the readers like them. Or they can be resolved within a chapter or two.

Whatever subplots you create, they should receive the same care and feeding as your main plot. You're not allowed to shortchange a subplot just because it's not the main story! They have the same rising action/climax/falling action structure as a main plot, complete with a complication or two along the way. They're just smaller in scope than the main plot.

SUBPLOT BONUS POINTS

Although subplots can exist separate from the main plot, you get bonus points from the reader if your subplots somehow connect to the main plot. When plot and subplot are woven together into a tight tapestry, the story becomes more compelling—it's essentially become a single story with multiple layers instead of several fragmented story lines connected by a single character. The reader isn't continually flipped from plot to subplot and back again because all the plots relate to each other, and that makes for tighter, easier reading.

In a paranormal novel, any real-world subplot should reach into the supernatural main plot and have an impact on it—and vice versa. A fine example of this is *Harry Potter and the Half-Blood Prince*. In a real-world subplot, Harry starts dating Ginny, the younger sister of his best friend Ron. Ron discovers the romance and becomes angry with both Harry and Ginny. Hermione, Harry's other best friend, tries to patch things up, but Harry and Ron continue to fight, and she eventually storms off, disgusted with both of them. As a result of all this, Harry spends a chunk of the book without his friends' help. This severely hinders his attempts to resolve his supernatural main goals for the book: shut the evil Lord Voldemort out of his mind and find a way to get at the magical memories stored in another wizard's head. It isn't until Harry has patched things up with Ron and Hermione that he's able to move ahead with his main goals. The subplots have a big impact on the main plot, which makes the book tighter. Whenever possible, your book should do the same.

CHAPTER 10:

Fight Scenes and Flashbacks: How to Handle Paranormal Pacing

I was in trouble. My current book was going to run long by 30 or 40,000 words. I phoned up my editor, and she said not to sweat it. "Finish the book and we'll worry about length later," she said. So I finished the book and sent it to her. A couple weeks later, she e-mailed back with, "It's too long. You need to cut 30 or 40,000 words."

After I got over my urge to strangle her, I continued reading. "Every scene needs to count," she wrote. "You have several scenes in which nothing really happens, and you can safely cut them." Then she proceeded to list each, with depressing exactness. I sighed and called up my word processing program.

Two weeks later, I had a cleaner, tighter read that clocked in at 120,000 words—much closer to my contracted length. The pacing had also picked up considerably. I probably learned more about pacing from that book than I had in the previous two I'd written, and we'll take a look at those issues here.

SETTING THE PACE

Pace is how quickly or slowly your story moves from one event to the next. Action-packed stories that fling the reader from conflict to conflict have a fast (or even breakneck) pace, while novels layered with a great deal of description, character rumination, and careful conversation have a slow pace.

Pace is, frankly, subjective. One reader's snappy pace is another one's breakneck. One author's leisurely pace is another's dragfoot. General tastes in pace also change. Nineteenth-century readers allowed a much slower pace in their fiction, and authors like James Fenimore Cooper and Victor Hugo thought nothing of stopping the plot dead to explain how to build a log cabin or to deliver a little lecture on the history of the Paris sewers. As society sped up, however, the demand for a faster pace in fiction grew and these little side jaunts became unfashionable. You'll need to decide what kind of pace you want for your book while keeping several factors in mind.

Many paranormal novels are flat-out adventure novels, and most of the remaining ones usually have at least a hint of adventure to them. Adventure lends itself to a faster pace, with the characters rushing headlong from one conflict to the next, with only brief pauses here and there to catch their collective breath. Young adult paranormal fiction also tends to move quickly, the theory being that younger readers will lose patience with a slow book and set it down.

On the other hand, paranormal books that focus more on characters or relationships will often have a slower pace. The author takes the time to explore emotional reactions, internal thought processes, and the characters' relationships, which slows down the overall plot. This is fine, as long as your audience is expecting character and relationship instead of adventure. So the pace will depend on what you're writing.

There are trade-offs among types of pace. Faster-paced books tend to give the reader quite a lot of action, since they concentrate more on plot. Even character development scenes tend to be conflict-driven, and a sense of urgency drives the book continually forward.

Slower-paced books tend to give the reader more language play. When less is happening, the author needs to keep the reader's interest in other ways, and one method is to use more figurative language and other stylistic tricks to pull the reader along. Faster-paced books often lack the lovely language not because the author necessarily lacks the skill, but because there isn't room—extra similes and metaphors and other careful descriptions eat up words that the author wants to use for action.

Note that this is a *tendency,* not a hard rule. We all know authors who are stylistic geniuses and who can keep a story moving. Shakespeare is the most shining example. Charles Dickens's *A Christmas Carol* is a stylish supernatural character story with a fairly fast pace, especially considering he wrote it in the Victorian era, a time when novels moved slower.

No matter what pace you settle on, however, your opening hook should be quick and snappy. As I said in chapter nine, you want to grab the reader right away, and a fast pace is the best way to do it. Once you've hooked the reader, you can slow down, if that's your intent.

Neil Gaiman's *Neverwhere,* for example, has an overall leisurely pace, but it begins quickly, with a paragraph about a girl fleeing from danger. Then it presents a creepy two-page conversation between two odd men named Mr. Croup and Mr. Vandemar. After that, things slow down considerably. Gaiman gives us a careful description of London along with a bit of the city's history, and then he slips into a long explanation of two characters named Richard and Jessica's relationship. Not much happens for several pages. The quick opening hook is meant to grab the readers so they'll stick around once Gaiman drops into the slower pace.

Naomi Novik does the same thing in *His Majesty's Dragon.* Temeraire, the dragon, doesn't hatch until page 17, and the preceding sixteen pages are filled with descriptions, character bits, and exposition. It's all exceedingly well written (which is partly how Novik gets away with it), but ultimately very little happens in those initial pages. The rest of the book has what I would call a slow-to-medium pace, until the climax, when she speeds up considerably. But Novik *starts* this slow-to-medium paced book with, "The deck of the French ship was slippery with blood," and the rest of the paragraph shows us how the battle ends. Because her book has a slower pace, she makes sure to start with a fast opening hook.

THE GREAT PROLOGUE DEBATE

Paranormal (and high fantasy) novels sometimes start with a prologue, a sort of chapter zero. I mention them here as a point of pacing. Authors, editors, and readers continue to debate them and their effectiveness. The first question is, what are they used for?

Some authors use prologues as opening hooks. They start with an action-heavy scene that usually ends badly for the main character, then they abruptly flash back to the past, where the events leading up to this scene begin. The theory is that the reader will be hooked by the action and then stick around to find out how we got there.

Prologues are also used to hand background information to the reader. See, paranormal novels often have a lot to explain. There's a magic system, secret history, cultural information, or any number of things that the reader might have to know in order to follow the main story, and a prologue can get that information to the reader quickly and efficiently, which makes them very useful. However, there are some problems inherent in prologues, too. Let's take a look.

PROLOGUE PROS

Prologues help authors and readers in a number of ways. If you're writing in a complicated or strange setting, the prologue can clue the reader in very nicely. A prologue can give a character's backstory or history by showing events from years before the main story opens. A prologue can also show us events from another character's point of view so when the main character arrives at these events, we're already armed with a certain perspective.

Terry Pratchett opens several (though not all) of his books with a prologue that describes the Discworld. In *The Fifth Elephant,* he opens with:

> They say the world is flat and supported on the back of four elephants who themselves stand on the back of a giant turtle.

They *say* that the elephants, being such huge beasts, have bones of rock and iron, and nerves of gold for better conductivity over long distances.

They *say* that the fifth elephant came screaming and trumpeting through the atmosphere of the young world all those years ago and landed hard enough to split continents and raise mountains.

No one actually saw it land, which raised the interesting philosophical question: When millions of tons of angry elephant come spinning through the sky, and there is no one to hear it, does it—philosophically speaking—make a noise?

And if there was no one to see it hit, did it actually hit?

In other words, wasn't it just a story for children, to explain away some interesting natural occurrences?

As for the dwarfs, whose legend it is, and who mine a lot deeper than other people, they say that there is a grain of truth in it.

After this, Pratchett shifts to the main characters. Later in the book, the existence of the crash-landed fifth elephant becomes extremely important, and the prologue helps the reader—weirdly—believe it a little more easily.

PROLOGUE CONS

Prologues come with certain baggage. Some readers (and editors) flatly dislike them, no matter how necessary or well written they are. They also jerk the reader around by starting the story in one place and then suddenly popping through time or space to another. The reader has to start over, reorient in a new setting or with new characters just after settling in with the old ones. (This is why some readers hate prologues.) Finally, prologues are extra work for the author. You have to hook the reader twice—once for the prologue, and once for chapter one.

THE FINAL ANALYSIS

In the end, use prologues with caution. A prologue will automatically alienate some readers, but opening with chapter one alienates no one. If you're thinking of using a prologue, keep in mind a few tips:

Writing the Paranormal Novel

First, keep it short. Say what you need to say, and get on to the first chapter. Terry Pratchett's prologue above isn't even 200 words long, and in the book it covers barely a third of a page.

Second, keep it extra-entertaining. You're starting with a potential strike against your book, so you'll need to give your reader a reward for putting up with it. It's often death to start with high-sounding language that sounds like it came out of a college textbook. Pratchett uses reader-grabbing humor in his, which has the additional advantage of letting the reader know that the rest of the book will be funny, too.

Before you start with a prologue, ask yourself if there's any way to avoid it. Can your reader follow what's going on if you just start with your story? Couldn't you fill in the information a little later with some well-placed exposition? If the answer to either of these is *yes*, don't use a prologue.

Another possibility to consider is renaming the prologue. Is your prologue really just chapter one in disguise? If you can call it chapter one and move on, do so. J.K. Rowling starts *Harry Potter and the Sorcerer's Stone* with the story of how Dumbledore brings the infant Harry to his awful aunt and uncle's house, and it's written in a fly-on-the-wall point of view. At the beginning of chapter two, we've jumped ahead ten years, and the story is suddenly told from Harry's point of view. We stay with Harry's point of view for the rest of the book, and we have no more giant leaps ahead in time. Rowling's opener, in fact, reads very much like a prologue, but it's titled chapter one. Hmmmm . . .

Finally, when in doubt, don't use a prologue. Jump right in and start your story.

PACING AND EXPOSITION

Exposition is the writer term for the process of explaining stuff to the reader. Paranormal novels have a problem endemic to all speculative fiction—there's so much more to . . . er, expose. The history of werewolves or how vampires are made or where fairies come from or how magic works all need explaining, and this comes in addition to all the "regular" exposition you have to sneak in, including character background, setting, plot setup, and so on. The problem is compounded by the fact that when you pause for exposition, the plot screeches to a halt and people often don't want to read it. So what's a writer to do?

AVOID THE INFODUMP

There's a terrible temptation to drop necessary exposition onto the reader in a big lump to get it out of the way or simply to make sure the reader has it. This is sometimes called an *expository lump* or *infodump,* and it makes for dull reading because the reader has nothing to do but "listen" to an author's lecture. You can avoid lumps and dumps in a number of ways.

First, you can break the information up into tiny pieces and scatter it into a scene where something else is going on. Spread those little lumps out, and readers scarcely notice they're reading exposition. Check out this passage from Philip Pullman's *The Golden Compass:*

> Lyra stopped beside the Master's chair and flicked the biggest glass gently with a fingernail. The sound rang clearly through the hall.
>
> "You're not taking this seriously," whispered her dæmon. "Behave yourself."
>
> Her dæmon's name was Pantalaimon, and he was currently in the form of a moth, a dark brown one so as not to show up in the darkness of the hall.
>
> "They're making too much noise to hear from the kitchen," Lyra whispered back.

Pullman gives three bits of exposition in this passage: Lyra has a dæmon, the dæmon's name is Pantalaimon, and Pantalaimon can change shape. The first fact he drops casually into the narrative by simply referring to Lyra's dæmon without comment. The second fact—the dæmon's name—he states directly. This is fine—it's short and quick, and we barely notice he's telling us something. Pullman puts the third fact—the dæmon's shape-shifting powers—in the context of what's going on: Pantalaimon has taken on this shape for camouflage so he won't be seen. (Indirectly, we've also learned that Lyra isn't supposed to be in the hall, so I suppose Pullman has actually handed us four bits of exposition.) Rather than stop the action to explain that all people in this world have dæmons and that children's dæmons can change shape, Pullman *shows* us a dæmon at work, and tells us only a couple tiny facts, barely pausing in the story to do so.

Another method uses dialogue to fill in expository blanks. People talk about the necessary information, and the reader eavesdrops. In the case of *The Lightning Thief* by Rick Riordan, Percy, the protagonist, eavesdrops, too:

> I inched closer.
>
> " . . . alone this summer," Grover was saying. "I mean, a Kindly One in the school! Now that we know for sure, and they know too—"
>
> "We would only make matters worse by rushing him," Mr. Brunner said. "We need the boy to mature more."
>
> "But he may not have time. The summer solstice deadline—"
>
> "Will have to be resolved without him, Grover."

We learn that something is strange about Percy's background. Not only that, his friend Grover and his teacher Mr. Brunner are in on it. A Kindly One, whatever that is, has appeared in the school, and although the summer solstice is important, Percy will have to miss it. We don't know all the facts, but we've learned enough to move the story forward, and the tension created by Percy's eavesdropping gives the reader a reason to stay interested.

A variation on this method is the necessary lecture. A character in the know explains to a less-informed character what's going on. Brandon Mull uses this technique in *Fablehaven.*

"What have they done to him?" Kendra asked.

"An act of vengeance," Grandpa said grimly.

"For trying to catch fairies?"

"For succeeding."

"He caught one?"

"He did."

"So they turned him into a deformed walrus? I thought they couldn't use magic against us!"

"He used potent magic to transform the captured fairy into an imp, unwittingly opening the door for magical retribution."

Here, Grandpa "lectures" Kendra about what happened to Seth, informing both her and the reader. Notice also how Kendra reminds the reader in her own dialogue that fairies theoretically can't use magic against humans (and that Mull stays within the limitations he set up for magic—fairy magic can't hurt mortals, but Seth changes the fairy into an imp, and therefore all bets are off).

This method works very well, but it does walk a fine line. You have to make sure the people who do the talking have a *reason* to discuss the topic. One of the bigger sins a paranormal novel can commit is an *As you know, Bob* moment. This is when two characters have a conversation about something they have no reason to talk about for the sole (and obvious) purpose of informing the reader. The term *As you know, Bob* got started in science fiction pulp magazines, but it's bled into other genres. It's a reference to bad dialogue that started with *As you know:*

"As you know, Bob, we now bring the automobile to a complete stop."

"Right, Dr. Zinger! Because the light turned red!"

"And after a suitable time has elapsed, what will happen?"

"The light will turn green and we'll be able go."

"That's correct. Oh look—it has done so. Now, as you know, when I press the accelerator . . . "

These characters have no reason to say any of this, and such scenes are nothing but blatant and bad attempts at exposition. At least one character in such a conversation needs to be ignorant of whatever it is the other character is explaining, or it turns into *As you know, Bob*.

Another method is to have characters find or stumble across reading material—books, diaries, magazine or newspaper articles, even Web sites—that you reproduce on the page. This can work well if it's not overused and if you have a nonfiction bent. Some writers like the chance to use a different writing style for a bit. J.K. Rowling pokes gentle fun at this method several times in the Harry Potter series. Hermione gleans enormous amounts of expository information from the book *Hogwarts, A History*. She relates the information to Harry and Ron (and the reader), and then grouses that the two boys could just as easily read it themselves. "What's the point?" Ron says. "You know it all by heart, we can just ask you."

You can also dip into a character's memory for exposition. This isn't quite as involved as a flashback (see below), but it works. Something conveniently triggers a memory about facts the reader needs to know. The technique shows up in *Fablehaven*:

> [Kendra] had overheard when Mom had approached Grandpa Sorenson about letting the kids stay with him. It was at the funeral.
>
> The memory of the funeral made Kendra shiver. There was a wake beforehand, where Grandma and Grandpa Larsen were showcased in matching caskets. Kendra did not like seeing Grandpa Larsen wearing makeup. What lunatic had decided that when people died you should hire a taxidermist to fix them up for one final look?

Here we learn that Kendra grandparents are dead and that her mother hit up Kendra's other grandfather about child care arrangements at their wake. We also get a bit of Kendra's reaction to the event, and that tells us something about Kendra.

Which brings us to the final bit about exposition—whenever possible, put it in terms of the viewpoint character. In other words, be sure your exposition shows up with the character's thoughts and feelings woven into it. Above, the wake and funeral are unpleasant for Kendra, and those feelings are part of the memory. This adds a human element to the infodump and makes it more interesting to read.

You may have noticed that I've spent an enormous amount of time telling you how to avoid expository lumps. This demands the question, "Can a straight infodump ever be done well?" And the answer is, "Certainly." Or rather, "Certainly, but . . . "

Imagine a group of a thousand professional actors. The vast majority of them could handle a role in an Agatha Christie murder mystery play. A minority could play Shakespearean leads like Hamlet or Julius Caesar. And maybe two could enthrall an audience just by reading the phone book aloud. Writers are the same. Most are pretty good at their craft and can keep a decent story going, while a very few could write a bestseller about the history of sawdust. Until you know for sure that you're part of the tiny minority, you're probably best off avoiding as many expository lumps as possible.

HOLDING OFF

World building is *fun*. So is creating character histories. The more you think about them, the more ideas you get, and the more elaborate the world and people become. And since you've put so much time and effort into the material, there's a completely understandable desire to put it all in. After all, it's interesting, it's fun, and it's informative.

Another temptation is to explain the entire world or character at once. Put it all in front of the reader and get it over with. If it's well written, people will read it just fine, yeah?

The fact is, you *can* hold off. In fact, you probably should. Your reader doesn't need to know everything up front, or even ever. Lots of your well-crafted world building and character histories will never show up in the book. Every author has pages of notes that never make it into the final book, and you will, too. Also, always remember that exposition slows the story down, no matter how well written it is. Ask yourself if the reader *really* needs to know a particular fact. If not, try holding off on it. You'll probably have a cleaner, faster read.

FLASHING BACK

You can also pop back in time to let your reader in on what came before. This is called a *flashback*. Flashbacks can run short or long, depending on how much information you need to convey, and they're very handy—they let you start in the middle of some action and then back up a little once you've gotten the reader's attention. In a paranormal novel, flashbacks become an extremely handy tool for handling the extra amounts of exposition these books often require. However, you can't just drop a flashback into any old scene. It has to be set up properly.

THE LEAD-IN

Something needs to trigger a flashback, create a reason for it to appear. Otherwise its appearance is abrupt and obvious. You want to lead readers gently into a flashback so they barely notice what's going on. The character might see or remember something that sends his mind back to an earlier event. Or another character might mention something that triggers the flashback. Or whatever's currently happening to the character might start the flashback.

J.K. Rowling needs to show us some of eleven-year-old Harry Potter's history with his dreadful aunt and uncle in *Harry Potter and the Sorcerer's Stone,* and she leads carefully into the flashback. The Dursleys are planning a trip to the zoo for Harry's cousin Dudley's birthday, and they're forced to take Harry with them. Uncle Vernon isn't happy about this.

> "I'm not going to do anything," said Harry, "honestly . . ."
> But Uncle Vernon didn't believe him. No one ever did.

> The problem was, strange things often happened around Harry and it was just no good telling the Dursleys he didn't make them happen.

From there, Rowling starts a series of flashbacks about Harry's odd childhood. She uses the current event—a trip to the zoo—as a trigger to set the whole thing in motion. And incidentally, she gets double duty out of this transition—it also lets us know that something's supernaturally strange about Harry.

SHORT FLASHBACKS

Short flashbacks are no more than a paragraph long and are meant to give the reader a little burst of backstory. If you're writing in past tense, short flashbacks are written in the past-perfect tense. This means you use the helping verb *had* and add the past tense of the main verb, as in *had killed, had written,* or *had hit.* Switch back to regular past tense to signal the reader that the flashback has ended. To continue with Rowling's example above, she writes when the lead-in is done:

> Once, Aunt Petunia, tired of Harry coming back from the barbers looking as though he hadn't been at all, had taken a pair of kitchen scissors and cut his hair so short he was almost bald except for his bangs. . . . Next morning, however, he had gotten up to find his hair exactly as it had been before Aunt Petunia had sheared it off. He had been given a week in his cupboard for this, even though he had tried to explain that he *couldn't* explain how it had grown back so quickly.

The verbs are all in past-perfect tense for this one-paragraph flashback. Rowling adds two other brief flashbacks, and then comes out of them with a new paragraph that starts, "But today nothing was to go wrong." The phrase *But today* leads us out of the past into the present, and the verb *was* (instead of *had been*) confirms the move.

Writing the Paranormal Novel

LONGER FLASHBACKS

Sometimes you might need to drop in a longer flashback, one that tells a story complete with dialogue and descriptions. They're helpful for introducing characters and explaining intricate or complicated story lines. Putting an entire extended section into past-perfect tense, however, makes for clunky, awkward reading, and you don't want to go that route. Instead, you lead the reader in with past-perfect tense and switch to normal past tense for the rest of the flashback. At the end of the flashback, you give the reader one or two more past-perfect sentences, and gracefully slip back into the present.

Brandon Mull does this at the beginning of *Fablehaven*. While riding in the family car, Kendra continues to remember her grandparents' funeral and Grandpa Sorenson's presence there:

> It had been more than eighteen months since either of the Sorensons had visited. [Grandpa Sorenson] had apologized that his wife could not attend because she was feeling ill. There always seemed to be an excuse. Sometimes Kendra wondered if they were secretly divorced.
>
> Toward the end of the wake, Kendra overheard Mom cajoling Grandpa Sorenson to watch the kids. They were in a hallway around the corner from the viewing area.

The flashback starts in past-perfect tense (*had been* and *had visited*), then shifts to regular past tense. (Notice also Kendra's reactions to the memory. Her musing about a secret divorce makes the scene more interesting—and tells us something about the way Kendra thinks.)

From there, Mull goes into a full page of flashback, complete with the dialogue between Grandpa Sorenson and Kendra's mother. Like the second paragraph above, it's all in past tense. When the scene nears its end, Mull writes:

> Kendra moved away from the hall at that point. She had quietly worried about staying with Grandpa Sorenson ever since.

Notice the first sentence uses past tense (*moved*), but the second sentence, which moves us out of the flashback, uses past perfect (*had worried*). After that, Mull returns to the main story in its usual past tense.

A SPECIAL CASE

If you're writing in present tense, flashbacks are done a tiny bit differently. In a past-tense book, the reader is in the present, the book is in the past, and flashbacks are in the distant past (before the events of the novel). However, if you set your book in present tense, you've moved everything forward one step. Your book is in the present with the reader, which puts flashbacks in the more recent past. That means your flashbacks will be in past tense.

Such flashbacks are handled with the same pattern as their past-perfect counterparts. You start with a lead-in written in your normal present tense, then switch to past tense for the flashback.

A FINAL FLASHBACK WORD

Avoid early flashbacks. New authors often try to start *in media res* with a single sentence of action—good idea—then ruin it by resorting to a flashback—bad idea—as in "Melissa faced the werewolf in the misty alley. She couldn't believe it had come to this. Just ten minutes ago she had been walking home with her boyfriend Zack. He had been joking about the eerie mist and how any second a werewolf would probably ambush them." A decent opening hook is sidetracked and ruined by a scene-slowing flashback. If the information in an early flashback is truly necessary, you probably started the scene too late. In the example above, it might be better to start with Melissa's boyfriend making a joke about the eerie mist (though better just to dump the information altogether—that werewolf is dying to attack).

FIGHTING

Paranormal books are given to fights. The idea of a fictional fight is nothing new, but in a paranormal book, things can get a little more complicated.

Writing the Paranormal Novel

The list of weapons is longer, for one thing, and the outcomes more varied. Writing for a fight also differs from writing for other types of scenes. All of this makes fights worth examining here.

GETTING INTO A FIGHT

Since paranormal books range across time and space, you might find yourself writing a fight that involves fist and feet, tooth and claw, guns of any sort, or a host of medieval death options such as knives, swords, staves, pole arms, hammers—and this doesn't begin to touch the weapons found in non-European cultures. Humans are very inventive at finding ways to injure and kill one another.

Assuming you aren't already an expert in violence, this means you have to do your research again. Among your readers will inevitably be a bunch of experts in using whatever weapon you decide to hand your protagonist, and you don't want to look foolish. You aren't alone. Shakespeare included a number of sword fights in his plays, but most of his audience knew how to use these weapons. This required the actors at the Globe to know proper Elizabethan sword work because any unrealistic moves would instantly stand out—and Elizabethan audiences thought it sporting to throw half-finished food at anything resembling bad acting. Your readers aren't likely to fling rotten oysters at you, but you don't want to let avoidable mistakes creep into your writing, either.

A BIT MORE ON RESEARCH

Although we already talked about research in chapter four, this particular area is specific enough to require its own discussion.

Several resources present themselves when you need to do research into combat. Books and the Internet are useful for looking up any number of weapons and combat techniques, of course, but the printed word isn't all that great for getting across how a joint lock works, say, or the way a pistol really feels when you fire it. Too many new authors rely on movies for this, and that's always a mistake—Hollywood is more concerned with what looks good than with accuracy, and a number of movie tricks have mistakenly made their way into polite society as a result. (Bullets, for example, don't spark when they glance off metal, and punches don't make a *pshh!* noise when they land.)

A number of online video sites have instructional videos on how to fight hand-to-hand and with various weapons. Another great place to ask is at a local martial arts school. Just walk in and introduce yourself using the rules in chapter four for interviews. You'll find quite a number of people willing to show you how fights really work—both teachers and students. (You may recognize the voice of experience here.) Martial arts schools will also have weapons instructors who may talk to you, but they'll often be limited to one type or style. However, if you need to talk to someone about fencing or broadsword work instead of short staff and katana, a martial arts instructor may know of someone in your area you can talk to, so they can be a good starting point.

Another good group to contact is the Society for Creative Anachronisms, or SCA. They're dedicated to the study and re-creation of certain aspects of medieval culture, including combat. If your town has a renaissance fair or similar festival, you can bet the SCA will show up. Local chapters are also readily findable online, ironic as that may seem. Most SCA members will happily give you information, tips, and even demonstrations on armed and unarmed combat—or other aspects of medieval culture that might creep into your book.

One time, I had the good fortune to join a group of writers who had persuaded a group of SCA folk to give us a daylong demonstration of several types of fighting, both medieval and modern. These guys were *experts*—many were former military. We were treated to a completely free set of workshops on knife fighting, using swords of many sizes, axe throwing, how to ambush and assassinate someone in a dark alley, and more ways to deal death than I knew existed. It was wonderful—and it came about simply because one of my friends asked if they'd be willing. The resources are often there if you're willing to speak up.

Some paranormal books involve hand-to-claw or hand-to-fang combat. On the one hand, this is a little trickier—you have no true frame of reference for how a normal human would fight a half-human, clawed, and fanged werewolf. On the other hand, this makes it more fun—you can experiment with your combat to see what works. Here again, a local martial arts studio can be a good resource, since experts in hand-to-hand combat have a better shot at extrapolating a realistic fighting style. It's also worth watching videos of normal animals. If you're writing about werewolves, look up shows on wolves. If you need information about claws, check out shows about tigers and panthers. Watching the original animal in action will give you ideas on how the animal moves, too, lending yet more verisimilitude to your fiction.

When it comes to local information about pistols, no one beats the police. They *have* to stay well informed about all kinds of armed combat—it's a survival thing. Some local law enforcement agencies also offer courses in civilian gun safety, and if your novel is going to include a significant amount of pistol play, you may find it worthwhile to enroll. Finally, modern-day supernatural protagonists may well run into the police in your book, and it's not a bad idea to know correct police procedures. (Cop shows on television almost never have it right—Hollywood strikes again.) If you want to find out about either police procedures or weapons safety, call up your local police agency and ask to speak to the public relations officer. It's that person's job to answer questions like yours, and he's glad to do it, especially if it means someone out there will get procedures right. Sure, you have a good imagination, but only a police officer knows how a cop would really react if confronted with a giant wolf, girl with fangs, or other threat that didn't fit the books.

STAGING FIGHTS

Deciding who stands where and moves in what way is called *blocking*. Blocking out a fight can be fun and challenging at the same time. Some people are good at doing it in their heads, but others (like me) aren't so talented, especially when more than two or three people are involved.

To help visualize how a particular fight would work, get two or three good friends to be stand-ins so you can see how things will work. (My sons love doing this.) You can also use those little lead figures for gaming to see who stands where, or, in a pinch, sketch out a little map on a piece of paper like theater directors do. Moving the fight from your head to a more physical location helps not only to make the combat more realistic, but can also give you ideas you hadn't thought of before. It also helps point out impossibilities—characters who couldn't reach that far or who can't be in a certain place by the time a fight ends.

FIGHT PROSE

Something else that Hollywood gets wrong—fights go *fast*. They start fast and they end fast. A fight that lasts more than thirty seconds is considered long. I hold a second-degree green belt in karate, so I have a certain amount of firsthand experience here. This was reinforced when I attended that SCA workshop—the ambush technique they demonstrated took down the victim in less than three seconds. Fights are also the epitome of an action scene. Quick, snappy pacing is what you need, and along with it, you need quick, snappy prose.

Your writing style may run gothic or flowery or downright poetic. But when the fight starts, a lot of those stylistic points need to fade into the background. In a fight—or any other action-based scene—pretty prose is a distraction. The extra words get in the way and slow down what needs to be a fast event.

Take a look at the words often used to describe hand-to-hand fights: *kick, punch, smack, hit, crack, break, slap, block, strike, slam, dodge,* and the list continues. Many of these words are onomatopoeic—they sound like what they mean—and they're a single syllable long. Quick, punchy prose indicates quick, punchy action. Words for sword fights go the same way. Steel blades can *ring, clang, slash, thwack, poke, score,* and *slice.* Okay, so *parry* has two syllables—the pattern remains. Words associated with guns continue in this vein: *fire, shoot, bang, crack,* and more. All these words have a violent connotation to them, meaning they're well suited to getting the point across. Use them, and be direct.

Fight scenes are usually best done with shorter sentences as well as shorter words. The quick sentence structure indicates quick action. Longer sentences, even if a lot happens, feel like they take up more time. Look at the difference:

> Ben's fist sank into the werewolf's gut, and the air whooshed out of the creature, flooding Ben's nostrils with the stench of foul, long-dead meat. The werewolf recovered quickly, leaping at Ben with bloody claws extended and slashing at the air, barely giving Ben time to duck out of the way. A growl of frustration rumbled in the werewolf's chest as Ben desperately searched the ground for the gun and the precious silver bullets he had dropped moments ago.

An okay fight scene, but it suffers from an abundance of long, clunky sentences. Now try this version:

> Ben punched the werewolf in the gut. Air whooshed out of the creature, and Ben smelled rotten meat. The werewolf recovered and leaped. It slashed the air—once, twice. Ben ducked beneath the bloody claws. A frustrated growl rumbled in the werewolf's chest as Ben desperately scanned the ground. Where the hell was the gun?

The shorter words and sentences move the fight along much better.

Within the same novel, fight scenes need a different pacing from "regular" scenes. For example, Ginn Hale uses a fairly florid style in *Wicked Gentlemen*, as this typical passage demonstrates:

> Roffcale's letters smelled of dried blood and very cheap cologne. I pulled in his scent while my fingertips brushed over the clumsy lines of his reform school script. He was young and passionate. He poured himself into each word with absurd intensity. With every

> letter he set down, he fell in love and was overwhelmed with rage. . . .
> Roffcale stacked cliché upon cliché until they achieved a stagger-
> ing tower of artless adoration.

The passage is heavy with metaphor and is fairly typical of Hale's writing style throughout the book—except when it comes to fights. Then her style shifts somewhat:

> [Scott-Beck's] hand crushed brutally around mine. I slashed my
> free hand up and drove my long nails into the flesh of his throat.
> His skin was like horsehide. My claws barely cut into it.
>
> In an instant, Scott-Beck stepped aside and twisted my hand
> violently. Cracking pain burst through my arm as a bone in my
> wrist snapped. He twisted my hand farther and I stumbled on my
> feet, dropping to one knee.

Only one bit of figurative language here—a simile—and the wording is punchier than her descriptive sections. The paragraphs are shorter as well. All of this adds to the faster feel of combat. Hale still manages to preserve her overall style, but the action and combat sections move faster than the other scenes, as they should.

MAGIC WANDS AND MAGIC WARS

Supernatural fights can introduce a dozen impossible things before combat, and they completely change the picture. Pitting a guy with a gun against a witch with a wand gets tricky—how do you know which one would go off first? Would the spell fly faster, or the bullet? Could the guy dodge the spell after he fired the gun?

Really, once you introduce a purely supernatural element into a fight, the result comes down to exactly what you decide the story needs. If the story requires spells to outspeed bullets, then so it must be. If the story requires the guy to dodge the spell, then so he must. However, as we saw in chapter seven, you must always remain consistent with it. Once you decree magic to be faster than bullets, you can't renege two chapters later.

THE NECESSITY OF SCENES

Every scene in a novel must have a reason to exist. Each scene must move the story forward, develop character in a specific direction, or give the reader specific information—and it's best if you combine these functions. Unnecessary scenes slow your pacing and hurt even a leisurely novel.

There's also a practical reason for writing shorter. A longer novel takes up more pages to print. More pages means more paper, and more paper drives up the cost of the book. (We're talking about print novels here, as opposed to electronically published books.) Publishers like to keep the cost to the reader as low as possible, especially with new authors. The idea is that readers view new authors with suspicion—they have no way of knowing whether they'll like this unknown entity's fiction or not. If the book's price is high, readers are unlikely to overcome their suspicion and buy the book. If the book's price is low, readers are more willing to take the risk. Shorter, less expensive books are therefore more likely to get a green light for a new author, so you'll want brevity over length.

When my editor returned that novel manuscript to me with 40,000 words to cut, I went though every single scene and asked myself, does this scene *really* need to appear? Can it be cut? If not, can it be shortened? Combined with another scene? Ask yourself the same questions.

One thing to remember is that you don't need to explain everything. You can imply certain things and let the reader fill in the rest. Some time ago I was critiquing Cindy Spencer Pape's manuscript for *The Gaslight Chronicles*, which was a paranormal work in progress at the time, but has since been published. During this read-through, I came across a set of scenes that I thought could be condensed. In the first scene, Merrick, the male protagonist, is dealing unsuccessfully with a group of magically talented street urchins whom he'd more or less adopted. In the second scene, Merrick's aunt, who knows the situation, spends considerable time convincing a governess named Caroline to come and interview at the house.

In the third scene, Caroline leans back in the carriage, wondering what this strange man and his street urchin children will be like.

I mentioned that the second scene could be cut. It didn't really do anything except show the reader how Caroline is persuaded to interview with Merrick. All Pape needed to do was show the children running wild through the house and end with something crashing to the floor. Merrick turns to his aunt and whimpers, "I think I need a governess." The aunt replies, "I know just the one." And then we jump to Caroline in her carriage. We don't *need* to see the persuasion scene—Caroline's presence in the carriage implies it for us—and removing it trims unnecessary wordage from the novel. Pape agreed and cut the scene.

This isn't to say that every scene *needs* to be cut or shortened. My editor put on the chopping block several scenes from my book that I insisted should stay, and I did keep them even as I cut several others. Just as in life, moderation is the key in fiction. You can't cut everything, but what you can cut, you probably should.

Writing the Paranormal Novel

CHAPTER 11:

Language and Dialogue

A character from Louisiana doesn't speak the same way as a character from London, and a character from three dimensions over won't sound like a native to this world. And imagine the slang that might spring up if elves publicly showed up and made themselves at home in Detroit. Introducing supernatural elements to a book naturally changes the way the characters speak and will likely have a significant impact on the narration. This chapter examines those issues in detail.

THE IMPORTANCE OF DIALOGUE

Human conversation grabs the mental ear—it's a chance to eavesdrop on something fascinating—and it's the reason dialogue remains the main thing readers want in a book. In fact, dialogue is one of the stronger opening hooks you can use.

Dialogue performs a number of functions. It moves action forward by telling the reader what's going on. It sneaks in exposition. And most importantly, it tells the reader what your character is like.

ESTABLISHING CHARACTER

Everyone has his own speech patterns. This means no two people talk alike, not even ones from the same part of the country. Part of it is upbringing, but part of it is also outlook. People's ideas and attitudes shape the way they speak. Someone who expects the worst will choose different words than someone who expects the best.

All your characters should be differentiated by dialogue, whether they're ordinary people or supernatural ones. If you can reassign the dialogue in a given scene to another character without changing any of the words, it means you haven't done your job well.

Dialogue differences can be very overt. Tony DiTerlizzi and Holly Black use wildly different forms of dialogue among their fairy characters in The Spiderwick Chronicles books. Thimbletack the brownie speaks in rhyming couplets. In *The Seeing Stone*, Jared meets a caged hobgoblin named Hogsqueal, and the difference between the ways the two characters speak shows clearly:

> "You're not very chicken-beaked for a nib-head," the hobgoblin grumbled. "I'm in [this cage] for letting out one of the cats. See, I like cats, and not just 'cause they're tasty, which they are, no mistake. But they got these eyes that are an awful lot like mine, and this one was real little, not much meat there. And she had this sweet little mewl." The goblin looked lost in his memory, then abruptly looked back at Jared. "So enough about that. Let me out."
>
> "And what about your teeth? Do you eat babies or what?" Jared had not found the goblin's story very reassuring.
>
> "What is this, an interrogation?" Hogsqueal groused.
>
> "I'm letting you out already." Jared came closer and started to cut the complicated knots on the cage. "But I want to know about your teeth."

The differences between Jared's and Hogsqueal's dialogue stand out sharply. Hogsqueal's word choices have a New Jersey flavor to them with some invented fairy slang (*chicken-beaked* and *nib-head*) mixed in. DiTerlizzi and Black are going for humor here, since no one would expect a fairy to talk like a New York cab driver, and the resulting dialogue very quickly

Writing the Paranormal Novel

paints a picture of a crude but crafty creature. We also learn that Hogsqueal likes to eat cats. Jared is meant to be a nine-year-old boy who could be from anywhere in the country (since the books don't get specific in their setting), so his dialogue is free of regional dialect.

Christopher Moore's characters in *A Dirty Job* speak differently from one another as well, though the difference is subtler. Here, Charlie is talking to Mr. Fresh about what it means to be Death—or *a* death.

> Mr. Fresh shrugged. " . . . Surely you've noticed that no one sees you when you're out to get a soul vessel."
>
> "I've never gone out to get a soul vessel."
>
> "Yes, you have, and you will, at least you should be. You need to get with the program, Mr. Asher."
>
> "Yeah, so you said. So you're—uh—we're invisible when we're out getting these soul vessels?"
>
> "Not invisible, so to speak, it's just that no one sees us. You can go right into people's homes, and they'll never notice you standing right beside them, but if you speak to someone on the street, they'll see you . . ."
>
> "So that's how you got to be a—what do they call us?"
>
> "Death Merchants."
>
> "Get out. Really?"

Here, Moore doesn't even need to tell us who's talking. Partly it's that he gives us a cue up front when he writes that Mr. Fresh shrugged and then slips in a cue when Fresh addresses Charlie as "Mr. Asher," but mostly it's the dialogue itself. Fresh has a more formal, polished mode of speaking. Later we learn he can drop it and speak much more informally—the polished dialogue is part of an image he tries to project. His attitude affects his dialogue. Meanwhile, Charlie's dialogue is peppered with fits and starts. He also uses *yeah* whereas Fresh uses *yes*. The differences are subtle but clear. You certainly couldn't put Charlie's words into another character's mouth without serious changes.

EXERCISE

Read the following dialogue.

> Evan strode into the dark room and flung back the curtains.
> "How much did you pay for this place?"
>
> "Enough." Abby set her suitcase on the threadbare
> carpet and glanced around the tiny cottage's living room.
> "Come on, it was a steal and you know it. It has a fireplace."
>
> "We only get a week together. I just wanted it to be
> someplace nice. Romantic. Not a . . . well, not here."
>
> "There's romantic and there's romantic," Abby said.
> "The place isn't important. We are."
>
> "I know. I do. I'm just worried." Evan checked his smart
> phone. "Six days, fifteen hours, and forty-two minutes be-
> fore full moon. You know what happens then."

Now rewrite it in two different ways, changing only the words of
the dialogue, not the interstitial material. You may not change the
overall intent of the dialogue, only the wording.

CHANGE #1

Evan is furious—but not with Abby. (Perhaps he's overt and straightforward, or maybe he shows his anger through sarcasm, or maybe
has another method.) Abby is on a hair-trigger herself but is trying
to hold it together.

Also, Abby and Evan should speak differently from one another.
Differentiate their dialogue choices in some way. Perhaps they're
from different regions, or even different countries.

CHANGE #2

Evan is frightened of Abby. Abby is in control of this relationship
and knows it. Continue to differentiate their word choices.

Writing the Paranormal Novel

> Now pick the version you like best and add several more dialogue exchanges.

WRITING GOOD DIALOGUE

Every year when we begin the Shakespeare unit, my ninth graders take one look at the dialogue and inevitably ask, "Did people really talk that way back then?" And my inevitable answer is "No way."

Characters in books, plays, movies, and TV shows don't talk at all like people in real life. Dialogue for real people is full of stammers, stutters, and verbal clutter such as *like*, as in "He was, like, no way, and I'm like, yeah we are." Real people ramble when they speak and natter over details no one cares about: "The bus was rushing straight toward me, and I didn't know what to do. I remember that it was Tuesday because my oldest has his lessons on Tuesdays, and I was taking his clarinet to him because he'd forgotten it *again*. The boy would forget his head if it wasn't attached. So anyway, the bus . . . " Yeah. Real people rarely say anything worth putting into a book—not without heavy editing, anyway.

But here's the thing—a lot of people *think* they speak well. They don't notice the annoying verbal clutter, the rambling, the number of times they say *um*, or the fact that they start every other sentence with *You know*. So when they read or hear dialogue that doesn't have any of that stuff in it, it sounds good and natural to them.

Good dialogue *sounds* natural without being the slightest bit natural. It's all part of that illusion of reality you're creating. There are a number of ways to create realistic-sounding dialogue, even for unrealistic characters, and a number of traps to avoid.

SPEECH TICS

All of us have little verbal tics we use when we speak. As noted above, we end our sentences in *yeah?* or say *Goodness me!* a lot or misuse the word *literally,* as in *My boss will literally kill me if I'm late again.* Our problem is we use these tics too often, and they would become annoying on the printed page.

You can and should assign speech tics to your characters. The key is to use them *sparingly,* as in no more than once or twice per scene. You want to give the flavor of a speech tic without annoying the readers with it.

Supernatural characters can have their own otherworldly speech tics. We already saw Hogsqueal's odd slang in The Spiderwick Chronicles. Gina, the fashionista vampire in Lucienne Diver's *Vamped,* has a number of teenage girl speech tics, including the words *like* and *totally.* In chapter four, Gina says, "What I mean is, we're, like, beyond the law. Renegades, right? No reflection, so probably no image left behind on pesky security cameras." The word *like* doesn't appear again in dialogue for the rest of the chapter—or in the next. Gina's dialogue retains the flavor of teenage dialect without actually *being* teenage dialect, and it gets the idea across in print very nicely.

In a more extreme example, Dobby, the house elf from J.K. Rowling's books, avoids pronouns for himself and other people, referring to himself as *Dobby* instead of *I.* He also addresses Harry in third person indirectly and by his full name Harry Potter. In *Harry Potter and the Chamber of Secrets,* for example, Dobby says, "Dobby has come to protect Harry Potter, to warn him, even if he *does* have to shut his ears in the oven door later . . . *Harry Potter must not go back to Hogwarts.*" This speech tic makes Dobby's dialogue quite distinctive and, as I said, a little extreme, but Rowling gets away with it because Dobby is an extreme character. She wisely avoids this with her main characters.

SUPERNATURAL SWEARING

Okay, this one can be a delicate topic, but it needs addressing. Some novels have explicit swearing in them, and some don't. Which it is depends on what the author has decided is appropriate for the audience. If your book doesn't use swear words, you can safely skip this section.

In English, swearing revolves around two things: bodily functions and religion. Other languages have other standards for swearing. In China, it's a dreadful insult to call someone a turtle, for example. Swearing is based on the forbidden—in English-speaking cultures we're not allowed to say our swear words because the concepts they're based on are considered impolite, disgusting, or profane.

This gets tricky when you have a character from another culture, say from the other side of a mystic gate. What if that culture treats sex as a public act but drinking is considered private, and even a little shameful? The tricky part isn't creating the swearwords, actually—the tricky part is getting away with having a character who stubs his toe and yelps, "Drink!" It can be done. You just have to use it consistently and have other characters react appropriately, forcing your reader to accept it.

One way to create new swearwords is to leave the powerful ones alone but create mild ones for your culture. *Oh my God* or just *God* are common mild swearwords in our culture (though they used to be much more powerful), and a number of paranormal books have characters swear in the plural, saying *Oh my Gods* or *Gods,* or mentioning deities by name instead.

Finally, in a supernatural setting, swearing might have consequences that go beyond social censure. Not that long ago, people were reluctant to mention the devil's name in case calling it out got his attention. ("Speak of the devil, and he is like to appear.") The ancient Greeks were equally reluctant to call on the death god Hades for the same reason. J.K. Rowling's characters dislike saying the name of the dread wizard *Voldemort* aloud, and everyone reacts as if it were a dreadful swearword. And in a world where magic or the gods are real, swearing might create real consequences. In *The Sword in the Stone* by T.H. White (which is high fantasy but still worth mentioning here), Merlin experiences a moment of frustration toward young Arthur and shouts, "Castor and Pollux blow me to Bermuda!" He instantly vanishes and reappears a moment later, hair and robe wildly disheveled. When

Arthur asks what happened, Merlin only replies, "Let that be a lesson to you not to swear."

SOUNDING REALISTIC

Conversation has a natural rhythm, a give-and-take that's not always easy to capture perfectly on paper. Your dialogue should always sound natural. One of the best ways to see if it does is to read it aloud to yourself. Does it sound natural? Could an actor say it on a TV show and sound normal? If not, go back and revise. Try saying the words aloud first and write them down second. Become a one-writer show. You'll need some privacy—or a lack of concern for what others think of you—but you might like the results. However, this rule applies more to human characters who live in our world.

OTHERWORLDLY AND INHUMAN DIALOGUE

Readers are willing to accept that characters who aren't human, or who didn't grow up speaking human languages, won't speak the way the humans do. (This is why Hogsqueal's speech patterns are funny—they're the opposite of what readers expect.) Dobby the house elf's speech patterns are outlandish and don't really pass the read-aloud test, but Rowling pulls it off because Dobby isn't human. The same goes for Thimbletack's rhyming couplets. These characters, however, can't occupy center stage for long because their strange dialogue tends to overwhelm everything else that's happening in the scene. There are ways to show odd dialogue without overwhelming the character.

One convention to show otherworldliness is simply to avoid contractions and add a touch of formality to the dialogue. This makes it sound like the speaker's first language is something other than English and the speaker is therefore speaking carefully. Look at the difference between these two sets of dialogue:

> Dennis stared up at the centaur in awe. "But how did you get into a public park?"

Writing the Paranormal Novel

> "I'm not certain," the centaur replied. "One moment I'm grazing, the next I'm here. Didn't you see anything?"
>
> "Er, no." Dennis glanced around uneasily. "Look, I'm supposed to meet my girlfriend in five minutes. Is there someone I should call? I have my cell."
>
> The centaur stamped a hoof. "What's a cell? You're trying to capture me? But I've done nothing to you!"

Here, the otherworldly centaur speaks like a modern American, despite his professed ignorance of American culture. But we can shift it a bit:

> Dennis stared up at the centaur in awe. "But how did you get into a public park?"
>
> "I am not certain," the centaur replied. "One moment I was grazing, the next I was here. Did you not see anything?"
>
> "Er, no." Dennis glanced around uneasily. "Look, I'm supposed to meet my girlfriend in five minutes. Is there someone I should call? I have my cell."
>
> The centaur stamped a hoof. "What is a cell? You are trying to capture me? But I have done nothing to you!"

This is serviceable enough—the lack of contractions makes his dialogue sound more formal, more careful, as if English weren't his first language. However, it still comes across as a bit stilted, so we can modify the centaur's dialogue a bit more:

> Dennis stared up at the centaur in awe. "But how did you get into a public park?"
>
> "I am uncertain," the centaur replied. "One moment I was grazing, the next I was here. You saw nothing?"
>
> "Er, no." Dennis glanced around uneasily. "Look, I'm supposed to meet my girlfriend in five minutes. Is there someone I should call? I have my cell."
>
> The centaur stamped a hoof. "A cell? You wish to capture me? But I have done nothing to you!"

The touch of formality in the third version adds yet more otherworldliness to the centaur's speech patterns. All we need is a touch, though. We don't want to go too far:

> Dennis stared up at the centaur in awe. "But how did you get into a public park?"
>
> "I am in doubt," the centaur replied. "At one moment I was grazing the tender shoots, the next I stood here on this fair plain. Did you not see the event?"
>
> "Er, no." Dennis glanced around uneasily. "Look, I'm supposed to meet my girlfriend in five minutes. Is there someone I should call? I have my cell."
>
> The centaur stamped a hoof. "A cell? You are attempting to seize my person? And yet I have done nothing to you!"

Too far. The near-Shakespearean language overwhelms the dialogue like too much garlic in a soup. A taste is plenty.

Naomi Novik uses this technique with her dragons. Most of her dragons speak with a formal lilt, but Temeraire, a Chinese dragon, speaks even more formally, which accents the fact that he's an alien among dragons as we see here in *Victory of Eagles*:

> "Well, old fellow, I am afraid we will have to swap."
>
> "Swap?" Temeraire said, puzzled, until he divined that Requiescat meant caves. "I do not want your cave," adding hastily, "not that it is not very nice, I am sure; but I have just got this one arranged to suit me."
>
> "This one is much bigger now," Requiescat explained, or by his tone thought he was explaining, "and it is much nicer in the wet; mine," he added regretfully, "has been full of puddles, all this week; wet clear through to the back."
>
> "Then I can hardly see why I would change," Temeraire said, still more baffled, and then he sat up, outraged ... "Why, you are a damned scrub," he said. "How dare you come here, and behave

like a visitor, and all the time it is a challenge? I never saw anything so sly in my life . . . you may get out at once."

Novik is one of the few authors around who uses semicolons in dialogue, incidentally, and this small touch serves to accent the fact that we're in a different time and place. In this passage, Requiescat's dialogue has a bit of formality to it, but it's not completely so—the phrase *old fellow* is slangy, or it was for the time. Temeraire, however, uses much more elevated dialogue, complete with extra-complicated sentence structure, as we can see when he says, "you may get out at once" (instead of a simple "get out") and "How dare you . . . behave like a visitor, and all the time it is a challenge?" (instead of "How dare you pretend to be a visitor when all the time you wanted to challenge me?"). Temeraire's careful speech doesn't fall into the ridiculous—Novik is too careful for that—but it does show us that he is neither human nor native to England.

You can also add elements from another language that you're familiar with. Play with grammar and word order to give sentences an exotic feel. Perhaps your dwarves have a Germanic bent and their sentences reflect Germanic influence. "Come you in. It will soon give rain" is German translated straight into English, for example, and could sound very much like a dwarf with a Germanic background.

EXERCISE

Pick a nonhuman character such as a dragon, unicorn, winged horse, elf from the fairy realm, or whatever you like, and pair it with a modern-day human. Write a dialogue in which the nonhuman speaks with the same speech patterns as the human. Then rewrite the dialogue so the nonhuman speaks markedly differently from the human in a way that also shows the character isn't human.

THEY SAID BEAUTIFULLY

There are a number of ways to indicate who said what, and since fiction writers spend a lot of time with dialogue, few mechanical aspects of writing generate more heated discussions. Let's take a little look at what's going on.

The little bits like "he howled" and "she murmured" that writers sneak into dialogue are called *speech tags*. The most common one of these is "said," as in *"Close the door before the werewolf gets through," Norman said.* There are a bunch of others: *growled, murmured, yelled, whispered, roared,* and so on.

For some reason, the speech tag *said* is much maligned. I once attended a writing seminar in which the instructor told the attendees that good writers never, ever use *said*. "It's boring, it's pedestrian, and it shows lack of imagination," he said.

Oops. Did I just use *said?*

And did you notice? Probably not. There's really nothing wrong with using *said* as a speech tag. It's quiet, it's innocuous, and it doesn't call attention to itself. There are really only two rules about using *said* in dialogue.

First, you don't want to *over*use it. If you use *said* for every single speech tag, you'll call attention to it by accident. Use it twice, maybe three times if you're stuck, and then avoid it for a bit before going back to it.

Second, you want to avoid *modifying* it, especially with an *-ly* adverb. Tags like *he said softly* are weak, and you're better off replacing it with something more specific such as *he murmured* or *he whispered*. Besides, *-ly* speech tags are prone to *Tom Swifties*. Tom Swift was a science fiction hero of the pulp era, and the books were written quickly, with little editing. It became a joke among readers to spot such lines as *"Cut the rope!" Tom said sharply*, which were unintentionally funny and became known as Tom Swifties. So avoid *said -ly* speech tags, but feel free to use *said* by itself in moderation (he said authoritatively).

Another way to indicate who's speaking is to use blocking within the same paragraph. Rules of grammar require a new paragraph every time you get a new speaker, so the identity of the speaker is easy to discern: *Tanya slammed the door and leaned against it.* "I think we're fine." We know Tanya is the speaker, since the dialogue comes in the same paragraph as her action. However, you have to be careful that only one person acts in the paragraph. Otherwise you can get confusion. *Norman pressed an ear to the wood. Tanya joined him.* "What do you hear?" In this case, either Norman or Tanya could be speaking, and you want to avoid such problems.

A third way is to let the dialogue run its course without any speech tags once you've established the back-and-forth pattern of the speakers. If the reader will know who the speaker is, there's no need for the author to interrupt for a reminder:

> "I can't hear a thing," Norman whispered.
>
> Tanya bit her lip. "Is that a good sign?"
>
> "Probably. We burned the stupid book and scattered its ashes over—"
>
> "Shh! What was that?"
>
> "I don't know," Norman said. "The stupid door's too thick."
>
> "What are we listening to?" whispered the werewolf.

Just make sure there are enough cues that we don't lose track of who's speaking. Drop in a speech tag every now and then to remind us, as the above example does.

USING CURRENT SLANG: OKAY OR GAG ME WITH A SPOON?

Paranormal novels that use a modern setting with modern characters naturally lean toward modern language. YA authors especially want to use up-to-the-moment words and phrases so they can identify characters with their audiences. The big question is: How far should you go?

When it comes to recent slang, you *have* to know what you're doing. If you aren't a member of the group who uses the slang, you need to *sound* like you are. Teenage readers especially will spot fake slang users faster than Holden Caulfield can finger a phony, and you'll instantly lose all credibility with your audience if you make a mistake. So if you don't have an absolutely sure hand with current slang, avoid it.

Another problem with current slang is that it dates your novel. You might be good with the idea that your book is firmly set in a particular year or decade, especially if you're writing an historical novel, or your story surrounds a famous event, such as a particular presidential election or the start of the Gulf War.

However, if your book is set in a timeless present (as most modern-day books try to be), you want to avoid anything that could date your book, including current slang.

Some slang has become eternal, and you can definitely use it without worry. Words like *yeah, okay,* and *cool* have been part of the American scene for so long, many people have forgotten they're slang.

REALLY FOREIGN LANGUAGES

Ranadar the elf drops into our world from his own. He's never visited this world before, and his culture has never crossed our own. How does he communicate?

This is kind of tricky. Realistically, Ranadar shouldn't be able to speak or understand English. Even gestures are culturally based. In America, we ask if someone wants to eat by miming a plate with one hand and scooping a handful of invisible food toward our mouths with the other. But in China, people mime a bowl with one hand and over it they waggle two fingers from the other hand—chopsticks. Would Ranadar, who grew up on another world entirely, understand either one? There's also the mirror image of this—the character from our world who goes to another world. The language should be nothing like English, or whatever the character speaks.

This causes major story problems. Your character will have to spend enormous amounts of time just learning to communicate in order to get the story going. Unless your book is about exactly this problem, you probably don't want to deal with it. Fortunately, you have a number of solutions available to you. One is simple, long-standing tradition. Authors since Homer have ignored differences in language and just got on with the story. (It doesn't seem likely that citizens of Troy, situated on the western coast of what's now Turkey, spoke the exact same language as the Spartans in the middle of mainland Greece, but that doesn't stop Paris from falling in love with Helen, and Homer didn't bother to stick in a translator.)

You can also slip in a magical solution. A spell or magical object might allow for instant translation or understanding. Or the transition from one world to the next might create an automatic understanding of the new language. You *are* allowed to do a little hand-waving here—most readers want the story and characters to move along.

Some authors like to create bits of language—or even the entire thing. The gold standard for this, of course, is J.R.R. Tolkien, who created over a dozen languages for his books. Richard Adams created a language for rabbits for *Watership Down* (which has definite supernatural elements) so successfully that when Bigwig faces down General Woundwort and snarls, *"Silflay hraka, u embleer rah"* at the climax, the reader has no trouble understanding him.

If you don't want to go quite that far for your werewolves or pixies, you can create pieces of a language—words or phrases that the character can use now and then to remind the reader that the speaker thinks in a language other than English. Again, you'll want to look to other languages for inspiration. If you just throw together some vowels and consonants and substitute them for English word-for-word, it'll come across as stilted and silly. Different languages have different word order and rules for grammar, which should show up in a language you create.

On the other hand, you don't want to create eye-twisting, impossible words for your readers, either. Some African languages use a sort of clicking sound that English speakers can't re-create, not even to write—the official western character for it is an exclamation mark. Creating a language with words like *tqigl!maf* might be fun for the author, but it turns readers away. Balance creativity with the reader's ability to keep up.

CHAPTER 12:
Paranormal Polish

Y ou've crafted the characterization, developed the dialogue, and worried about the world building. You've spent hours, days, weeks, and months at the keyboard, and now you have a first draft. Hooray!

Now the revisions begin.

The revision process ranges from painful slog to fascinating revisit, depending on the writer—and the novel. Revision is an enormous topic, one that could fill an entire book of its own. But paranormal novels have specific challenges, and we'll examine a few here.

GENERAL TIPS

Some ideas apply to novels of all stripes when you're going back over your stuff. This list isn't comprehensive, but it touches on some ideas that may not have occurred to you.

LET IT SIMMER
You may feel a terrible temptation to start revisions the moment you've finished the first draft. Don't give in. The material is too fresh, too green. You need to forget what you've written—at least partially—to give yourself a new perspective for revisions. Set the work aside for a few weeks. Don't look at any part of your book, not even your favorite bits. The mistakes will stand out better once time has allowed you step back and look at the material from a distance.

REREAD OLD NOTES

Very few people can keep everything in their heads, and most authors scribble notes to themselves about their characters, worlds, and plotlines. But as the book progresses and you get to know everyone and everything more intimately, you probably stopped checking your notes. Here's the thing: A hundred thousand words later, you've probably modified a few things on the fly or dropped some old ideas. Check your original concepts and see if there's anything you intended to do that fell by the wayside—or that could be worked into a sequel.

KEEP IT

Smart authors keep everything. You never know when an old version of a story will turn out to be useful—or might unexpectedly become your only surviving backup. When you start revising, take a moment to save your first draft in another computer folder. If you remove a scene or cut a character or slice out a subplot, keep that material in a separate file, too. Paranormal novels often spawn sequels, and cut material is great fodder for future story ideas.

WHEN IN DOUBT, CUT

I've already mentioned why shorter is better, yet new writers tend to write long. It's not a bad idea to cut, especially during the final polish. If a scene doesn't need to be there, cut it. Where you used ten words, use nine. The technical word for this is *tightening,* and it makes your book a much better read.

HOW MANY DRAFTS?

There's no magic number for drafts. Hell, in the age of computers, it's hard to know what a draft *is.* You finished chapter six, then changed a few sentences in it before going on to chapter seven. Is that a new draft?

The answer: Who cares? The only draft that matters is the final one, the one that you show to an editor or agent.

However, at some point, you do have to say, "I'm done." You can't spend your time with endless rewriting and polishing. If you've gone over it six or seven times, ask yourself if you're really rewriting, or putting off sending it out for fear of being rejected.

PARANORMAL TIPS

Some rewriting challenges are specific to paranormal books. Let's take some time to examine a few.

CHECK THE MAGIC, CHECK THE WORLD

During the writing, it's quite likely your concept of magic and the structure of the world you built shifted from your original concept. This is good—ideas need to grow and change organically. However, changes mean the magic you're using in chapter twenty may be rather different than the magic you started with in chapter one, and I've harped on keeping your magic and your world consistent so your readers will come along with you. During the revisions, make sure your magic and your world remain consistent from beginning to end.

MORE CONSISTENCY

Double-check your characters. As we mentioned in chapter six, supernatural characters often have odd names, so make sure you keep them the same. While you're writing those early drafts, it's very easy to accidentally change the spelling of an odd name, or change it on purpose and then fail to catch all the incidences.

The same goes for changing background and characterization. Characters change and grow in a book—and in the writer's mind. When you're rereading your own work, keep a special eye out for people who act out of character.

THE GREAT EXPOSITION

Letting your novel sit for a while first will allow you to come to the rewrites pretending to be a new reader, someone who doesn't know anything about this supernatural world or these supernatural characters.

This is good for checking your exposition. Have you overexplained? Under-explained? Did you delete a scene that also had some necessary exposition in it?

As an example, I realized I had started my novel *The Doomsday Vault* too early, so I scrapped the first several scenes I'd written and jumped ahead to a more action-based scene for the opening hook. The new beginning was much tighter, with a faster pace. Perfect! However, when I was going over the rewrites, I discovered that along with those early scenes, I'd inadvertently cut the introduction of an important character. As a result, this character just showed up in a later chapter, with no rhyme or reason. Oops. I had to sneak him into an earlier scene during the rewrites.

AND DON'T FORGET

These apply to anyone and everyone, but it's amazing how few people bother with them, so I'm giving them their own section.

SPELLING

When you're done, run a spell-check. No matter how good a speller or typist you are, you *will* make some errors. A spell-checker won't catch all your mistakes, but every one it *does* catch is one fewer mistake an editor will see.

GRAMMAR

If you know you're prone to mix up *its* and *it's* or *their, there,* and *they're,* beg someone who knows better to go through your manuscript for grammatical mistakes. Because every editor and agent in the world has his or her grammatical pet peeves (such as starting a sentence with the word *because*), and you don't want to look like an idiot in front of someone you're hoping to impress.

CHAPTER 13:
The Real Challenges

Now we come to some of the hard stuff—and some of the most valuable. It's the stuff that separates the good from the great, the decent from the powerful, the fine from the freaky. We're talking about theme, symbolism, and voice. This is where your true power as a writer lies, so let's dig in.

THEME

There are different ways to define *theme*. One way to look at it is as what your book is about, and I don't mean the plot or the story. The story is what happens, one event building on another. The theme is the idea your book explores. It can be a big concept like *love* or *death* or *war* or *choices*, or it might be more specific, like *defying authority* or *loss of love* or *restriction of choice*.

Once a big idea appears, it usually needs to be narrowed even more. This is what the book is *saying* about the big idea. It can—should—be extremely specific, like *No one finds his dreams* or *Death finds everyone* or *Everything has its opposite*. J.K. Rowling and Christopher Moore both write about the desire to avoid death, for example, but their actual themes are much more specific. Rowling wrote about the search for immortality. Lord Voldemort wants it in a literal sense. Harry and Dumbledore gain it in the metaphorical sense. Harry's parents give their lives to deny it to

Voldemort and ensure it to Harry. On the other hand, Moore writes about the futility of fighting or avoiding death, and how by giving in to it, you conquer it. Charlie loses his wife to death and tries to fight death. He ends up fighting death gods quite literally. He tries to avoid becoming death, and only wins in the end when he gives in not only to his role as death, but embraces death itself.

Narrowing the idea, having something to *say* about it, is what separates the ordinary from the extraordinary. It's easy to claim your book is about life and nature. Heck, just about every book in existence talks about one or the other. Exactly what is your book *saying* about those two concepts?

These ideas are abstracts, something that readers can't see or hear. They touch emotions and spirits and resonate there. A powerful theme stays with the reader after the book ends, and makes the reader want to return to it. A masterful book has themes woven into many layers so readers can read the same book more than once and discover something new about the themes—or maybe find an entirely new theme the second time around.

THE NECESSITY OF THEME

Actually, you can get away without putting a theme in your book. But your book will be the poorer for it. It's like making a cake entirely out of frosting—it might look good, but there won't be much substance there. Theme shows deeper thought, richer layers of reading. Even if readers aren't fully aware of all the themes, they'll be still touched by them on other levels.

A theme holds a story together on a more abstract level. When most—or all—of the plots and subplots and images work toward a single theme, the book comes together more powerfully than does a book without a theme. Theme unites the book.

It's actually not difficult to include theme. In fact, it's almost impossible *not* to include at least one theme in your writing. You can't avoid the "big idea" ones—any book with human beings in it will at minimum discuss the themes of life and humanity struggling to survive physically or emotionally.

Sometimes the difficult part is actually noticing the themes in your own work. Even experienced authors can miss them. I once interviewed award-winning science fiction and fantasy writer Octavia E. Butler for a magazine, and I asked her about a recurring theme in her work—the idea of people being forced to make tough, rock-or-hard-place choices. The idea appears in nearly all of her work, both short and long. She blinked at me in surprise for a few moments, then answered, "Well, we don't always have choices. . . . And all too often even when we do have choices, they're not necessarily the ones we want." In other words, the idea was part of Butler's worldview, and she had never noticed she had incorporated it as a theme into the body of her own work. (I feel I should point out that Butler, a master of the craft, also inserts a number of themes into her work on purpose, which makes the appearance of an accidental theme all the more interesting.)

This has happened to me, too. One of my books was reviewed in the *Library Journal*, and the reviewer pointed out that the theme of the book was loss and reconciliation, since several characters in the novel came from broken families and were trying to reconnect. I stared at the review and realized she was right, even though that hadn't been on my mind at all when I was writing. I'd been thinking about escaping physical and emotional slavery, and of the relationship between the real world and the world that makes up dreams. However, I'd written the book just after a tremendous upheaval within my own family, and the loss and reconciliation idea had clearly crept into the story as well.

I wish I had noticed this theme myself—I would have changed parts of the story to reflect it more powerfully. It's overall much better if a theme is developed on purpose. That way, the disparate elements in the story will point toward the theme in a more unified, careful way instead of by accident. It's also one of the better ways to help your book get published—as a new writer, you need a theme to help your book break in. Your book needs to be *better* than normal to get an editor or agent's attention, and a powerful theme that stays in the editor or agent's head is the perfect way to show your book's worthiness. If the editor can't get your book out of her head (for good reasons), you've probably got a sale.

Usually it's a matter of whether you want theme to be under your control or not. And you *do* want it under your control. An accidental theme is a kid learning to ice skate. His main goal is to make it across the arena without falling over, and he doesn't notice the patterns he draws in the ice as he skates. Once or twice, he skitters sideways and wrecks part of the pattern, but his parents still applaud when he arrives. Such a good boy!

A controlled theme is an Olympic skater, leaping and spinning with precision, and leaving exact swirls and cuts on the surface of the ice. He goes exactly where he wants to and concentrates on both the individual moves and the overall pattern. When he's finished, a stadium filled with people thunders in appreciation and the judges award him a medal. Both skaters have accomplished something worthwhile, but the second touches more people and has a better chance of being remembered. Even if you feel like a kid learning to skate, aim for the Olympics.

THEMES AND THE PARANORMAL

Paranormal books have the power to explore themes that "normal" books can't. Normal books (i.e., books that have no impossible elements to them) are locked out of a number of themes. Werewolf novels often look at themes of controlling that inner beast, or about forces of nature and their inescapable impact on our existence. The better novels about vampires explore a number of themes—the downward spiral of the dead feeding off the living, the living world's dual fascination with and fear of the dead, the war between light and darkness, faith and skepticism, domination and submission. Octavia E. Butler's final novel *Fledgling* delves into the relationship between vampire and prey. Is it domination and submission, or symbiosis and interdependency?

This theme isn't something easily explored outside the paranormal genre. Philip Pullman explores several themes relating to humanity's fall from grace and the desire to redeem itself, as well as the more down-to-earth theme of using knowledge to gain freedom. Although the latter theme can appear in any book, the former is particularly well-suited to a supernatural setting.

Paranormal novels can also explore normal themes using supernatural means. This harkens back to the ordinary subject matter with a supernatural twist added to it. The children of Edward Eager's *Half Magic* feel their family has been split in half after the death of their father, which has also left them with only half a mother. The book explores their attempts to create a whole family again, with and without a half-magic charm. This theme allows the book to transcend its 1920s setting and resonate with children and adults decades after the book was written. Terry Pratchett puts a con man in charge of the Ankh-Morpork mint in *Making Money* to take a hard look at how frighteningly ridiculous—and delicate—our own entire banking system is, how much of it is based on con games and illusion. In the end, he uses an army of solid gold golems to show how money can *really* work for you, something you couldn't really do in a novel set on real-life Wall Street.

You have the power to use any number of resonant themes in your own book, whether they're supernatural or not. To make your good book great, you need to keep theme uppermost in your mind.

NOW OR LATER?

So this brings up a big question: Do you start with a theme or add one later? And the answer is: whichever one makes you happy as a writer.

Really. It may sound counterintuitive after that long harangue about having theme under your control from the start that I'm now telling you that theme can show up early or late in the process, but this is indeed the case. It's because everyone's writing process is different. Some writers can start with a theme in mind while others need to wait for one to show up.

As long as it's there and under control by the time the book is finished, it doesn't matter how or when it arrived.

I've actually done it from both ends, myself. The story "Thin Man," which I've mentioned before, has a theme that showed up late. The story was nearly finished when I realized I had a recurring theme, the idea of people being tricked into believing they had no choices when actually they had several. I also saw that I had the ideal vehicle for this theme—the chimneys that Dodd is forced to climb into and clean every day. The chimneys give Dodd only one way in and one way out, with hard, unyielding bricks on every side to enforce the singleness of the direction. Once I realized this, I was able to go back and ensure that the events of the story and the settings and even the dialogue tilt toward this theme. I'm convinced the presence of this theme is the reason Marion Zimmer Bradley bought the story for her magazine, even though she specifically stated in her guidelines that she didn't want dark fantasy or stories with child protagonists. She broke her rules on the strength of the story's theme, a theme that showed up late in the writing process.

On the other hand, when I wrote the first word of my novelette "The Soul Jar," a sequel to "Thin Man," I already had the themes firmly in mind—every person and event has multiple parallels, and every choice destroys a thousand pasts even as it creates a thousand futures. When I started the story, I had only the idea of a set of identical twins who perform in a clown act by mimicking each other on either side of an empty mirror frame. I also knew that one of the clowns was going to die, unbalancing the mirror gag and destroying everything the surviving brother knew. But as I wrote the story with the themes in mind, it changed. I saw that I was also exploring the idea of the foil, a character's opposite, and I wove that into the story as well. I saw that I needed to kill another character, one who had survived in my original concept, which changed other parts of the story. A caged mechanical feline that I'd thrown in for background color became a central focus of two key scenes—and turned into a parallel for Schrödinger's cat. The themes became more

Writing the Paranormal Novel

and more intricate as I wrote, and made the story far more powerful than I'd even planned it.

Overall, starting with a theme in mind is better for the simple reason that it's easier to incorporate one into the book as you go rather than go back and rework material to reflect a theme you discover later. (I say this as someone who's done it both ways.) But however you work it is up to you, as long as the theme is ultimately under your control.

Besides, as I've already pointed out, some themes will escape your notice. In chapter four I mentioned the saying *Write what you know.* There's a corollary: *You may as well write what you know—you will anyway.* In other words, some aspects of your worldview and real-life experiences will inevitably sneak into your fiction. You won't be able to keep them out. After a while, your readers may notice a pattern to your work as I noticed with Octavia E. Butler's. Since themes will appear whether you want them to or not, do your best to find as many as you can and tame them into serving the book instead of letting them run wild across your pages. Becoming aware of your themes will also prevent you from writing the same story over and over again.

FINDING YOUR THEME

You do have a theme in your book somewhere. We just need to find it. The first step is actually an exercise.

EXERCISE

Read the following question, then set this book aside and write down your answer separately:

> What is your book about?

Now check. Which of the following two statements does your answer most resemble?

1. It's about an ordinary young man who trades his last posses-
   sion for a magical plant that transports him to another world,
   where he finds wealth—and danger.
2. It's about how poverty creates a world in which theft and even
   murder can become sympathetic acts.

If your answer is more like number 1, you're thinking more about
the plot. If your answer is more like number 2, you're thinking more
about the theme.

If you answered like number 2, you have at least one theme. If
you didn't, let's look at a few ways to draw your theme out.

First, go back and try to answer the question so it's more like
number 2 above. Don't talk about the plot—talk about *ideas*. Love,
hate, religion, nature, power, sex, money, cruelty, yearning—what
is your book *about?*

Should you get stuck, make a list of words that describe your
book. Use free association and let your mind wander within your
story. Generate a list of twenty or thirty words. Using that list as a
starting point, see what sort of theme you can generate.

Themes can also ask questions. Perhaps your book asks questions about the nature of life or human nature or God. Why do bad
things happen to good people? Why do smart people make stupid
choices? Is there a plan behind the universe? You don't necessarily
have to posit an answer, either—the fact that the question has no
answer can itself be a theme.

YOUR COMFORT LEVEL

Themes vary wildly along the comfort continuum. Some themes are safe,
some are risky, some are frightening, and some are taboo. You'll need to
decide where your book will land on that continuum.

Safe themes abound in fiction. *Good triumphs over evil. The son becomes the father. True love wins in the end.* Safe themes produce safe books.

Writing the Paranormal Novel

They make readers feel good, and no one challenges them in school libraries. There's nothing inherently wrong with this, and you can make a decent living writing safe books. The danger is that safe themes have been so widely explored, you run the risk of boring yourself. Safe themes don't go anywhere new—if they did, they wouldn't be safe. It's difficult to challenge yourself as a writer with nothing but safe themes, since you have thousands of years of examples behind you.

Risky or challenging themes also abound: *No one gets their dreams. Challenge authority. Religion promotes ignorance.* Risky themes are harder to write about. They have the potential to make readers uncomfortable or angry—or maybe just challenge them to think. People remember them after they've put the book down. Risky themes also tend to stretch you, since they're harder to address, perhaps even uncomfortably so. If a theme drags you out of your own comfort zone a little and makes you think a little differently, you've created a risky theme—and you'll grow as a writer. For a real challenge, try writing about a theme that runs counter to what you believe.

Taboo themes lie at the far end of the continuum. *Abuse portrayed in positive terms. God is secretly evil. Racism is a good thing.* And others even more explosive. These themes are difficult to handle—readers who enjoy being pushed or challenged may only go so far. They'll be distracted by how upset they are about your theme and not be thinking about how good the writing is. Editors know this and are often reluctant to buy explosive books from first-timers—or even established authors. Books with taboo themes that do get published can get quite a lot of attention, both positive and negative.

In the end, your themes will outlive you. They're what touch people, move them, pull them into new places, and make them remember your story forever.

WORKING WITH YOUR THEME

Once you and your theme have been introduced to each other, it becomes a matter of working your theme into the story obviously enough so readers can pick up on it but not so heavily you seem to be working with a sledgehammer. There are a thousand ways to pull this off, some obvious and some more covert. Here, the best way to learn is by example. Read, read, read, and read some more. As I mentioned above, Octavia E. Butler's novel *Fledgling* deals with the relationship between vampire and prey. It also examines building communities out of nothing. Shori awakens at the beginning of the novel naked and suffering from amnesia. In other words, she has nothing at all, not even her own memory. She meets Wright Hamlin and from that base begins to build a community. Read the novel with that theme in mind to see how Butler does it.

Ray Bradbury's classic and scary paranormal book *Something Wicked This Way Comes* deftly and darkly explores the conflicting fears and desires related to growing up—and growing old. It also looks at the power that belief and fear hold over the human mind and body and how to conquer both. There's also a parallel to *Peter Pan* by J.M. Barrie (sometimes known as *Peter and Wendy*), another paranormal novel worth reading in the original.

Outside of the paranormal genre, I suggest looking at John Steinbeck. *Of Mice and Men* is a short read packed with theme and symbolism, and if you haven't looked at it since high school, now would be a good time to take a look at it again. Steinbeck weaves several themes into the novel: people trying to find their dreams, the consequences of giving up a dream, the idea that everyone is lonely, and that to be a real man, you need a full name and two hands (or perhaps that real men have two hands and a full name). He does all this and more in a compelling story that takes up less than 120 pages.

VOICE

Almost every set of submission guidelines from agents and editors says they're looking for authors with a *strong voice*, a *unique voice*, or a *powerful voice*. Guidelines for everything from thrillers to cookbooks mention the importance of voice. My own agent's Web page mentions *original new voices*. But none of them says exactly what that means.

Voice is a little hard to pin down. It basically means *how you write*. It involves the words you choose and the rhythms you write in. It's how your writing sounds on the page. I know, I know—these descriptions actually sound a bit like writing *style*. Style is related to voice. Voice goes deeper. Voice is also the persona you put on when you start writing.

When you put words on paper (yeah, yeah—or on computer screen; work with me here), you aren't really being *you*. You aren't showing the world your true face or personality, though glimmers of your true self will show through. Like an actor strolling onto the stage, you're adopting a different persona, one that combines elements of yourself with a bunch of stuff you've made up. This persona, this *voice*, is the one who tells the story.

FIRST PERSON

An author who writes in first person very naturally slips into a particular voice, since the main character speaks directly to the reader, and the main character will speak differently than the author. Let's compare three different first-person vampire novels. In *The Vampire Lestat*, Anne Rice writes:

> I turned my back on it and let out a terrible roar. I felt its hands close on my shoulders like things forged of metal, and as I went into a last frenzy of struggling, it whipped me around so that its eyes were right before me, wide and dark, and the lips were closed yet still smiling, and then it bent down and I felt the prick of its teeth on my neck.
>
> Out of all the childhood tales, the old fables, the name came to me, like a drowned thing shooting to the surface of black water and breaking free in the light.
>
> "Vampire!" I gave one last frantic cry, shoving at the creature with all I had.
>
> Then there was silence. Stillness.

Octavia E. Butler's vampire in *Fledgling* speaks very differently:

> I stared down at the bleeding marks I'd made on his hand, and suddenly I was unable to think about anything else. I ducked my head and licked away the blood, licked the wound I had made. He tensed, almost pulling his hand away. Then he stopped and seemed to relax. He let me take his hand between my own. I looked at him, saw him glancing at me, felt the car zigzag a little on the road.
>
> He frowned and pulled away from me, all the while looking uncertain, unhappy. I caught his hand again between mine and held it. I felt him try to pull away. He shook me, actually lifting me into the air a little, trying to get away from me, but I didn't let go. I licked at the blood welling up where my teeth had cut him.

And the voice of Lucienne Diver's young vampire in *Vamped* plunges into a completely new direction:

> "You're right," I said, thinking feverishly. "I do need a bite to eat. And I know just the thing.
>
> Based on how quickly [Bobby] stepped back, I'm pretty sure he thought I meant him, but that wasn't it. Mom and Dad had been big with the child-rearing clichés. *When life gives you lemons, you make lemonade* had been a favorite of theirs, and I guess it must have sunk in a little. All I needed was a place to shower and change, a stylist, a mani-pedi, and some skin cream and I'd be as good as new. I could even start my own entourage for touch-ups. Better than any mirror. I tried to believe it.

Three vampires, three voices. Rice, writing as Lestat, uses an abundance of figurative language. Similes and metaphors dominate her work, competing with an abundance of adjectives. Her word choice leans toward florid. Butler, writing as Shori, uses a more spare, straightforward voice with little in the way of description and more focus on action. Shori speaks with more verbs than adjectives. Her words are plainer, leaner. Diver, writing as Gina, tends to speak in short, punchy bursts. Her clauses are short, and she avoids prepositional phrases that might lengthen her sentences, giving Gina a breathless voice appropriate to a teenaged fashionista.

Did Diver think in those terms? I'm imagining her sitting at her keyboard, brow furrowed, finger hovered over the Delete key. "Oops," she mutters. "Used too many prepositional phrases in this section. Need to cut out a few."

I doubt it. More likely, Diver (and Rice and Butler) did her best to think like her main character, learn how to speak like her main character, and put her main character's words on paper. The words came out that way because Diver (and the others) knew her character so well, she could speak in the character's voice.

A unique voice evolves from creating a unique viewpoint character and then getting to know the viewpoint character from the inside out. You know how some married couples can finish each other's sentences? That's the kind of relationship you need with your main character. That deep understanding will allow you to develop the voice.

And no, you don't need to have that understanding before you start writing. Your first draft is all about getting to know your main character (or characters). As you progress through the draft, your knowledge of the character will deepen and the voice will strengthen. Then, when you go back for revisions, you'll be able to catch inconsistencies and change what the character or narrator says so the voice becomes consistent.

THIRD PERSON

There's certainly a voice for third person novels, too. It's sometimes called the *author voice* or *narrator voice*. It's not that different from a first-person voice—the person is a narrator who's telling the story, and this narrator has a voice. The narrator may or may not be the author of the book. Usually it isn't. The narrator voice is often similar to the viewpoint character.

Naomi Novik demonstrates a mastery of third-person voice in her Temeraire books. She uses two distinct narrator voices, one for the dragon Temeraire and one for Will Laurence. It's easy to tell them apart at a glance. This passage from *Victory of Eagles* comes from Temeraire's point of view. The young dragon has been imprisoned for treason:

> [Temeraire] was quite sure he and Laurence had done as they ought, in taking the cure to France, and no-one sensible could disagree; but just in case, Temeraire had steeled himself to meet with either disapproval or contempt, and he had worked out several very fine arguments in his defense. Most important, of course, it was just a cowardly, sneaking way of fighting; if the Government wished to beat Napoleon, they ought to fight directly, and not make his dragons sick to try to make him easy to defeat; as if British dragons could not beat French dragons, without cheating.

Compare that to this passage a few pages later from the point of view of Will Laurence, imprisoned for the same crime:

> There had been no defense to make, and no comfort but the arid certainty that he had done as he ought; that he could have done nothing else. That was no comfort at all, but that it saved him from the pain of regret; he could not regret what he had done. He could not have let ten thousand dragons, most of them wholly uninvolved in the war, be murdered for his nation's advantage.

In these two passages we have the same event told from two different points of view, and two different voices. The narrator who tells Temeraire's story speaks with Temeraire's voice, really. Novik injects a naïve arrogance into Temeraire's point of view. Temeraire also thinks about the cowardly sneakiness of using plague in warfare. Laurence, on the other hand, speaks with an older, more cynical voice. Novik—or Laurence—avoids self-congratulatory language, and his thoughts wander to the fact that he had done the right thing but was still going to pay for it. Temeraire is outraged at their situation where Laurence is resigned to it, and it shows in their individual voices.

You don't *have* to switch voice whenever you switch point of view. However, different voices within the same book is one of those things that can distinguish a good book from a great one, or make it more memorable in the mind of an editor.

I was going to say that switching voices in a book will *always* distinguish a good book from a great one, but really, plenty of authors maintain a single narrator voice throughout their work. Terry Pratchett's voice never wavers in any of his Discworld novels, no matter what character he's writing about, and the style of humor is distinctly his own. Philip Pullman also uses the same voice whether he's writing from Lyra's or Will's point of view in *The Subtle Knife*. The real key is to make your voice distinct, which we'll talk about in a moment.

FIRST AND THIRD PERSON TOGETHER

A few authors inject themselves directly into their books. They make it clear that they're telling a story by addressing the reader directly or using a narrator *I*. This usually shows up in books aimed at younger readers, since it creates the illusion that someone is telling the reader a story instead of the reader actually reading it. Edward Eager uses this type of voice in *Half Magic*:

> Katharine was the middle child, of docile disposition and a comfort to her mother. She knew she was a comfort, and docile, because she'd heard her mother say so. And the others knew she was too, by now, because ever since that day Katharine would keep boasting about it, until Jane declared she would utter a piercing shriek and fall over dead if she heard another word about it. This will give you some idea of what Jane and Katharine were like.

Eager is talking to us. His voice is casual and uses the repetition common to oral storytellers. The last sentence clinches it—we're listening to a story, not reading.

Eager addresses the reader rarely throughout the book: just often enough to remind us he's telling us a story, and not so often that his voice becomes intrusive.

THE INVISIBLE NARRATOR

One of the harder voices to pull off is the *invisible narrator.* Sometimes called *transparent prose,* this is an author voice that tries to fade into the background. It's kind of the opposite of the combination first and third person above—the author tries to disappear as much as possible.

Brendan Mull uses this voice in *Fablehaven,* as we see here:

> Seth set the mug on the dresser. Taking a calming breath, he silently prayed that the tarantula would be gone and the fairy would be there. He slid the drawer open.
>
> A hideous little creature glared up from inside the jar. Baring pointy teeth, it hissed at him. Covered in brown leather skin, it stood taller than his middle finger. It was bald, with tattered ears, a narrow chest, a pot belly, and shriveled, spindly limbs. The lips were froglike, the eyes a glossy black, the nose a pair of slits above the mouth.
>
> "What did you do to the fairy?" Seth asked.

Mull doesn't talk to the reader and doesn't adopt a particular point of view with his voice. He barely gets inside *Seth's* point of view, in fact, with only a single reference to what Seth is thinking or feeling. The advantage to this voice is that the narrator never gets in the way of the story. The disadvantage is that transparent voice can come across as dry. Writers who use it need to make up for the dryness by adding other color. Mull uses plenty of magic and action to keep his story moving so his readers don't notice the transparent voice.

KEEN ON VOICE

As I said above, almost every agent or editor will say they're looking for fiction with a unique or interesting voice. Several say that a good voice will grab their eye above anything else. Why are they so keen on voice?

The reason is that a unique or interesting or quirky voice can really make a book. In chapter five, I pointed out that the hero's quest is nearly ubiquitous in paranormal (and a lot of nonsupernatural) books. A lot of other elements crop up over and over again. Regardless of what twist you put on your vampires, they're still vampires. No matter what new element you introduce into your ghost story, it's still a ghost story. One thing that *can* be unique, regardless of the story type, is the author's voice. A fascinating voice can get the reader to overlook other problems, or even fail to notice things like clichés entirely. Remember back in chapter five when we talked about reasons editors buy clichés even when they claim they don't want any? A cool voice is another reason an editor will overlook clichés and buy a book. The unique voice overcomes the tired clichés.

So you really do want to work on creating and developing a fascinating author voice for your book. It's your main selling point.

HOW TO FIND A VOICE

There's no one way or formula to finding a voice. This process is mostly a matter of experimenting, playing around until you find something that clicks or makes sense to you or just hangs together in a way that sounds great. Here are some things you can do to find that voice. Some are exercises, some are techniques.

LET YOURSELF WRITE BADLY

Ray Bradbury, famous for both his supernatural and his science fiction work, once said that there are a million bad words in every writer—you just have to keep writing until they're all out of your system. So give yourself permission to write badly. Get those words down, even if they're crap. Don't judge what you've written yet. Keep going and see what you're going to say next. A voice will begin to emerge.

WRITE FAST AND SEE WHAT HAPPENS

Bull-rush your way forward. Pound those words out and don't look back. Write quickly, even if it's nonsensical. Don't edit (yet). Write like you're writing journal entries or a letters to a friend under deadline—no time to stop. Maybe some quirky turns of phrase will come flying out of your fingers and develop into the voice you're looking for. Or maybe a character will develop in an unexpected and interesting direction. In any case, save the editing for later and see what you can come up with *now*.

LET YOUR CHARACTERS TALK TO YOU THROUGH THE COMPUTER

Pretend you're the character and start typing in that character's voice, even if your novel is going to be in third person. Don't worry about developing the story yet—just let the character ramble at you while you write down what you hear. (And don't fret if you find yourself talking back, either. A number of my writer friends do it, as do I. In fact, you'd might be surprised at how many professional authors sit in little rooms talking to people who don't exist.) Write letters, journal entries, trial transcripts, sessions with the character's therapist, or what the character says aloud when no one is listening. You might develop a voice by becoming someone else for a while.

EXPERIMENT

Go there. Do that. Be silly. Be stupid. Be florid. Be pretentious. You won't know what it looks like until you write it down. No one will see it except you, so why should you care if your second-grade niece could probably have done better? Every bit might be dreadful, or one of the experiments might turn up something worth keeping—but you'll never know unless you give yourself the freedom to try it.

SAVE EVERYTHING

Never, ever throw anything away. Early notes, character sketches, the material you generate doing any of the above—keep every word. I can't count the number of times I've gone back through old material on a work in progress and realized I'd overlooked something good, whether it was an idea, a turn of phrase, or a bit of characterization. Ultimately, it all contributes to voice, so keep it.

CHANGE THE POINT OF VIEW

If the writing seems dull or stale, try a shift in the viewpoint. If it's first person, change it to third and let you, the author, speak. If it's third person, change it to first and let the character speak. See what impact it has on the story—and on your voice.

You can also try shifting to a different *character's* point of view. Since every character has a different way of seeing the world and a different voice, try writing the same scene through the eyes of two different characters. Make sure the voice is different, and see which one you like better.

WRITE WHAT YOU
REALLY WANT TO WRITE

Write the themes you *really* want to explore. The stuff that gets under your skin, or makes you giddy, or pisses you off. Too many new writers try to gauge the market and only write what they think is commercial so they can break in. This is usually a bad idea—the book produced by this kind of thinking will probably be dull and lackluster. Don't dance around what you really want to say, and don't worry what your family or friends or co-workers will think about your book. Should anyone ask why you wrote such a thing, you can say, "Hey, I wrote a book. What did *you* do last summer?"

If you need to, switch genres. If you don't think that relationships can have happy endings, don't try to write a paranormal romance. If you secretly think everything will come out all right in the end in real life, what are you doing trying to write horror? Figure out what idea revs your motor and then build a story around it. The emotional response from you, the writer, will stimulate voice—and engage the reader.

PART IV:
BANISHING
THE
BOOK

CHAPTER 14:

The Reality

Even the most high-flown paranormal novel has to deal with the real world eventually. We need to get that book out the door and into the hands of someone who will publish it. There are a number of points and pitfalls in the process to examine.

Years ago when I started writing novels, you hit up editors with a proposal package that included a twenty-page synopsis and the first three chapters. If you were lucky, the editor wrote back and said, "Send me the full manuscript," which you did. If you were really lucky, the editor called you to say, "I want to buy your book." You thanked the editor profusely, hung up the phone, and hunted madly for an agent.

Things have changed.

Before we go any further, I'm assuming you've finished your first novel. You've done the first draft, second draft, more rewrites, and a final polish, and your book is ready to go. This is a requirement before you can send anything out because it's pretty much a given that no editor will offer a contract to a first-timer who doesn't have a full manuscript yet, and no agent will offer to represent one, either. There's a simple reason for this—no matter how strong your initial proposal may be, the editor or agent has no way of knowing if you have the staying power to finish the whole thing. A lot of new authors—in fact, the vast majority of them—never complete a book. (This means that actually finishing a novel puts you ahead of 90 percent of everyone else, so once you finish, you're allowed a few moments of self-congratulation.)

Once your book is the best you can make it, you're *not* going to submit it quite yet. First, you need to put together a short treatment.

HOW TO TREAT A TREATMENT

Computers and the Internet have largely destroyed the twenty-page synopsis. Word processing made the physical act of writing much easier, and people who wouldn't have the patience for it before are now producing 100,000 words. And they all want to send them out. Editors and agents are inundated with more submissions than ever. Couple that with massive layoffs in publishing that require everyone in the business to do the work of three people, and your average editor has much less time for reading. Treatments have become much more common as a result.

A treatment consists of three to five double-spaced pages. It sketches out in broad terms what happens in your book. Think of it as an expanded version of the back-cover blurb. You don't have much room, so you need to hit the ground running. It might begin:

> Life is conspiring against Henry Bayfield. His ex-wife has filed for sole custody of their daughter, he was recently bitten by a werewolf, and the guy in front of him at the bank has just pulled a gun. As the customers dive for cover, Henry fingers the gun in his own pocket and wonders why be bothered to get up this morning.

You'll notice the total lack of explanation about who Henry Bayfield is. It's death to start with something like *Henry Bayfield is a new werewolf with a nasty ex-wife.* Instead, a treatment focuses on what the character *does,* as in the above example.

As the treatment progresses, you'll have to condense greatly:

> ... Henry barely escapes the bank, but now the SPCA is hounding him. Some time later, he meets Farrah Finn, an old high school flame who seems ready to reignite. They hide out together in a series of bad motels while dodging the SPCA and the hit men sent by Henry's ex-wife, and their relationship deepens ...

The ending can be done in broad terms as well:

> ... In the end, as the hit men close in, Henry is forced to choose between Farrah, his daughter, and his new feelings of self-worth.

In three to five pages, you don't have much room to explain symbolism, theme, or character development. That's the way it goes. Focus on the main plot points and count on the sample pages to draw the editor in.

SAMPLE PAGES

You'll need to send a certain amount of your manuscript as a sample to showcase how fantastic your book is. Usually this consists of the first three chapters or so, but in case your chapters are extra short or long—or you don't use chapters—we're looking at the first fifty or sixty pages, or about 15,000 words.

Here's a big tip: End your sample chapters in some kind of cliffhanger. You don't have to leave your protagonist dangling over a pit of lava, but try to end with something that makes the reader naturally want to continue. You could leave off in mid-dialogue, or with something interesting just about to happen. The goal is for you to make the reader try to turn the page and be annoyed that there's nothing left to turn. If you get that reaction, you're likely to get a request for the full manuscript.

Format your sample manuscript as follows:

- Double-space it. Don't use 1.5 spacing to save paper or space. Double-spacing makes your manuscript easy to read for people who read all day. 1.5 spacing will put the reader in a cranky mood, and that's the last thing you want.
- Put a 1" margin all around the page. Be careful—some word processing programs have a 1½" margin as a default, so check.
- The only acceptable fonts are Courier (or Courier New) and Times New Roman. That's it. Some people will go so far as to claim that Courier is the One True Font. I've never heard of anyone getting rejected because they used Times New Roman

(I use it myself), but I *have* heard of plenty of people who got rejected because they used Arial, Verdana, or Love Potion Number 9. Don't use them. Editors hate Arial because a *1, j, l*, and *i* all look alike. They hate other fonts because they're flat-out hard to read.

- To indicate *italicized text*, you should <u>underline</u>. Bolded text should be done in **bold**.
- In the upper left corner of the first page, put your real name. Under that, put your address. Under that, put your phone number. Under that, your e-mail address. It doesn't matter whether this particular section is double-spaced or not.
- Space down a couple times. In the center of the line and in all capitals goes THE TITLE OF THE BOOK. Beneath that in normal text goes the word "by" and your name—or your pen name, if you're using one, as in "by Steven Harper."
- Skip another line, then start your sample pages.
- In the upper right corner of every page except the first goes a header with the following information: Last name/<u>Part of Book Title</u>/page number. An example looks like this: Harper/<u>Paranormal Novel</u>/12. The page number goes at the top of the page in case someone drops your manuscript and accidentally mixes up the pages. It's easier to reorder loose pages when the numbers are at the top.
- Do *not* bind, clip, staple, or otherwise fasten your manuscript in any way. Editors and agents don't want to fold pages over a staple.
- Use the same format for your treatment.

Now that everything is formatted and ready to go, you're actually going to hold off on submitting it. Save it on your computer, but don't print it out yet. Why? Because not all agents or editors will want to see the whole thing. Set it aside—we're going to figure out who might want to read it.

FINDING SOMEONE
TO SUBMIT TO

At one time, few agents read unsolicited manuscripts. (*Unsolicited = one they didn't ask for.*) Then came the Great Anthrax Scare. Remember those days? Two people got anthrax packages in the mail post-9/11, and the FBI told us to be suspicious of strange packages. The odds that any of us would actually receive anthrax were worse than winning a multistate lottery, but never mind—we needed to be scared.

One group that regularly receives strange packages by mail is (was) book publishers. Aspiring authors sent them boxes and padded envelopes every single day. Claiming to be fearful of employee safety, nearly all publishers announced their editors would no longer accept unsolicited manuscripts.

A few weeks later, the anthrax scare died down. The FBI said the mail was safe. But mysteriously, editors didn't resume reading unsolicited manuscripts. With amazing deftness, they foisted that little chore onto agents, who became the new gatekeepers to publishing.

Pre-anthrax, you submitted to an editor first, got an offer, and then found an agent. Nowadays things have largely reversed themselves—you submit to agents, find one who'll represent you, and then get an offer from a publisher. This is not a hard-and-fast rule, though. A few publishers still accept unsolicited manuscripts, and you can submit to them, too.

The question is, how do you find an editor or an agent?

AGENTS

One way to find an agent is through the Association of Authors' Representatives. As of this writing, their Web site can be found at http://aaronline.org. A great feature of their site is a search function that lets you hunt agents by what sort of material they represent. You can type in *urban fantasy* or *vampire* or *YA fantasy* and it'll generate a list of agents who handle that genre, along with their contact information. You don't have to be an AAR member to use their site.

All members of the AAR have to conform to certain business practices. They don't charge reading fees, they don't charge commissions in advance, and so on. AAR agents aren't necessarily *good* agents, but they're more likely to be *honest* agents. Many AAR agents have their own Web sites, so you can check to see if they're taking submissions, what format they want, what sort of stuff they do and don't want to see, and so on. Always, always check the agent's Web page if she has one and follow her submission instructions *to the letter.*

Another place to look is among authors. Authors will sometimes mention their agents' names in acknowledgments or on their Web sites. If your genre and/or writing style is similar to a particular author's, search around and see if you can figure out who the author's agent is—you might be a good fit. Don't ask the author for an introduction, though. That's a social no-no unless you and the author are already good friends and/or the author has reason to think his agent might be interested.

PUBLISHERS AND EDITORS

A few publishers still take unsolicited manuscripts. A quick way to figure out who might take your novel is to examine your own bookshelf—most authors write the sort of thing they like to read. Grab three or four books similar to yours. By *similar* I mean "in the same genre and style." Lots of publishers put out vampire books, but is yours a horror novel, a vampire romance, a vampire historical, an urban vampire, vampire humor, or what? You wouldn't want to send a vampire horror novel to Harlequin, for example, even though Harlequin publishes vampire stories; Harlequin wants vampire romance. When you have a handful of books similar to yours, check the inside cover or the spine to see who the publisher is. Warm up your Internet browser and hit their Web site. Somewhere on their site, they might have a *contact us* or *submissions* or *author information* link that will lead you to information on how and where to send a submission. You can also just check publisher Web sites cold and see if they take submissions.

If you strike gold, make sure you get the name of a specific person to send the manuscript to. In cases where no name is listed on the site, you're allowed to call the publisher's office to ask. You won't talk to the editor anyway—you'll talk to a secretary or assistant: "Hi! Your Web site says you accept unsolicited manuscripts, and I wanted to know the name and title of the person I can send one to." You want a name because nameless manuscripts go to the bottom of the mailroom pile, while named manuscripts are more likely to hit a specific person's desk.

The publisher's Web site will also list what genres they accept and whether or not they take (or prefer) electronic submissions, as opposed to print ones.

Once you have your list of potential agents and editors, you start the query process.

QUERIES

For agents and editors, the query process is much the same, though for simplicity's sake, I'm going to talk as if you're hunting down an agent. If you've gone through the steps above, you've already checked each one's Web site and you know what they want to see. The vast majority will want a query letter first.

Query letters are shorter than treatments. You describe your book and introduce yourself; the agent can decide whether the project is worth pursuing. Query letters save everyone time. The agent can read a dozen queries in the time it takes to go over a single synopsis, and queries are a handy way to weed out inappropriate material. See, overeager authors hit up the wrong agents all the time, and agents who don't handle science fiction and clearly say so on their Web sites still end up fielding manuscripts with hyperspace in them. Query letters let agents weed that stuff out faster.

A query letter follows standard business letter format. After the "Dear Ms. Smith" greeting, plunge right in with a one- or two- paragraph description of the book. This is back-cover blurb stuff, and you want to hook the agent's interest right away. Don't start by introducing yourself. That's dull and boring, and the agent wants to see if you can grab an audience. Introductions don't grab anyone.

In the next paragraph, explain why you're sending the query to this particular agent. See, you always want to tailor the query letter to the agent so the agent knows you're not just mass-blasting queries (even though you probably are—it keeps up a polite fiction). You can say you found the agent's Web page and figured the agent might be interested. Or if you know the agent represents a particular author whose fiction is similar to yours, you can say, "I like what you've done for Mercedes Lackey's career and thought you might be interested in my work as well" or "I really enjoy your client Esther Friesner's books, and I write in a similar vein." If you met the agent at a conference or convention, now's the time to bring that up. ("It was a pleasure meeting you at MegaCon last month. We talked about my book after the 'Where Have All the Dragons Gone?' panel, and you gave me your card.")

In the final paragraph, give info about yourself: "By way of introduction, my short stories have appeared in . . . " If you have no writing credits or anything about yourself that relates directly to your book, skip this part. The agent doesn't care that you live in a tree house or that your dog is named Mr. Wuzzles. It's okay if you don't have any short story credits. Really. Time was that magazines were considered the training ground for novelists, and short story sales were just about the only way to get anyone to look at your novel, but once again times have changed. Agents only care how good your writing is *now*, not how good it was last year.

Close with something like, "I have a synopsis and full manuscript for the book if you'd like to see it. Thank you for your time. Sincerely ..."

And you're done.

Here's a sample query letter for a paranormal novel:

Dear Ms. Smith,

Hot young attorney Jonathan Harker just wants to marry his beloved Mina and run a legal practice in peace. Unfortunately, a terrible monster has followed Harker back from a recent trip to Transylvania, a monster that visits Mina at night and drinks her blood. In desperation, Harker enlists the aid of Abraham Van Helsing and, using clues supplied by a lunatic imprisoned in an asylum, they set out to track down the evil vampire Dracula before he turns her into an undead slave.

I love the novels of Robert Louis Stevenson, especially *The Strange Case of Dr. Jekyll and Mr. Hyde,* and my work follows a similar vein. When I learned you represented Mr. Stevenson, I thought you might be interested in seeing my work as well.

By way of introduction, my romance novel *The Primrose Path* was serialized in *The Shamrock*, and *The Shoulder of Shasta* came out just last year. I have a complete manuscript for *Dracula*, and I'm working on another gothic romance.

If you're interested in seeing *Dracula,* please let me know. I have enclosed a self-addressed, stamped envelope for your convenience. Thank you for your time.

Sincerely,

Bram Stoker

INSTANT DEATH

There are certain things you want to avoid in queries. Including any of the following will get you rejected, and rejected fast.

- *The wrong name.* I already mentioned how query letters should be personalized to the agent or editor, even when you're mass-blasting them out by e-mail. It's really, really easy to put the wrong name into a query letter when you click that Paste icon. Triple check. The fastest route to rejection by Ms. Smith is to send her a query addressed to Mr. Brown.
- *Biographical information.* At the query stage, the agent only cares about your writing. Once she agrees to take you on as a client,

she'll be fascinated to know that you grew up in Borneo or that you have forty-six cats. Until then, keep your mouth shut about anything that doesn't involve the book.

- *Your research.* No one—and I mean *no one*—cares about this. Agents and editors assume you've done proper research or you wouldn't have written the book. Telling them you did research is like telling them you learned to type.

- *What rights you want to sell.* The query letter stage—or any part of the submission stage—is not the negotiation stage. Once the agent calls to say she wants to represent you or the editor calls to say he wants to buy the book, you can talk numbers and percentages. Any earlier than that sounds pretentious.

- *How cool a movie this would make.* Sure, it's fun to cast the movie in your head. But it's not a selling point for a novel. Movies aren't books. Once your manuscript is published, you can talk to Hollywood (or, more realistically, hope that Hollywood talks to you).

A NOTE ABOUT SEARCHING AND YOUR WEB SITE

Internet searches are *de rigueur* these days. Any editor or agent who thinks your query is worth investigating further will turn to the Internet and run your name through a search engine before asking to see the full manuscript. If you're shopping a book around, check your Web site, your blog, and the social places where you hang out online. Are your posts something you'd want an agent or editor to see?

> Okay, sent out fifty-five query letters this week after getting twenty-six rejections last week. Stupid agents wouldn't know a good book if it leaped off the shelf and sank its fangs into their ugly throats.

Or perhaps:

> I hate my life. Everything is horrible all the time. All I see is darkness
> and despair closing in on me like a hellmouth of doom. Sigh.

Stuff like the first entry tells the agent you can't act professionally in public. Stuff like the second entry tells the agent you won't be any fun to work with. You can be sure rejection is forthcoming.

E-MAIL OR HARD COPY?

A great many agents now take queries by e-mail. Take care that you follow the agent's guidelines. Some will want the query letter pasted into the body of an e-mail, and others will want it as a separate file. If the agent wants your treatment and/or samples, send it the way the agent wants. As with queries, some want the material pasted into an e-mail and others want a file. You don't need to put your address and phone number at the top of an e-mail query letter.

If the agent wants a paper query, send it with a self-addressed stamped envelope for the agent's reply. The same goes if you send a treatment and/or sample chapters. You can add "The manuscript is recyclable, and I have enclosed a business-sized envelope for your convenience" to avoid paying extra postage for the manuscript's return.

EXTENDED QUERIES

Some agents may want more than just a letter with the initial query. Their Web page or writers guidelines may say they want:

- a treatment AND/OR
- the first five pages of the manuscript OR
- the first twenty pages of the manuscript OR
- the first fifty pages of the manuscript OR
- the first chapter OR
- the first three chapters

I've even run into a couple of agents who ask for the first page only, though this is rare. (And, I feel, a little mean-spirited, like someone who says, "You

Writing the Paranormal Novel

have ten seconds to impress me, starting five seconds ago.") Yes, you can cheat a tiny bit. If page 20 ends in mid-paragraph, you can send twenty pages plus half a paragraph.

If you can, still try to end with that cliffhanger, however small. You want to finish with something that makes the reader *need* to turn the page.

PITCH SESSIONS

A number of writers conferences around the country give potential authors the chance to attend *pitch sessions.* A pitch session is essentially a short one-on-one interview between you and an editor or agent. You have a short period, usually around ten minutes, in which to convince the other person that your book is worth reading. It's sort of a combination of job interview and speed dating.

Before you sign up for a pitch session, do your homework. For an editor pitch session, find out what publisher the editor works for and what sort of fiction he edits. (Usually this is listed in the conference's programming information, but you may need to do some Web surfing, too.) There's no point in pitching your haunted detective series to an editor who handles memoirs and how-to books, for example. You'll also want to know if the publisher is a real publisher. (See the section on scams on page 246.) Find out what else they've published. Can these books be found in stores? Have you heard of any of their authors?

For an agent pitch session, the approach is much the same. Find out what sort of fiction the agent handles, who is on her client list, and to what publishers she has sold books. If things seem acceptable, sign up.

Some conferences charge extra for pitch sessions; others include them in the price of attendance. Be sure the price, if there is one, is something you feel you can afford. It's a gamble, since there's no guarantee you'll sell the book or sign on with the agent. If you can't afford to lose the money, don't play.

Before the pitch session, figure out what you're going to say about your book. Prepare the sort of thing that might appear on the back cover. Include the overall concept of the book and the basic plot idea. Be brief and succinct, like you would in a query letter. Yes, it's perfectly okay to use notes on a card—the agent/editor knows you're a writer, not a public speaker.

The pitch session is basically a job interview, so treat it as one. Dress professionally to show that you are a professional. (Jeans, T-shirts, and tennis shoes are a bad idea.) Bring with you:

- your business card
- a pad of paper
- a pen
- any crib notes about your book you might need
- a treatment
- sample chapters

It's extremely unlikely (though not impossible) the editor/agent will ask for a copy of your treatment or your sample chapters, so you're bringing those just in case. They flat-out won't want your manuscript; don't bother bringing it to the conference. The reason is actually logistical—they won't have time to read it at the conference, and they won't want to haul a four-hundred-page pile of paper home on an airplane when you can simply mail it to them.

When you walk into the pitch session, shake the other person's hand, make eye contact, introduce yourself—and *don't* plunge right into your pitch. Talk to the other person for a moment about something else; make a connection. This makes you more memorable and shows that you're interested in the person, not just in whoever happens to be sitting at that table. Let the editor/agent take the lead and say, "So tell me about your book."

Toward the end of the session, ask if the editor or agent would like to see sample chapters or the full manuscript. If she doesn't accept this gracefully, thank her for her time, and leave. If she does, ask for her contact information and whether she wants it electronically or in hard copy. Once you're safe outside, allow yourself a little joyful jump—the whole thing might still end in rejection, but you've gotten someone's attention.

One last tip: Hang out in the hotel bar later. If you see someone you pitched to, walk up, reintroduce yourself, and offer to buy the editor/agent a drink (assuming she doesn't seem to be occupied with someone else). *Don't* bring up your book again. You're trying to connect with the person and become more memorable. (And authors who buy drinks for agents are memorable indeed.)

THE FIRST RESPONSES, INCLUDING REJECTIONS

Four weeks is a reasonable time to wait for a response on a query letter. If you haven't heard back after about a month, you're justified in dropping another e-mail or letter that basically says, "On [date] I sent you a short query letter about my book [title]. Approximately four weeks have passed and I just wanted to check on its status." If you still don't hear back, it's safe to say the agent isn't interested—don't waste your time with further inquiry.

Most of the responses you receive will be "no thank you" rejections. That's the way it goes, and there's no remedy except to develop the hide of elephant and keep submitting queries. (Meanwhile, you're also working on your next novel, right?)

But one or even more agents may express interest. If you only sent a query letter, they may want to see the treatment and sample chapters—or even the full manuscript. Since it's already formatted, you're ready to send it. Once you've done so, about six weeks is a decent time to wait for a response. If you haven't heard back by then, drop that "I just wanted to check on the status of my book" letter.

Again, most responses will still be rejections. Some may come with suggestions for revision. Since one of the steps to becoming a professional writer is a willingness to learn, I suggest you consider their comments carefully. Editors and agents are extremely busy people, and anyone who takes the time to give you pointers is doing you a huge favor. The last thing you should do is write back with a snarl. That sort of behavior is unprofessional and will get you blacklisted by other places—agents and editors talk to each other and love to share horror stories.

Incidentally, although you can mass-blast queries and samples, you can only send a full manuscript to one editor at a time. (The same applies to agents, but since editors and agents are separate parts of the industry, you can send the full manuscript to one editor and one agent at the same time.) This is because you can only *sell* a book to one publisher at a time. If you send your full manuscript to two editors and both offer to buy it, you'll have to turn one down. The one who loses out will realize she spent all that time reading your book and getting the go-ahead from her superiors for nothing. She won't appreciate it and she *will* remember you. Later, you may find yourself wanting to switch publishers, or that editor may come to work for your current publisher right when you're trying to sell another book. The publishing industry is actually very small, and the segment of it that publishes paranormal fiction is even smaller.

If more than one editor asks to see the full manuscript, however, it's perfectly acceptable to send a second copy of the full manuscript out as long as you say, politely, in your cover letter to the second editor that someone else is currently considering the book. In other words, don't surprise the second editor and you'll be okay. (And if multiple editors are asking for your work, you really need to step up your efforts to find an agent.)

A SIDE NOTE ABOUT WRITING IN GENERAL

There's a saying among writers that it takes a novel to learn to write a novel. A great many professional writers have at least one novel sitting in their desk drawers (or these days, hard drives) that they can't sell. I certainly do. My first novel is still tucked away in its file, completely unsalable. I also have about three-quarters of my second novel. My "first" novel is actually my third. But I *learned* from that first book I wrote. I learned about plot structure, character development, and how to carry a story through 100,000 words. If your first novel doesn't sell, don't despair—you're in good company. Your next novel will be better anyway, and then you'll show them all.

DEALING WITH ACCEPTANCE FROM AN AGENT

When an agent calls or writes to say she enjoyed your book and would like to represent you, feel thrilled, but don't celebrate quite yet. You'll need to talk—probably on the phone if you don't live nearby—to do a little interviewing. Ask the agent exactly what sort of services she provides, what experience she has, and what books she's sold. (The latter are likely listed on her Web site, too.) You're perfectly within your right to ask for references. You also need to ask about the commission.

The agent's job, you see, is to negotiate on your behalf with publishers, editors, and anyone else who wants access to your work. It's her job to know what rights are acceptable to sign away and for how long. She knows what undesirable clauses the publisher is likely to slip into a contract and how to get them removed. She argues about money, royalties, percentages, and the dozens of other details with the editor or publisher, leaving you, the writer, free to enjoy a purely artistic relationship with these people. You don't have to worry about arguing money for half an hour with someone and then having to talk with the same person about rewrites for chapter seven.

In exchange for all this, the agent takes a *commission,* which is a percentage of everything you earn on any book she negotiates for you. Most agents charge a 15 percent commission on domestic sales and a 20 percent commission on foreign sales. Good agents do not charge for phone calls, copying, or other office costs. Since the agent's income is tied to yours, it's in the agent's own interest to work out the best contract possible for you.

Once you've interviewed the agent and decided you want to sign on, the agent will send you a contract. One tip: Avoid a clause that ties the agent or agency to you for a certain period of time. The agent may leave the agency or the industry, or you might discover you don't like the agent's work after all, but you'd be stuck there until the contract ran out. Instead, make sure the contract allows you or the agent to end the relationship with appropriate notice, usually thirty days. However, the agent will still collect commissions on any books she negotiated for you before you terminated the contract.

DEALING WITH ACCEPTANCE FROM AN EDITOR

If an editor calls you to say she wants to buy your book, thank her profusely and say your agent will call her. When the editor asks who your agent is, tell her you're in negotiation with someone right at that moment (if you have any queries out with agents, you'll be telling the truth), but you don't want to give a name until the negotiations are final. Thank the editor again, get off the phone, and contact the agent at the top of your wish list either by phone or e-mail. Tell the agent about the offer, and I guarantee you'll get a fast read on your book. Don't worry about losing the editor's offer—publishing moves slowly, and the editor's offer will be good for weeks.

Then go celebrate.

GOING IT ALONE

There's no law that says you have to use an agent, and some authors choose to operate without one. Some do it because they can't find an agent they like, and others because they don't mind handling the bargaining and the paperwork themselves, and would rather save the commission. If you're well acquainted with contract law and the publishing market, enjoy haggling, and don't mind spending lots of time on the phone, you can go this route perfectly well. Frankly, I don't recommend it unless you have no other choice. My own agent writes novels of her own, and even she hired an agent to represent her work.

SCAMS

True story, though the exact details have been changed for anonymity's sake: A few years ago, I was browsing through a bookstore with fellow writer Sarah Zettel, who happens to be one of my best friends. We were talking about fantasy novels in general, and one of the clerks overheard us. "I've written a fantasy," he said. "I've got an agent, too. Things are going great—she hasn't charged me very much."

Sarah and I exchanged *uh-oh* looks. After more than two decades of friendship, we've developed a working mental telepathy, and both of us knew the other was thinking: *Which one of us should break the news?* I finally took a breath and asked a quiet question. "How much have you paid her?"

"Only about a thousand dollars," he said.

"Okay," Sarah said gently. "Here's the thing. Your agent isn't aboveboard. She's scamming you. Real agents don't charge up front. They only get paid when you do."

"She's right," I said. "If you pay an agent up front, she has no incentive to sell your book—she already has the money."

The guy looked like I'd just kicked his puppy. "That's not true," he said. "That's not what she told me."

Sarah pointed to the bookshelf. "Well, those are my books, and those are Steven's. We really do know what we're talking about."

"Here's what you do," I said. "You write that agent a letter demanding your book back and ending your relationship with her. Then you look for a *good* agent or publisher."

He still didn't want to believe us. Who could blame him? He'd already sunk a thousand bucks into his belief that his agent was doing right by him, and believing us would mean he'd wasted all that money. Sarah and I gave him a little more information about finding an agent and then fled the bookstore. Even though we hadn't done anything wrong—in fact, we'd helped him out—Sarah and I felt horrible. At least we'd stopped the guy from sending that crook of an agent more money. I hope.

There are a lot of con artists out there just waiting to pounce on you and your manuscript. You can avoid almost all of them by remembering one ironclad, never-break-it rule: ***The money flows toward the writer.***

Never, ever write a check to an editor or an agent. Here's how the real thing works:

When a publisher owes you money, the accountant sends a check for the full amount to your agent. Your agent cashes the check, deducts her 15 percent, and *on the same day* sends you the rest. By overnight mail, if you request it.

Publishers also send you free copies of your book, usually between ten and twenty. (The exact number will be specified in your contract.) If you need more, you can usually buy them at cost, not retail. Some publishers will even send you more free copies, if you ask nicely.

Con artists will tell you all kinds of sweet lies: Established authors do their best to keep new talent out of publishing because they see you as competition. (Actually, the prevailing attitude is "The more, the merrier!" and every editor in the business is dying to discover the next J.K. Rowling.) Authors must "share the risk" in putting out a book. (Actually, if an editor thinks your book is financially too risky, she'll simply reject it.) Everyone charges reading fees these days as a price of doing business. (Actually, no one charges reading fees—except the crooks.)

Remember, you don't send a check to your publisher any more than you'd send a check to your boss. Anyone who tells you otherwise is either ignorant or lying.

SELF-PUBLISHING

A number of tools exist these days to publish a novel yourself, both in print and electronically. Although self-publishing is an option, keep a few things in mind before deciding to go this route.

First, you may have heard about some authors who have found great success through self-publishing. Some of these stories are true, some are exaggerated, and some are untrue. However, even the true stories are the exception, as in "winning the multi-state lottery" exception. The vast, vast majority of self-published books sell a handful of copies, maybe enough for beer money. Be ready to accept that for your book.

Also, be sure that you've run through the venues of agents and editors first. Since self-publishing reaches fewer people (and I'm assuming you want your book to reach as many readers as possible), you really don't want to turn to it unless all other venues have been exhausted. And even then, perhaps you'd be better off spending your time and energy taking what you learned from the book you couldn't sell and writing another book you *can* sell.

If you decide you do want to explore self-publishing, you'll also need to do more research into the type of self-publishing you want to use. There's the *print model*, which produces physical books. You hire a company to print your novel, buy a bunch of your books from them, and sell them to readers and to bookstores. There's *print on demand model*, which creates a book that's ready to go, but only prints one up when someone orders a copy. There's also the *electronic model*, in which you create and upload a version of your book to an online service for sale, and they typically take a certain percentage of the price every time someone buys and downloads a copy. In any of these cases, be absolutely sure that you maintain control over your book and its copyrights. Also be sure that you can pull your novel from publication at any time. This area of publishing is rife with the con artists I mentioned above.

You'll also need to create a cover, have the book copyedited, design the interior, decide whether or not to buy an ISBN (the unique number booksellers use to identify your book), learn to create the various file formats for the different types of electronic book, figure out how to deal with accounting issues, ship books, and handle all the other bits and pieces that crop up when you go into self-publication.

Finally, you should have a marketing plan. Booksellers almost never carry self-published books unless the author personally visits and persuades them. This means you'll need to get out there and meet booksellers, talk to them, persuade them to carry your book. If you're going the electronic route, you need to ensure Web surfers find out about your book in a way that makes it stand out above all the thousands and thousands of other self-published e-books out there. Just uploading it to an online bookseller won't be enough. And through all this, you're still working on your next book, since a single novel usually isn't enough to sustain a career.

Some writers welcome all of the above as an invigorating challenge. If that's you, self-publishing is definitely your place. But if any of it makes you cringe, you're probably better off exploring the route to traditional publishing.

No matter which route to publishing you take, there are some things you can do to help your career—and others you can do to destroy it. We'll examine those in the next chapter.

Writing the Paranormal Novel

CHAPTER 15:

Destruction and Creation

A great deal of a writer's career lies outside of his control. Publishers have quite a lot of power over it. So do book distributors, booksellers, and, of course, readers. However, there are a number of things that *are* under the control of the author. Some will destroy your career just like magic, and some can build it up with a little hard work.

HOW TO DESTROY YOUR CAREER LIKE MAGIC

It's easier to destroy than create in any business. A number of opportunities present themselves in publishing, too. You can wipe yourself out before you even get started, or wreck a fledgling career just as it's getting off the ground. I've seen a number of potentially brilliant authors crash and burn, taking some wonderful books with them. Here's how you can do the same thing.

GIVE UP

No one will make you write. There's no boss, no punch clock, no stockholder. There's also no one to cover for you. If you get sick, no writing fairies will magically crank out a thousand words in your absence. The same goes if you have to plan a wedding, have a child, or have a really stressful month at work. And here's the harshest part—no one will care. Not one person will care that you didn't make your personal writing goal for the day or week. Not one person will care that your novel goes unwritten. Not one person will care that you don't become an author. *You* have to care, because no one else will. (Well, maybe your significant other will care, but we all know the reaction people get when they say to the husband/wife/girlfriend/boyfriend, "Honey, don't you think you should be working on your novel?") If you can't make yourself work on your book, you're in the wrong business.

Most people wouldn't dream of quitting their day jobs because of personal problems, but a large number of people set aside writing careers for them. In other words, they give up. This is the fastest way to end your career.

You can't finish a novel you never start—or never write.

QUIT SENDING IT OUT

True story time: Brenda Clough, another author friend of mine, was attending a large book festival where she came across a woman holding a book signing for her fantasy novel. Intrigued, Brenda stopped to have a look. At first glance, the novel seemed to be fairly well written, but the imprint page listed the publisher as a company well known in the writing community as a scam/vanity press, a place that sells a pile of books to the author and no one else. Brenda asked the woman why she had selected this particular company to publish her book.

The woman admitted that she had submitted her novel to a major New York publishing house, but the book had languished for too long, so she had given up and submitted to the scammers instead.

"Which New York publisher did you submit to the first time?" Brenda asked. The woman told her, and it happened to be Brenda's publisher. Suppressing a start, Brenda said, "How long has your book been there?"

"A few months," the woman replied.

"My god," Brenda blurted, "you were on your way! If they were going to reject it, they would have bounced it back to you in a week, a month tops. If it was there for months, it was working its way up the decision chain, sitting in people's inboxes, getting considered!"

The woman had given up way too soon. Who knows what would have happened if she'd had a little more patience?

I narrowly escaped the same fate. My first novel—the third one I'd written—went to over a dozen publishers. The very last one (Baen Books) took six months to look at the proposal and sample chapters I sent them, and finally asked to see the full manuscript. Six more months passed before they offered to buy it. Good thing I didn't send it to a vanity press.

A fantastic way to end your writing career is to stop sending your work out too soon. The time to stop sending your novel out is after it's been to every paying market, not before. Sometimes it just takes patience.

REFUSE CRITICISM

We can all name a few writers who've gotten too big for their britches. You know whom I'm talking about—the big gun who turns out thrilling or fascinating novels early in his career and then seems to slide. You pick up his latest book, realize it's awful, and wonder how someone so skilled could turn out something so dreadful. What usually happened is the author got lazy and used his best-selling clout to introduce a "no-edit" clause into the latest contract. A no-edit clause means the editor can't criticize the book or recommend changes—she has to accept it as-is. And this is always a mistake, even for the best of writers.

Listening to criticism about your writing isn't easy. It's not so much that the person is saying bad things about you—she's saying you have ugly children. The instinctive response is to snap something back in defense or storm away in a huff. What the heck does *she* know, anyway? Writing is art, and no one has the power to say what's good and what's bad.

Once you've calmed down, though, take a good look at the comments you got. I pointed out earlier that agents and editors are extremely busy people, and anyone who takes a moment to critique your work must have seen something worthwhile in there—it's much easier to hand out a form rejection. And if you submitted your piece to a workshop or other critique group, you asked for a much-needed fresh pair of eyes.

Look at the comments you received. Would they improve your writing? Are you avoiding them because it would be too much work to do the rewrites? As you read them, are you saying, "Well, yeah, but . . . "? *Yes* answers mean it's probably time to incorporate those comments into your work. Ignoring them is a perfect way to short-circuit your work—and your career.

Because we can all get better.

RESPOND BADLY TO REJECTION

No one enjoys rejection. But no matter how ticked you get, the only appropriate response is . . . no response. You can destroy your budding career by responding with anger, sarcasm, or snark. The editor or agent will remember you, he won't be inclined to read anything else you submit, and word will get around faster than a curse. Instead, file rejections away and keep submitting your work with the thought that someone out there will eventually like your stuff.

BADMOUTH BY NAME

You can really wreck yourself by howling about publishing industry people online by name. If you have a beef (legitimate or otherwise) with someone, gripe with face-to-face friends, complain to your dad about it on the phone, and mutter about it to your dog, but don't put it in print or post it online. Once those words get out there, they get away from you. Not only might there be legal ramifications, but you can get a worldwide reputation as a whiner or troublemaker and no one else will want to work with you. Professionals avoid slinging dirt at each other, and you definitely want to keep a professional face in public.

Writing the Paranormal Novel

GIVE IN TO WRITER'S BLOCK

None of the professional writers I know believes in writer's block. It's an excuse, really. Complain that you have writer's block, and your friends feed you tea and cookies (or maybe scotch and soda), pat you on the head, and make sympathetic noises. It also ends your writing career.

When the work in progress won't move, change the point of view, skip ahead to another scene, write something really stupid that you know you'll delete but will get the story moving, or work on something else for a few days. Go for a walk, see a movie, work out for an hour, learn how to bake a soufflé. And then get back to the keyboard.

ISOLATE YOURSELF

Writing is a solitary business. You can't do it in a group setting, with others talking to you or constantly distracting you or otherwise expecting social give-and-take. But isolation leads to mental stagnation. Other people generate new ideas and new perspectives. They keep your knowledge of the human condition current. Much as you might want to be a recluse, you also need to get out into the world. J.D. Salinger and Harper Lee produced great literature in seclusion, but only one time each.

HOW TO BUILD YOUR CAREER WITH A LITTLE HARD WORK

Enough of the tearing down. There are lots of ways to build yourself up, too. None of them are magic, but these little extras can help push your career forward.

USE SOCIAL NETWORKING

Get your name out there in as many ways as you can. Learn to use social networking sites on the Internet. If you aren't Internet-savvy, pick one site and master it, then figure out another. Many of them can be linked to each other so you don't have to post the same newsworthy nugget about yourself five different times.

Once your book gets published, arrange online interviews on other people's sites. (And be willing to return the favor.) Talk yourself up to build an audience. Host discussions about writing or topics related to your book. Hold contests for giveaways.

The main thing to remember, though, is to do what you feel comfortable doing. No one really knows how much of an impact a writer's Internet presence has on book sales. Some writers swear they'd have no career without the Internet, and some highly successful authors have almost no Internet presence whatsoever. Using the Internet can't *hurt*, which is why lots of writers use it. But if you find yourself spending more time online than writing, or if you cringe at the thought of putting together online profiles and constantly updating your status, I have one word of advice for you: *don't*.

READ, READ, READ

Read everything you can get your hands on, and not just in the paranormal genre. Read mysteries, science fiction, romance, historical fiction, literary fiction, and best-sellers. Read nonfiction in every field and genre. Not only does reading feed your internal idea generator, it teaches you how to write.

At a conference I once met a guy who told me that he avoided reading because he didn't want to be influenced by other writers. He wanted to be sure his writing was "pure."

Rubbish.

Art students study great paintings and sculptures to see how artists create. Acting students attend movies and plays to see how great actors perform. And can you imagine a culinary student who refused to try a master chef's recipes?

As a new writer, you need to study how other authors put words together so you can learn from their example.

ATTEND CONFERENCES AND CONVENTIONS

If finances and location allow, go to literary events. Writers conferences abound in this country, and they're easy to find thanks to the Internet. And any given weekend, there's a fantasy/science fiction convention taking place somewhere in the United States. Since you're writing a paranormal novel, you'd be a natural attendee. Such conventions (or *cons*) are easy to find online. Some cons are big, some are small. Some are great for making professional contacts, and some are only good for socializing. However, showing your name and face among the people who have the greatest chance of buying your book is always a good idea.

If you've never attended a con before, don't worry—fantasy and science fiction fans are generally very welcoming toward newcomers, and many cons even hold a little orientation meeting for first-timers. Find one and go!

LEARN PUBLIC SPEAKING

Public speaking terrifies a number of people, but being an effective speaker is a valuable skill for any writer. Once your book comes out, you'll want to talk about it, and it's much better if you can manage to be interesting and engaging when you go about this. Local libraries, schools, book clubs, and other venues are often interested in having local authors come to speak for them, and some of them pay rather nicely. Conventions and conferences want speakers as well. Some only give free admission to the event, and others pay an honorarium. Quite a number of writers make some decent pocket change as speakers, in fact, and good speakers are in high demand. Most speaking events will let you hold a signing afterward, which lets you get your book out there.

JOIN A PROFESSIONAL ORGANIZATION

A number of professional organizations exist to help writers further their careers. They exchange information about markets, editors, and agents, hold conventions, give awards, help with publicity, or even assist with legal issues. Dues are often nominal. Since contact people and addresses change, I don't want to list exact information here, but these organizations are easy to find online. Not all of them require professional sales for membership, either.

The Romance Writers of America accepts writers of all stripes, but mostly exists for writers of romance, including paranormal romance. Those who write paranormal mysteries should look into the Mystery Writers of America. The Horror Writers Association helps writers of horror. The Science Fiction and Fantasy Writers of America looks out for writers of any kind of paranormal fiction, and their Writer Beware program has exposed a number of crooked publishers, editors, and agents.

JOIN A WRITERS' GROUP

Writers' groups, or critique groups, exist to help members improve their writing. The basic format is that members usually exchange their work (either by handing copies around or by reading them aloud) and then everyone gives *polite* comments of the "I liked this" and the "I think this part needs improvement" variety. Some groups take place online, and others meet face-to-face. A good writers' group gives you both an audience and feedback, and can give you a reader's perspective on your writing—very helpful if you've read your own work so many times, it's become difficult to see mistakes. It'll also get you used to accepting criticism.

You can find face-to-face writers' groups by checking out your local community college or university, local bookstores, or even local newspapers that post notices about such things. You can also try starting your own group by posting notices yourself.

The main thing to remember about being in a writers' group is that it needs to help you improve your writing. If your writing isn't getting any better (that is, it isn't getting any closer to publication), look for another group.

KEEP WRITING

It may seem obvious, but some new writers forget it. When Book One is finished, move on to Book Two, and then Book Three.

THE FINAL WORDS

Never give up, never quit.

Persist.

And one day your book will be done. Just like magic.

ACKNOWLEDGMENTS

*Thanks must go to the Untitled Writers Group
(Christian, Cindy, Mary Beth, Richard, Sarah, and Steve)
for reading so many early drafts on such short notice.*

Index